A Pastor's Profession

Gerald Thomas

A PASTOR'S PROFESSION

A Profession of Faith, Innocence, and Hope

GERALD THOMAS

Cadmuspublishing.com

A PASTOR'S PROFESSION

A Profession of Faith, Innocence, and Hope

GERALD THOMAS

Manufactured in the United States of America. Copyright 2024 by Gerald Thomas. All rights reserved. No part of this book may be reproduced in any form, audio, digital, or in print, except excerpts by reviewers, without written permission from the copyright holder or Cadmus Publishing LLC. The Scripture quotations contained herein are from the New Revised Standard Version Bible, copyright 1989 by the Division of Christian Education of the National Counsel of the Churches of Christ in the U.S.A. and are used by permission. All rights reserved.

DISCLAIMER:

The thoughts, opinions, and expressions herein are those of the author and do not reflect those of Cadmus Publishing LLC. Any similarities to actual events or people are purely coincidental. Names and distinguishing characteristics have been changed to preserve identities of any individuals.

Published by Cadmus Publishing LLC. P. O. Box 8664. Haledon, NJ 07538
Web: Cadmuspublishing.com

ISBN# 9781637514498
Library of Congress Control Number: 2024949407

Book Catalog Info Categories:
Personal Memoir, Christian Ministry/General, Christian Life/Personal Growth.

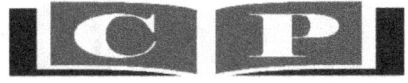

Dedicated to Mom and in Memory of Dad

Also dedicated to Pastor Dave and Martin

"I am the Way, and the Truth, and the Life."

-John 14:6

". . . and you will know the truth, and the truth will make you free." Jesus

-John 8:32

A PASTOR'S PROFESSION
TABLE OF CONTENTS

Author's Note vii

Prologue 1

ONE: "A PROFESSION OF FAITH" .4
Chapter One: The Call To Ministry 5
Chapter Two: Preparing for Ministry 43
Chapter Three: Public Ministry of Word and Sacrament 108

TWO: "A PROFESSION OF INNOCENCE" 136
Chapter Four: Pretrial 137
Chapter Five: The Trial 187
Chapter Six: Pursuit of Innocence 241
Chapter Seven: Listening for God 289

THREE: "A PROFESSION OF HOPE" 331
Postlude 365

AUTHOR'S NOTE

This is not my story. I am convinced that it is God's story. Perhaps I have the starring role, the lead role in this story, but sometimes I'm not so sure. All I am sure about is that it happened in this way, and I am the only person who knows the entire story, which is made up of many parts and many people, taking place over many years. Therefore, I am obligated to write it down. The story is amazing, although it didn't seem so amazing at the time. The fact is it often felt the exact opposite of amazing. Only in retrospect, can I truly use the word "amazing" to describe this story.

I also understand the hardships caused by the sexual abuse of young people perpetrated by clergy, teaches, coaches, and other people of authority, and if you are a victim of such a crime, I offer my heartfelt and sincere apology to you. At the same time, it has become far too easy to convict someone of these sorts of crimes, partly because of our society's disgust and disdain towards the people who have violated the trust that we have given to the leaders of our communities, but also partly because it is politically correct to pass laws making it easier to convict a person of these types of crimes, and political suicide to take a stand against such laws.

The laws to convict someone of a sexual assault are as easy as saying the words, "he did that to me." No other evidence is necessary these days to put someone in prison for the rest of their life on a charge of sexual assault. Unlike a murder trial, where we would expect some evidence in order to convict, a sexual assault charge needs no evidence, no corroboration evidence, merely an allegation and twelve people to believe that allegation. It is in many ways reminiscent of the Salem Witch Trials where an allegation of being a witch alone could lead to a conviction and was often punishable by death.

What are we to do? We want to be tough on punishing people who have abused the trust we have given them, but we also need to be tough on protecting those who are wrongfully accused. This story doesn't address this social issue. That is perhaps a discussion for another day. This is just the story as it was handed to me through what I lived.

I wrote the entire story down while still in prison, except for the very last chapter, of course. That part is not yet known. I believe that God wanted this story written from the perspective of faith and hope for what God has yet to do, rather than writing from the perspective of reporting what happened after the fact.

In that sense, this is first and foremost a story of faith, redemption, hope and life. It is a pastor's story. It is a story of God's greatness. It is a Pastor's Profession.

######

A PASTOR'S PROFESSION

A PASTOR'S PROFESSION

PROLOGUE

It took the jury all of ten minutes to return a guilty verdict on the eleven-count indictment. Deliberate? They couldn't sign each guilty verdict fast enough. Four counts of sexual assault, three of which were first degree aggravated charges. Sexual performance of a minor, and a slew of others. Next came the Punishment Phase. A mere formality, really. Maximum sentences and fines on each charge. The judge stacked each charge, one on top of the other to total 397-years. The joke was on them, though, I'd never be able to do that much time.

"It is the opinion of this court," the judge barked, "that no more just verdict has ever been handed down than this verdict here this afternoon. You have as good and as well have murdered and killed and maimed with what you have done with these lives." I felt a little sorry for them to have been fooled so easily. Don't show them any emotion, I told myself. They don't deserve it. I went to trial because I was innocent, not because I was guilty.

They made a big scene of handcuffing me in front of the jury and escorting me out; a Texas tradition. I was stopped in the back hallway by a newspaper reporter and photographer. The jail guards told me I could make a statement if I wished. I did. The reporter wrote frantically as I spoke until I said something she didn't like. She stopped writing instantly when I began to tell her that my conviction was based on lies and greed for settlement money from the civil lawsuit that was already pending.

But she had the story written already; she was just looking for a sound bite to fit into her story.

At the jail they put me on suicide watch. Standard procedure when someone gets more time than they could ever do. Innocent people don't commit suicide, do they? I was not about to give them the satisfaction.

God will speak when God is ready to speak. I've preached on this before. On Good Friday, when Jesus was crucified, all signs pointed to this as being the end for Jesus. But on Easter Sunday God spoke loud and clear. Jesus was raised from the dead. It wasn't the end at all, but the beginning of a new era. I knew that God was yet to speak on my behalf. Note to self: Must be patient.

I also remembered another theme that I had preached on. Praise God at all times. In good times and in bad times. The ancient Old Testament story of Job came to mind. Job was doing pretty well for himself. He had land, thousands of animals, a big family, all of the things that made for a successful man in those days. Then, one by one, Job lost everything. First, the Sabeans stole the oxen and donkeys and killed the servants. (Job 1:14) then fire fell from heaven and burned up the sheep and servants. (v. 16) Then the Chaldeans stole the camels and killed the servants. (v. 17)

Finally, a great wind knocked over the house and killed his sons and daughters. (v. 18). But instead of cursing God, verse 20 tells us that "Job fell on the ground and worshipped God. ' The LORD gave, and the LORD has taken away, blessed be the name of the LORD.'"

A PASTOR'S PROFESSION

But Job was not finished with his hardships yet. In Chapter Two Job is "inflicted with loathsome sores from the sole of his foot to the crown of his head." (v. 7) Job's wife looked at Job's misery and told Job to "curse God and die." (v. 9) But Job replied, "shall we receive the good at the hand of God and not receive the bad?" (v. 10)

Verse ten says that "in all this, Job did not sin with his lips."

We often refer to Job as being a patient man. But I would suggest something different. It's not so much that Job was patient because he had no idea how this string of calamity would end, or even if it would end at all. Instead, I suggest that Job endured faithfully throughout his entire ordeal.

In the end, God did speak, and God replenished Job with more than he had in the first place. Chapter 42, verse ten says that "The LORD gave Job twice as much as he had before." Note to self: Keep the faith.

GERALD THOMAS

PART ONE
A PROFESSION OF FAITH

A PASTOR'S PROFESSION

CHAPTER ONE

THE CALL TO MINISTRY

IN THE BEGINNING

The first time it happened was during my second year being a church-camp counselor. It was July 1983. The previous year I had quit my well-paying job at the grocery store to go away to college. I had already put in two years at the local university, Wayne State, in Detroit, while living at my parents' house. Their rule was, as long as I was attending college full time, I could stay under their roof free of rent. It was their way of helping their kids with school because with six of us kids, there was no extra money available for tuition.

I lived at home, went to Wayne State University, worked at the grocery store, and socked some money away. My heart was set on graduating from Central Michigan University, with a degree in broadcasting and journalism. So I quit the grocery store job a little early to spend the summer being a camp counselor. The summer salary was about the equivalent to a week's pay at the grocery store, but it was never about the money. It was more of a calling.

After the first year of camp counseling, I started Central Michigan University in the Fall of 1982 and then got my first real-paying radio job after Christmas at the Country King, in Harrison, Michigan, working there on the weekends and attending school during the week. I had bought a decent car, a hatchback Chevy Monza, perfect for a college kid. It proved to be great transportation to Harrison, sixty miles one-way from C.M.U. to the Country King in Harrison. I was able to pay cash for it, but not from my wages at the radio station – that was minimum wage, $3.35 per hour at the time. The money for the car came out of my little stockpile I had saved from working at the grocery store.

Summer was coming up and I wanted to return to church camp one more time. Heck, I was a college kid. I had my whole life ahead of me to work a real job. I decided to take on the camp counselor role one last time. My boss at the radio station was supportive, as long as I could find a replacement for the summer, I could have the job back in the Fall. So I asked around the university, people I knew in the broadcasting program, and found someone who promised to relinquish the job once I returned after the summer. I gave my boss a quality person who wanted the work, only for the summer.

Summer 1983 camping season got going in June. Five of the six male counselors were back for a second summer. The staff was well seasoned. Kids started coming in for a week of church camp from Lutheran churches from around the state and from northern Ohio. We hosted between 100 and 130 campers a week, and our staff provided a wonderful Christian experience for the kids. There were two separate groups of campers. Confirmation camp was for campers aged 12 to 14. The Pioneers were younger, aged 10 to 11.

For the week of July 4th, 1983, we had no kids at all on the schedule. For the staff, it would be a week of camp improvements. Painting, light carpentry, taking care of the grounds. But five of us were chosen to travel to Saginaw, Michigan, across the state, to do a day camp for some of the inner-city kids. They were not affiliated with the church, just neighborhood children who came to the Catholic Church for a free lunch. Our job was to gather the children up after lunch and play camp games with them and sing camp songs with them. I brought my guitar along for that. We took some of them to a retreat center, owned by one of the churches in the neighborhood to do a day-camp for them. The retreat center was outside the city by a lake. It was a very unique experience working with these kids from the inner-city of Saginaw. We shared with them something of our Christian camping experience. They otherwise would not have the opportunity to go to church camp.

But the week quickly came to an end and after thanking our hosts, we headed back to Stoney Lake Lutheran Camp for the rest of the summer. We arrived on Saturday and quickly learned of all the work we had missed out on. And, "Oh, yeah," one of the guys said to me, "We worked out a plan to do a Passion Walk. We're going to act out the life and ministry of Jesus. We even built a removable cross for the crucifixion scene," he told me. Then he added, "everyone decided that you would be the perfect Jesus."

"What?" I answered. "I'm supposed to be Jesus? Hold on a second. Don't I have a say in this?" Apparently not.

GERALD THOMAS

"The kids will be here tomorrow. Our first Passion Walk will be Wednesday. We'll time it so that the crucifixion scene is at dusk," I was instructed, "so you better start learning your lines."

So I had until Wednesday to come up with the Jesus part. They had the scenes figured out, and where on the camp property each scene would be played out. Except for that, the speaking parts still had to be worked out.

On Wednesday, we put on the very first Passion Walk at Stoney Lake Lutheran Camp, and it got great reviews from the pastors attending camp with their kids. We had a baptism scene in the lake with an awesome John the Baptist, who baptized me each Wednesday in Stoney Lake. We had some scenes of Jesus' miracle healings. I memorized the beatitudes, "Blessed are the,..." as an example of Jesus' sermons. Our King Herod was wonderfully done, complete with a Burger King paper crown. (Camp is a lot of improvising). And yes, every week at dusk, the staff put me on the cross and "Crucified" me.

######

BACK TO SCHOOL

After the summer camp had ended a successful season, I returned to Central Michigan University and my Deejay job at the Country King. Later that year I moved up the dial to 94-Country, the local radio station in Mt. Pleasant. It was a powerhouse 100-thousand-watt station, (the maximum power for an FM radio station) broadcasting to a very large area, basically the entire middle of the state. But because such a large portion of the middle of the state is agricultural, corn and sugar beets, it

A PASTOR'S PROFESSION

was still considered a small market. The pay was a little better than the minimum wage of the Country King; it paid a whole $4 an hour. The other benefit was that I didn't have to put 240 miles on my car every weekend going back and forth, that 94-Country was in the same town where I was attending school. The radio station also had an AM Sister Station, which was geared to a more local audience. The two stations together kept me busy with on-air work, commercial production and filling in when one of the full timers was sick or on vacation. It provided good part-time work for a full-time college student in the field of his studies.

I no longer had to take the 60-mile one-way drive to Harrison's Country King to put the station on the air at six AM every Sunday morning, so I had time to go to church. I attended the Lutheran Church in Mt. Pleasant, Emmanuel. I had met the pastor at camp the first summer. His church was really growing. Many professional people from the university attended Emmanuel as did two of the radio station staff. I volunteered to lead the music for the mid-week school. (Mid-week school is just like Sunday school, only it's on Wednesday evenings.) I taught and led music, many of the songs that I knew from summer camp. There were about 50 children in mid-week school, and they loved to sing!

They sang and they sang loudly, at the top of their little lungs. One Wednesday while I was putting everything away after our singing session was over, a fourth-grade boy came up to greet me. He had a smile on his face from ear to ear. I greeted him saying "Hi," and without saying one word, he reached into his front pocket of his jeans, struggling to get his hand fully inside, and after a little squirming around, he pulled out a candy Easter egg and offered it to me with a giant grin.

"For me?" I said. "Well, Thank you." The boy was still speechless and grinning. He was so proud of himself. I didn't have the heart to tell him that I really couldn't eat it knowing that this unwrapped piece of candy was probably in his pocket all day, but I had graciously accepted the gift. It was the best gift that I didn't use, because the thought was greater than the gift.

It was a great senior year. I was working at 94-Country, finishing college, sharing camp songs with the Mid-week children at Emmanuel Lutheran Church. I graduated that May 1985. My parents, brothers and sisters came to the ceremony and watched me walk across the stage of the football field to receive my diploma. Later in the month, my parents threw a big party for me back home. I'm the oldest of not only brothers and sisters, but also of my cousins. So it was a big deal in my family. I wouldn't be the only kid in the family to graduate from college, but I was the first.

In a college town, rent is very cheap in the summer months due to so many apartment vacancies. So I stayed in Mt. Pleasant for the summer after graduation, worked a little extra at the radio station filling in for vacations, but I knew my days were numbered. I needed to find a job and move out by August, before the next school year began. The clock was ticking. That's when it happened again.

A PASTOR'S PROFESSION

I did not participate in the church's Vacation Bible school, but two women who were in charge that year needed someone to play the part of Jesus. On Sunday they approached me after church to ask me if I'd play the part. Little did they know that I had already played the part of Jesus in the Passion Walk at camp two summers prior. Making a single appearance should be a snap.

I accepted the women's offer with one condition. I wanted them to assure me that they would tell the kids that I wasn't really Jesus, just a guy playing the part. They agreed to my stipulation and so I showed up on the day that they had scheduled for this to happen. When I arrived, they had a white robe and a pair of sandals for me to wear and I walked into a room of 75 children sitting on the floor, obviously prepped for my arrival.

I sat on the floor facing them and began speaking to them about the life and ministry of Jesus. I'll never forget what happened next. A little four-year-old boy who was sitting near the back of the group stood up, his big brown eyes locked onto me. He then walked around, sometimes over the rest of the group still sitting, his eyes locked on me alone. He didn't care what anyone else thought of him, his only mission at that time was to sit on the lap of Jesus. He made a beeline to my lap, never looking back at anything else around him.

I continued my talk about Jesus with this little guy sitting on my lap. I don't remember what I said. He probably didn't hear a word I said anyway. As far as he was concerned, he was sitting on the lap of Jesus, and that's all that mattered to him.

As the summer rolled on, I was busy sending out my demo tapes to bigger radio stations. I got a bite, a radio station in Saginaw wanted to talk to me.

######

LIFE AFTER COLLEGE

The Program Director at Stereo Country had received my demo tape and was in need of additional on-air personnel. I took the trip to Saginaw, a 60-mile trip to the east, interviewed with him and was offered the job. At $5.25 an hour I was slowly working up the broadcast wage-scale, but still only a little more than half of my hourly wage at the grocery store a few years earlier. But it was a step in the right direction.

Saginaw was a step up. It was considered a Medium Market because it is in the top 100 largest markets in the country. The market actually consisted of the Tri-Cities: Saginaw, Bay City and Midland. Stereo Country also penetrated Flint, Michigan, which is itself a market larger than Saginaw/Bay City/Midland. When I went to announce my intention to quit 94-Country in Mt. Pleasant, the owner offered me an additional quarter an hour to stay. But I had already made up my mind. It was time to move on to bigger and greener pastures.

The problem was that even at $5.25 an hour, the job was only part-time weekend and fill-in work. In broadcasting, you take the part-time gig because it's a step towards the next full-time opening, which may be next week or years down the road. So I needed to find another source of

A PASTOR'S PROFESSION

income in order to support myself. I called on my supervisor from the camp to inquire if he knew of any churches in Saginaw that might like to have a Youth Ministry Director.

Saginaw was originally a German settlement so there was a Lutheran Church on every corner, so it seemed. In the late 1800's and into the early 1900's, Germans settled the area around the logging industry. There were plenty of trees to cut down and lumber barons were created everywhere. There were old photographs from that era where a person could walk across the Saginaw River on the freshly cut logs floating their way down the river to the lumber mills. And the German immigrants who settled the area brought with them their Lutheran brand of Christianity.

My Camp Supervisor gave me the names and contacts of some of the churches he thought would be interested in the work that I was looking for. Armed with my list and the blessing of the Director of Camp Ministries, I went knocking on church doors. The first church that I went to seemed interested in my services and I set up a time with the pastor to meet with their Youth Ministries Committee. I planned on attending church there one Sunday and met after the worship service with the people who made up the Committee. They were indeed interested in hiring me, and once the church council approved it, the church hired me to be their Youth Ministries Director at Grace Lutheran Church.

Meanwhile at the radio station, a full-time position opened up in the sales department and I became an ad-man full time, selling radio advertising for Stereo Country's sister station, an AM Oldies format playing music of the 1950's and 60's. I still filled in on-air at Stereo Country, the leading Country Station in the market, as needed, and began my Youth Ministry at Grace Lutheran Church.

Little did I know what I had jumped into. At the church, not the radio station.

######

THE NUMBERS GAME

I was told that earlier in the year there was a sort of schism in the congregation. A member of the church was a rostered pastor, although he wasn't the pastor of that church; he was on leave from the ministry. Apparently, he brought up issues regarding the direction of the nationwide church. Church members took sides and debated biblical interpretation. The ongoing debate became very heated and in the end it boiled down to a vote over which side would retain the church property and which side would have to leave. He didn't have enough votes to take over the property, so he and his followers left the congregation and started their own independent Lutheran Church down the road.

And all of this turmoil began in the high school youth group.

This was the situation that I stepped into when I accepted the newly created position of Youth Ministries Director. More than half of the high schoolers and their families had left the congregation. I inherited what was left. But it was an opportunity for a new beginning. At least I thought

A PASTOR'S PROFESSION

so. But the Youth Committee's expectations were perhaps a little too high for what I could accomplish.

The pastor of the congregation gauged success by the numbers. I began to cringe every time he would ask me, "how many showed up for the youth meetings?" My boss at the radio station had a saying, "If you live by the numbers, you'll die by the numbers." He was referring to the Arbitration Ratings, the company that determines through survey, exactly how many listeners a broadcast station has, and what the demographics of the radio listeners are. If an advertising salesperson uses the Arbitron numbers to say, "We're number one," the next month he might wish he hadn't said so, because the numbers might not be as favorable.

The pastor finally realized that I didn't like talking about the numbers. So one day he directed the question differently. "I know you don't like talking about the numbers," he said, "so just tell me who was there?"

"That's basically the same question," I replied. "We're going to have to come up with a different way of gauging the success of this program. It can't be about the numbers, because the numbers will never be what they used to be."

There were successes, to be sure. A Halloween Party was well attended as was the New Year's Eve Overnight Lock-In. But otherwise, the High School Youth Program remained flat. The high schoolers didn't even want to attend the state-wide High School Gathering, held every year in Lansing. A thousand Lutheran High School Youth meet at a hotel for a three-day convention. It would have been a great Christian experience for them, and I tried to sell them on the idea, but they were sour about it. I went without them because I was on the planning committee that year. I was helping to run it.

At the convention I ran into a number of my camp kids who were now in high schools around the state. I was pleased to see that they were active in their faith since their confirmation camp days at Stoney Lake.

I began to realize that the future of my High School Group was in the Junior High Confirmation class. So I began creating opportunities to foster a sense of community with them. They were attending their confirmation class with the pastor, so I organized some fellowship events for them. I took them on the annual CROP Walk, raising money for local food pantries by walking a 10-mile course through the city. I initiated other fellowship outings for them. And although the pastor wasn't going to do it, he at least blessed the idea, I took the younger confirmation students to church camp. Those are the kind of experiences that build a sense of belonging in a youth group. The kids need a sense of ownership in order for the Youth Program to be successful. It's not about the numbers, it's about the experiences and the Christian friendships they form through those experiences.

At the radio station, everything was going well. My client list was growing and that year I won the local CLEO Award for the best radio commercial of the year. The Cleos are like the Oscars, but for advertising. I submitted a commercial that I had written and a co-worker at the radio station produced. It was not your run-of-the-mill local radio

A PASTOR'S PROFESSION

ad. It was about a host at a party who ran out of beer, the partygoers weren't too happy about it, but a particular party store would have exactly what he needed.

I went to the awards banquet which was attended by about 500 advertising people in radio, television, print, and ad agencies. I was asked to stand while my commercial was played. The ad people laughed at the commercial, good, it was intended to be funny. Then they applauded me for writing the best radio commercial of the year. They gave me a plaque with the name of the commercial on it and my name engraved in it. I took the plaque back to the radio station and we hung it on the wall. Perhaps it's still hanging there today.

I received a phone call one morning at 3:00. It was during the week. The Program Director who had originally hired me was also the morning deejay. He was sick and could hardly talk. Could I get to the radio station and do his 5 to 10 AM show? Of course I could. Doing the morning shift is hectic. Commercials to be played. News. Weather. People coming in and out of the studio. Hitting the network news at the top of the hour. All while sounding bright and cheerful and totally in control. It was a thrill.

It was right up there with my one experience deejaying at a major market station. While still attending Wayne State, I interned at a Detroit radio station at a time when Detroit was the fourth largest market, only behind New York, Chicago, and Los Angeles, and the station was the fourth the most popular station in the market.

GERALD THOMAS

It was New Year's Eve, 1982. Apparently no one wanted to work on air that night and the Program Director couldn't find anyone to fill in. "I'll do it," I said enthusiastically. It wasn't as though I didn't have the experience. My high school had a radio station and I worked at the campus station at Wayne State. Besides, it was New Year's Eve, how much harm could I really do?

The Program Director must have been desperate enough. He let me do the on-air shift. Wow! State-of-the-Art equipment on a Major Market radio station! Doing the morning shift at Stereo Country was right up there on my "Yeah, I did that" list. And advertisers love dealing with an ad rep who is actually on the radio.

At the church the pastor was still playing the numbers game and so was the Youth Ministries Committee. They weren't patient enough to wait for the program to naturally develop when the younger group became the older group. We were on different pages when it came to expectations. So after eighteen months they cancelled the Youth Ministries position. They asked me to stay on, but I felt it was best to make a clean break. I took my membership to a different church.

Since I was now back in Saginaw and learning my way around the city, I thought it would be fun to try and find the places where I had been when we were working with the inner-city kids at the day camp three years prior. The camping program had been sponsored jointly by the area Catholic and Lutheran churches. I found the Catholic Church where the neighborhood kids would stand in line for their free lunch. That had been our starting point. I didn't know it back then, but this was a rough part

A PASTOR'S PROFESSION

of the city. The Catholic Church was closed down now, and the rectory, where I witnessed one of the nuns hand out a sandwich to a homeless man at the back door, was now police sub-station.

I recognized a few other places, like the Catholic Rectory at another church across town where the five of us spent the nights that week and eventually I recognized one of the houses where we went to dinner. A different host would have us over for dinner each night of the week. It was always fun to recognize one of the sites of our stay.

One day at the radio station our news director asked me, "You look familiar, Jerry, where do I know you from?" I wasn't exactly sure.

"Well, I was a camp counselor at Stoney Lake Lutheran Camp, but I don't remember seeing you there." I said.

Then it clicked for him. "That's it! I haven't gone to camp in a while, but you and some others from the camp came to dinner at my house that week you were in Saginaw."

"Yes, I remember you now. We had pizza." Yes it was true. Our News Director was a Lutheran minister, but he wasn't pastoring a church. I later learned that he did pulpit-supply preaching now and then but worked full-time at the radio station. What a small world!

I bumped into one of the kids from the day camp. I was working the radio station's booth at the County Fair when I spotted him across the aisle. It was the kid with the birthmark on his face. He was twelve then, now he was sixteen. He was easy to spot, and he gave a big smile back when I waved. He remembered me. He was the kid who told me that in order to go to our day camp at the lake, he would have to earn the church's one-dollar charge by doing extra work around the house. Nothing wrong with earning your way. The dollar went for the transportation cost. He was with some friends, so he didn't come over to talk, but I imagine that seeing me brought back some good memories for him.

I never saw him again or recognized any of the other children from that week at our day camp, for that matter. I suppose we do our ministry in its time and place, then we leave the rest to God. Part of me wanted to know the outcome, the other part of me said, "Let it go."

######

BACK TO BASICS

I already knew the two pastors at Resurrection Lutheran Church. The older of the two, the Senior Pastor, had come to camp back when I was a counselor. The younger pastor, Pastor Dave, was fresh out of seminary serving at his first call as an ordained minister. While the Senior Pastor was polished due to being in professional ministry for some time, Pastor Dave was still a little inexperienced. He was energetic, he preached well, and he had a love for Jesus and the people of the church. I had already worked with Pastor Dave on some mutual youth programs for the area churches as well as the state-wide high school convention, "The Gathering" held every year in Lansing.

A PASTOR'S PROFESSION

I decided to join Resurrection and just become a good church member. No pressures, just do what I wanted to do. I joined the choir. They had a very nice music program and a wonderful choir director. Pastor Dave started a Young Couples group and although I was single, I tagged along for that too.

Of all of the churches that I had attended, this was the first time I had a pastor who was straight out of seminary. It was refreshing to witness a pastor ministering who was just beginning his professional ministry. All of my previous pastors were a little more refined. Perhaps even a little "stuffy." But Pastor Dave was different and for the first time, I thought that maybe even I could pastor a church. It would take a little more though, to push me over that edge and actually decide to do it, but I was headed in that direction.

After a couple of years, Pastor Dave left the congregation to pastor a church in Northern Ohio. I keep fond memories of my friendship with him and his lovely wife. We kept in contact since they left Saginaw. Pastor Dave has never missed an opportunity to send me a birthday card or a Christmas card, a monthly newsletter, shipments of crossword puzzles and notes of encouragement. We could all learn a thing or two from Pastor Dave about how to care for someone who is incarcerated.

The summer after Pastor Dave moved on, it happened again. I wasn't involved with the church's Vacation Bible school, but the organizers needed someone to play the role of Jesus and make a personal appearance. Just like it happened in Mt. Pleasant, two women approached me on a Sunday after church and asked me if I would play the part of Jesus and visit the children to talk to them about the life of Jesus. I told the women that I could do that, but I requested that they instruct the kids that I wasn't really Jesus, just a guy playing the part. Once more, I donned the white robe and robe cincher, sandals, and visited about 50 children at Vacation Bible school.

Do I look like Jesus? I didn't think so. I don't wear a beard or long hair. Quite the contrary. An Adman must have a clean business-like appearance. This was now the third time that I was asked to portray Jesus, from three different groups of people who certainly did not know each other.

"What's going on here?" I asked myself. "Why is it that everywhere I go, people ask me to portray Jesus?" I would like to think that perhaps I remind people of what they think Jesus would be. How Jesus walks, how he talks, especially how he treats others, loves others, respects others. But that's really for others to decide. If people see something about Jesus in me, then praise God! That is our mission in life as Christians. To portray Jesus to others. To be the hands of Jesus, the voice of Jesus, and to be the love of Jesus.

Our church was down to only one pastor now, so I took on a few other responsibilities. I taught one of the two Confirmation classes which met weekly. It would have been the class that Pastor Dave taught. One summer I chaperoned five high schoolers to the National Lutheran Youth Convention. That year it was held in Dallas. Fifty thousand Lutheran High School Youth from around the country converged on Dallas for

A PASTOR'S PROFESSION

five days. We literally took over the city! We traveled there with the other Lutheran kids from Saginaw and Midland, filling two tour buses. We planned a couple of side trips on the way there and on the way back.

The National Youth Convention is held once every four years. That gave us time to prepare. We did car washes and bake sales to raise much of the money needed for the trip. The Convention goes all out to bring some of the best key-note speakers in, the best in music and plenty of activities. Maya Angelou was one of the speakers that year, author of "I Know Why the Caged Bird Sings," and who later became poet laureate for the Obama Administration. The convention books every hotel room in the city and the surrounding suburbs. It's a very big deal as it allows Lutheran Youth to see something of the National Church and meet other High School Youth from Lutheran churches all around the country.

It was the following summer that I chaperoned the Confirmation class to church camp. Stoney Lake, where I had been a counselor eight years ago.

######

A CAMPING REUNION

On a sunny, summer Sunday afternoon, I packed the trunk of my car at the church parking lot with the luggage and sleeping bags of six kids from the congregation and we traveled West, across the state for a week of church camp at Stoney Lake Lutheran Camp. It was a three-hour journey and a sort of homecoming for me.

Stoney Lake is a small lake that connects to Lake Michigan via a half-mile winding creek. It is a beautiful, picturesque lake dotted with cottages and lined with trees. The campground itself is small in comparison to most camps, but it is functional and serves the needs of the campers well. The newest building is the kitchen and dining hall which also serves as a multi-purpose room when the tables are folded up. There is also a fireplace and a sitting area around it which also has served as a campfire circle on rainy nights, and there is a porch off the front of the building with built-in benches for congregating.

On the east side of the property are six cabins for the girls. The boys' six cabins are on the west side of the property. Each side has its own bathrooms and shower building. All twelve cabins were built within the trees. The middle of the property is a large open space for all-camp activities. There is a cinderblock building at the edge of the field which is used for arts and crafts and a basketball court closer to the boys cabins.

And then there's the "White House." Named so only because it is painted white, it was the original building on the property before becoming a church camp. In the 1920's, this was the summer cottage of a lumber baron from Chicago, who vacationed here in the summer with his family. It was a beautiful house in its day, with four bedrooms and a bathroom upstairs, a living room and kitchen downstairs, and a full wrap-around screened-in porch. The camp property is situated on high ground

A PASTOR'S PROFESSION

so the house would have had a spectacular view of the entire lake from its high perch, but now the trees and brush have obstructed that view.

Today the White House is used to house the weekly guests who accompany the campers to camp. Pastors, Chaperones, like me this week, who will be responsible for teaching their church groups a catechism class for two hours each day. Next to the White House are the stairs to go down to the beach. One hundred three steps made from railroad ties make a path down the hill to water level. There is a small sandy beach with a swimming area in the lake which is roped off for the swimmers. Beyond the beach is an area reserved for the campfire circle.

Then there is the bell. Every camp communicates through the clanging of a bell. Ours was suspended by a steel tripod, twenty feet into the air between the Arts and Crafts building and the White House. A continuous clanging called us to breakfast and dinner or to camp activities. But three clangs followed by silence, continuously, meant that a camper was unaccounted for. In that case, each counselor was to immediately bring their campers down to the beach and sit them together by cabin group until every camper was accounted for.

Because the swimming area was in the lake, it was particularly important that the lifeguards kept a close eye on the swimmers. So the campers were taught how to use the buddy board. Each camper was assigned a number on the first day. Their number corresponded to a numbered tag on the board. In order to enter the swimming area, a camper would first need to find a buddy. Both campers would take their numbered tag off of one side of the board and hang them together on the other side of the board to signify that they were in the water. When the lifeguard blew the whistle and yelled, "Buddy Check," the pair would find each other and hold their hands up in the air. The pairs of swimmers in the water must match the number of buddy tag pairs on the buddy board.

But sometimes a camper might forget to take the tag off of the board after getting out of the water and the number of pairs in the water didn't match the number of pairs of tags on the board. If the problem couldn't be resolved instantly on the beach, the bell began its three-clang-followed-by-silence routine. Campers realized the serious nature of the buddy board system when they came down to the beach to see the lifeguards dragging the bottom of the lake in search for a potentially missing camper, until the tag problem was resolved. If this routine happened at all during the week it rarely happened again.

Downtown Stoney Lake consisted of a park, a gas station, convenience store and a Bar and Grill that the owners called the "Yacht Club." Apparently they had a sense of humor because there were no yachts on Stoney Lake. The pastors who came to camp for the week referred to the Yacht Club as "The Library." They would meet there occasionally to "talk shop" with their pastor colleagues sometimes over a pitcher of beer.

Once back when I was a counselor, a pastor was walking with me and my campers back to the camp after an overnight camp out. The pastor told me about a new video arcade game they played at "the library." One of the campers was apparently listening in on our conversation. He piped in, "They got video games at the library?"

"What can I say," the pastor responded, "it's a small town." That seemed to pacify our ear-hustling camper well enough, while I thought to myself, "Busted!"

We finally arrived at the camp. It was great to be back to a place where I loved to be. I was eager to share this Christian camping experience with these six young people from my Saginaw church. I got them registered on the front porch of the dining hall where they would soon meet their counselors for the week. I helped them get their luggage and sleeping bags from the trunk of my car and soon they were off with their counselors and the other newly arriving campers that formed their cabin groups.

After the entire cabin group settled into their living space for the week, they would go down to the beach for their swim tests to determine who could swim in the deep end and who would only be allowed to swim in the shallow end and the staff would educate them on how to use the Buddy Board. Then they would go up for a quick dinner, and finally to the opening campfire to meet the entire staff and get a feel for how the week would unfold. I was free of responsibility until the next morning when I would teach a two-hour catechism class with the kids I had brought with me.

######

GERALD THOMAS

PROGRAM OR EXPERIENCE?

While the campers were meeting their cabin mates from other Lutheran churches around the state and going through their first-day routine, I was meeting the pastors and catechists who brought them. We were all settling in at the White House.

On Monday morning I noticed that two of the six male counselors had been campers eight years ago and I had been there counselor. Cool! I remembered their names, where they were from and even some of the camp activities that they participated in. I would have to talk to them individually when they had a free moment to see what they remembered. One-by-one they both confirmed my memory that they had been campers here when they were younger. One-by-one they both told me that they didn't remember me.

"Really?!" I thought. Here you are camp counselors and you both don't remember your camp counselor? I was a little shocked, and perhaps even a little hurt. I remembered everything and they both didn't know me from Adam.

I told one of the pastors there for the week about this injustice. He said, "Well, that's good!"

"Good?" I inquired further, "How so?"

"You pointed them to something greater than yourself," he told me. "They're here because you pointed them not to you, but to Jesus." I hadn't thought of it that way.

Well, I didn't raise them, I knew that. I was just their camp counselor for a week, eight years ago. Apparently they had a good enough Christian camp experience to go on and become counselors. But now I understood. Our mission is to further the mission of the church and to further the mission of Jesus, which is to show others the love of God by being a living example of the love of Jesus. Being remembered for it is immaterial to that mission. I now realized that.

I was given a new perspective. Let those guys do what they were called to do; I'll stay out of the way. After all, we're all on the same team. This was never about me, rather it was all about the mission of the church. It was all about pointing young people to Jesus.

I started to hear a phrase repeated over and over again by some of the camp staff and I cringed every time I heard it. They would tell the campers, "We put together this program for you," and they insinuated that the campers ought to plug themselves into the program and appreciate it. Since when did camp become a program to be plugged into? I always thought of camp as a Christian experience to learn and grow from. Some of the staff were missing the point and that would play out later in the week.

Every morning when I met with my church kids for catechism class, I would ask them how things were going. I wanted them to have a line of communication with me to discuss any problems they might be facing. On Tuesday, my girls, who were in the same cabin together, reported to me that there was a lot of tension in their cabin between them and two Black girls. They weren't getting along. I watched them at lunch time. There were icy stairs between these girls and their cabin mates.

GERALD THOMAS

Something would have to be done to unite this group or else these girls would leave camp with a bad campaign experience.

I remembered my camp counseling days. I worked very hard to bring my cabin of boys together. The kids came to camp and didn't know one another. They would soon come to understand that the church they belonged to was bigger than just the congregation that they came from. I wanted to create an environment in my cabin where each camper would feel accepted, loved, and be an important part of the group. After the opening campfire on Sunday night, I would immediately go to work with some get-to-know-you games and a couple of group-building activities in my cabin. Throughout the week I was always assessing the group, making sure that no one felt left out. Everyone was important in my cabin.

We would cook lunch over a fire. There were plenty of cookout pits throughout the camp property. I'd begin the week by teaching the boys how to work together to make a fire and how to make our lunches. I wanted them to have an ownership in the outcome. Tuesday and Thursday nights were camp-outs off of the camp property. There were two campsites that we could hike to and camp out on the shore of Lake Michigan. There was a hay barn, a pretty good hiking distance away we called "Grandma's Barn." An elderly woman at the area Lutheran Church allowed the camp to use the barn as an overnight spot. I enjoy taking my campers to the "Back-40." Called so because it was a 40-acre site in the woods, we could hike there, or we could canoe across the lake to get there. The canoe trip was a lot more fun and adventurous. It meant

A PASTOR'S PROFESSION

a canoe trip across the lake and entering a winding creek. If you didn't know where the landing for the Back-40 was, you'd pass right by it. I'd make sure we found some time during the week to teach my campers how to paddle a canoe for a Thursday night overnight.

By Thursday's overnight, I felt it was time to put my cabin of boys to the ultimate test of working together. Once we got to the Back-40 and settled in and ready to start our cooking fire to make our dinner, I would make the announcement.

"Oh no," I began, loud enough to get their attention. "I meant to pick up a new book of matches, but I forgot. All we have," and I pulled out a used book of matches from my front pocket, "is three matches to start our fire."

There were looks of disbelief. "Na-uh," someone would say.

"Afraid so," I would answer, "but I've taught you all week how to build a fire, and I've taught you how to work together. I know you can build this fire with only three matches. Now, everyone has to work together to make this fire so we can eat something tonight. I don't want to hear anyone blaming someone else, so work together, make it happen."

One of the boys would grab the matches from me, and then they would all go to work. It was as though once one boy took the matches from me they all took ownership of the project. They would all own the outcome and they all started to go to work. Some of them gathered firewood from the surrounding forest while others gathered kindling.

Another two boys began by assembling the pieces in the fire pit. Once the wood and kindling were all arranged, they would all gather around, and one boy would strike the match. The flame didn't take. Two matches to go. They brainstormed and rearranged the kindling. Match two. The wind would blow out the match. Down to the last match.

"Everyone get closer," one would say. Now everyone moved in closer to protect that last match from the wind. All hands on deck. They couldn't afford another dud.

Every week for the entire summer it got down to the last match. And every time the last match started the fire. You've never seen a group of boys working together so hard towards a common goal as when their dinner depended on it. I often wondered what would happen if I had to eat my words and retrieve the book of matches I hid in the first-aid kit. I would never know the answer because every week it was the same. They'd get down to the last match, and then they would pass the test. High-fives all around.

"I knew you could do it," I would tell them. "A little bit of teamwork goes a long way. Now let's make some dinner!"

Now, I was contemplating what I could do to help these girls out. That's when the same pastor who had given me a new perspective on the meaning of Christian Mission approached me. He had two girls in the same cabin and had received the same report from them as I had received from mine. There was a high degree of animosity between the different races of girls.

A PASTOR'S PROFESSION

"We have to do an intervention," he said. "There's still time to salvage the week for them." I agreed. But I didn't know what to do, or how to do an intervention. He told me that prior to becoming a pastor, he was a youth counselor at a youth home. He knew exactly how to do it. "We just need to get the OK from the counselor, figure out a time for when we could do it."

That didn't seem like a difficult task, so we approached the girls' counselor with our proposal. I let the pastor do all the talking, he knew what he was doing. I just tagged along.

Things weren't going too well with our discussion. "How about after beach time?" He asked the counselor.

"No, that's Arts and Crafts time," she replied.

"OK, how about after Arts and Crafts?" the pastor asked.

"No good. Then it's time to get ready for dinner," she answered to the pastor's frustration. She couldn't fit us into the schedule.

Just as I had suspected. The camp program had become more important than the Christian experience. The pastor was striking out and became more frustrated, so I figured I would give it a try.

"These girls are either going to have a good camping experience, or they're going to go home with a bad experience," I said. "I want my girls to have a good experience. They can learn and grow from this, or they'll go home with a hatred for one another. There are some issues that I believe we can help address, and these issues are way more important than any Arts and Crafts item they bring home with them." She contemplated this for a moment and silence filled the air around us.

Then she agreed with me. "Go ahead and take them at Arts and Crafts time." With that she turned and walked away leaving the two of us standing there. We had gotten our intervention time.

"You missed your calling," he whispered to me.

"I saw this happening from the beginning of the week," I said. "The Program has become more important than the Experience."

"You should have been a pastor," he replied. "I was losing my patience. I didn't know how to get her to see what was happening. But you saw a way. Yeah, you missed your calling."

I knew he was right, partly. It wasn't that I missed it so much as I ignored it. Every week while I was a camp counselor, pastors would approach me at the end of the week. Sometimes two or three of them at a time. They would tell me, "We have watched you this week, and we talked among ourselves. You ought to consider going into the ministry. We think you'd make a very good pastor."

No, I didn't miss my calling. I was too busy doing what I wanted to do. I wanted a career in radio broadcasting, and it was waiting for me to go back to when I started back to school in the Fall. But God is patient and God can wait you out. And in the end, God will get what God wants.

That's when I knew what I needed to do. It was time to do what God had called me to do. I was going back to school to seminary, eight years after I graduated from college. I was going to become a pastor.

A PASTOR'S PROFESSION

Pastor and I did the intervention with our girl's cabin. He did it, I just watched. He got the girls talking with one another, letting down their defensive guards, opening up and understanding one another's culture, likes and dislikes. In about an hour, they were laughing together.

That evening I watched them skipping and singing to the dining hall with their arms hooked together at their elbows. It was a beautiful sight. For the rest of the week that cabin of girls was inseparable.

In the end, my girls went home with a good Christian camping experience. I went home with a renewed sense of my call to become a minister. It was time to do what God had called me to do.

######

JONAH AND THE WHALE

(Hint: It's not about the whale)

The shortest book in the Bible, Jonah is only three pages long. It's a popular story to teach children in Sunday school about a man who gets swallowed by a giant fish and taken to shore. But the story isn't really about the encounter with the whale. It's an ancient story about rebellion and obedience to God's call.

According to the four chapters that make up the book of Jonah, God called Jonah to a very specific mission. God wanted Jonah to go to the eastern city of Nineveh and preach to them giving the Ninevites an opportunity to repent from their sinful ways and receive God's forgiveness.

But Jonah didn't want to go. Instead, he went to the coastal city of Joppa, got on a ship and sailed West in the exact opposite direction. Jonah did not like the Ninevites and had no intention to offer them God's forgiveness. So Jonah rebelled against God. Instead of doing what God called him to do, he did what he wanted to do, and he went in the opposite direction to avoid God's call.

That's when things got messy. The ship he was on encountered a storm and the shipmates blamed Jonah for the storm because Jonah had disobeyed God. They ended up throwing Jonah overboard to drown in the sea.

But God brought Jonah right back to his starting point, the point of Jonah's rebellion, and then God simply recommissioned Jonah. "Yes, Lord, I shall go," Jonah basically replied. Then Jonah obeyed God's calling and journeyed East to the city of Nineveh to preach and seek the Ninevites' repentance and receive God's forgiveness.

With very little effort and no enthusiasm, Jonah preached and all of the Ninevites were saved. They repented from their sinful nature, and they received God's forgiveness. Although Jonah didn't think it was fair that God would forgive them, God still used Jonah to preach God's message and through Jonah the Ninevites came to know God.

I can relate to Jonah's rebellion. It was at this very spot eight summers earlier that God had called me to go into the ministry. God's call came through the many people of God who had seen something in me that I didn't want to see myself. And through these people, God was calling me into the mission of God's church. But, like Jonah, I had rebelled and went in the opposite direction. I wanted to do what I wanted to do, and I had rebelled against God's call. And just like Jonah, God had brought me right back to the point of my rebellion. Then the Holy Spirit showed me a few things this week. And just like Jonah, I finally replied, "Yes, Lord, I shall go."

The opposite of obedience is not simply disobedience. The opposite of obedience is rebellion. Disobedience is simply not doing what God tells you to do. Rebellion is, like Jonah, making a conscience effort to go in the opposite direction. I'm such a rebellious Child of God. But God can use our rebellion to God's own advantage. Perhaps to gain insight and knowledge or learn and pick up some tools for the task.

The story of Jonah is not so much about how the whale brought Jonah back to the shore. The point of the story is that God brought him back to the point of his rebellion. Now, God had brought me back to the point of my rebellion. And just like Jonah did, I finally heeded to God's call to ministry.

######

FORKS IN THE ROAD

"AM radio is dead," my boss at the radio station would tell us privately, "but you'll never hear me say that in public."

It wasn't because he didn't try. The radio station had a highly professional sound that anyone in radio would be proud of. He had even made a large investment to broadcast in AM Stereo at a time when the public lacked AM stereo receivers. There were a number of AM radio stations across the country that were invested in AM Stereo. It was supposed to be the answer to the problem of competing with the higher quality sound of the FM band.

There were announcements from major car manufacturing companies that the new models would be equipped with AM Stereo receivers. That would give the AM radio industry a boost. Large corporations were involved to make AM stereo broadcasting possible, but the various systems they came up with were not compatible with one another. For a while, things were looking promising for the AM radio broadcasting industry.

But under the Reagan Administration's policy of "Let the Marketplace Decide," the Federal Communications Commission (FCC) refused to choose any one particular system and the large corporations involved were not willing to invest billions of dollars on a system that could end up on the losing side of the market. So the whole idea of AM Stereo fizzled out completely. AM radio would stay inferior to the higher quality sound of FM Stereo for good.

I was originally hired to sell commercials on the AM station, but my boss never complained when I brought in an ad contract for the more listened to FM station. He knew as well as I that it would be tough trying

A PASTOR'S PROFESSION

to make a living selling commercials only on the AM station. But I was still responsible for selling primarily on the AM station.

The new sales manager came in with new formulas in an attempt to assess the sales staff. "Your average sales per client is very low," he would tell me. Of course it was. I was still straddled with the AM station which had fewer listeners and cheaper ad rates.

The decision was made to sell both stations in combination. Sell the FM and upsell the AM, just like in the fast food industry, as in "Would you like fries with that, just a nickel more." So, for an additional five dollars, I'll throw in the AM station with that. Two commercials, two stations, for a mere five bucks more.

Unfortunately for me, there were eight sales reps in total, now all selling both radio stations in combo and under the new sales method we were already tripping over each other on the streets. Eight reps would be too many for selling these stations and someone would have to go. I was at a disadvantage because my sales numbers, compared to the reps who had been selling the FM station exclusively, were low. I and another rep got the axe.

I drew some unemployment benefits for a while and one day I received a phone call at my house from the manager of the classic rock station in the market. How he got my unlisted phone number will always be a mystery. How he even knew who I was and what my situation was is also unknown. But he wanted to meet me about hiring me for advertising sales at his radio station.

GERALD THOMAS

We all have those forks in the road of our lives, where if we decide one thing our lives will turn out differently than if we decide on the other. This was one of those forks. I turned down the job opportunity at the classic rock station. I was headed to seminary.

After living in Saginaw for eight years it was now time to pack up. Saginaw was a great place to be, but I had finally given in to what I felt was God's purpose for my life. Perhaps I had to get radio out of my system and now I had. It was really a stumbling block to what God had called me to do in this life.

I decided to take up my parents' offer once again and stay with them for the summer, save up some money, and prepare for the fall semester at seminary. There was a temporary job available at my dad's work; they needed extra help for the summer. I would be working in the shop refurbishing vending machines – coffee machines, snack and soda machines – preparing them to go out to new accounts in new condition. A couple times a week I'd go out on an install to set up a bank of vending machines in lunchrooms all across the Metro Detroit area. Six bucks an hour and all the overtime I could handle. My goal was to go back to school in the fall with a little bit of cash in my pocket.

I announced my intentions to go to seminary at my home congregation. They weren't at all surprised. "We knew that this was going to happen," they would say. These people had known me since I was a little kid. They seemed to know where I was eventually headed way before I wanted to acknowledge it. I was a son of the congregation, and they were proud. They offered to pay my entire tuition bill for my seminary education. What a blessing that would be!

The next step was to begin the admission process. The seminary expected a major essay, transcripts from college, letters of recommendation from pastors who knew me as well as letters of recommendation from non-pastors. One pastor from Saginaw was on vacation for an entire month, another letter got lost and had to be rewritten. Wayne State University wouldn't send the transcripts because they said I still owed them five dollars for a lab fee. It took the whole summer to get everything in order for the admission packet.

Then there was the Candidacy Committee. This was a group of people who would oversee my seminary career. The committee was made-up of clergy as well as lay people. I would meet with them throughout the summer and throughout my time at seminary. They were tasked with making the final decision on whether I would be approved for the ministry.

As part of that process the committee sent me to a psychologist. I met with him three times throughout that summer. He interviewed me and I took a battery of psychological tests. The Candidacy Committee didn't take their job lightly. They wanted to be as sure as they could that their candidates for ministry were mentally and psychologically sound.

One test I took was an aptitude test. I would read a word and then choose its opposite meaning. I had never seen these words before! Were they even in the English language? If I didn't know the meaning of most of these fifty words, how in the world would I be able to choose the opposite meaning? I didn't know these words either. The outcome of that test was that I may have a difficult time with advanced academics. OK, thanks for the warning. If this test was any indication of how tough seminary would be, I was in for a real challenge.

I worked throughout the summer at the vending machine company to save some money for the Fall semester. I got the approval from the Candidacy Committee and the admission packet was complete. With my home congregation behind me I was ready to embark on a new chapter in my life.

In my last week at the vending machine company, I asked my boss, whose family owned the company, if he knew of any vending operators in Ohio where I might find some part time employment.

"I know one," he said, "but it's in Columbus."

"Perfect," I answered, "because that's exactly where I'm going."

God closes some doors, but where doors are closed, God always opens others, especially when those doors open up to the opportunity to further God's Kingdom on Earth.

A PASTOR'S PROFESSION

CHAPTER TWO

PREPARING FOR MINISTRY

BACK TO SCHOOL . . . AGAIN

I arrived at the seminary in Columbus, Ohio, a week before classes were to begin, meeting the other Ministry Candidates who would make up my class. There were forty-five of us starting our first year. Not all of us would make it all the way through to the end for one reason or another but we all would begin with the intention of becoming ministers. All of us had a story to tell and a sense of calling to the ministry. The next four years of seminary would test whether or not that call was really of God.

A seminary education is a graduate program. A candidate would first be required to earn a Bachelor's Degree at a four-year university. Graduating from seminary would earn a Master's Degree, specifically, a Master of Divinity. The M. Div. is comprised of biblical studies, theological studies, church history and ministry classes, and a proficiency in biblical Greek. The third year is an internship at a church, and the fourth year includes some advanced studies. There are other requirements along the way, like a four-hundred-hour Clinical Pastoral Education, which involves a chaplaincy at a hospital. The church wanted smart, educated pastors leading their people in congregations, and the seminary learning experience would be exceptionally challenging. Like any graduate program, a student would pass with eighty percent.

Anything less was unacceptable. In graduate level studies, a "C" is a failing grade. So would it be for us as well.

The week before classes began involved registering for classes, getting a financial-aid package together and meeting the people who would make up our class. Besides having my home congregation's backing to pay my tuition bill, I received a smaller scholarship from another congregation. That would cover the textbooks I was required to purchase. I also called on my contact at the local vending machine company. Using the name of my boss in Detroit, I was hired instantly to work part-time, servicing some vending machines at a local trucking company. The job would provide not only a small steady income, but also would provide a break from my daily studies. I was now ready to start classes.

Our professors knew their studies well. It wasn't long before my classmates and I were swimming in more knowledge than we could keep up with. It was an almost impossible pace and we quickly formed study groups to survive. Our Old Testament class was especially difficult. Not only did we have the Primary Text, which is what we referred to as the Bible, but there was also a textbook to keep up with, which is what we called our Secondary Text. Then there were the lectures on Biblical Interpretation, and Scholarship on Old Testament Theology. We studied frantically to get a handle on so much material being thrown at us at such a rapid pace.

With our mid-terms around the corner, a classmate asked our Old Testament Professor what we should know for the exam.

A PASTOR'S PROFESSION

"Everything," she answered matter-of-factly. She was a brilliant Old Testament scholar, who specialized in the book of Isaiah, one of the most difficult books in the Bible, and she expected her students to be brilliant as well. She told us that she would feel she had failed as a teacher if one of her students got a perfect 100% on one of her tests. Most all of us failed that first mid-term exam because she was so nit-picky on minute details both in the Bible and in the textbook. She had to retest us and perhaps ease up just a bit. I ended up failing the class and had to retake it. The second time I took the class it was with a different professor. I passed.

We were all required to study a year of Biblical Greek, the language of the New Testament. Understanding the original language of the New Testament unlocks a great deal of meaning that would otherwise be lost in English translation. We would be required to pass a standardized exam of Greek vocabulary and verb parsing. The class required a great deal of studying. We had a wonderful, patient Greek instructor and when it came time to take the final exam, we all passed. The second year I would take Hebrew, the language of the Old Testament.

And so it went for the first two years of study, learning a great deal of Biblical Scholarship, a class on preaching, a class on Worship, another on Evangelism, an elective class on the Gospel of Mark, and other Theology, Bible, and Ministry classes.

The seminary assigned each member of the class to one of the Lutheran churches in and around the Columbus area. Like Saginaw,

Columbus was originally settled by Germans so there were plenty of Lutheran churches to pick from. The congregation each of us was assigned to would be our M. I. C. Church, or Ministry in Context church. Our assignment was low-key, attend the church services there, be in communication with the pastor, and plug into ministry opportunities in the congregation. At the end of the year, the pastor would write a report about his Candidate for Ministry, which would be a part of the student's file.

I was assigned to a large well-established congregation in a community twenty minutes outside of Columbus' city limits. It was far enough outside of Columbus that the community would have its own identity, yet close enough to be considered a part of the Columbus area. This church had two-thousand members, two pastors, an intern, and three youth ministers on its staff. It was a busy place with activities and programs throughout the day and evening. My supervisor was the senior pastor, a very generous, outgoing, gracious person who any student of ministry would love to emulate.

I would look forward to our weekly visits where he and I would meet for lunch and then drive around to the hospitals to visit his members. He was close to retirement and here I was just getting started and I tried to soak up as much wisdom as he was willing to give. I believe he enjoyed our exchanges as much as I did.

Around the church I assisted with the Saturday evening worship services; They had three services on Sunday as well, but that was already taken care of by other staff members. I led a Bible Study with the Senior

A PASTOR'S PROFESSION

Citizens and poked around in their gigantic Youth Ministries programs. The whole church ministry seemed to be a well-oiled machine, well run and well received.

The congregation was well established in the community, and because of its giant youth program, the Youth Minister had forged a relationship with the Buckeye Boy's Ranch which was located in the community. The Ranch is a famous home for children, mostly boys, with serious personal issues to work on. These children were usually placed there by the courts or Protective Services, and they came from all over Ohio, Kentucky, and Indiana. The Ranch consisted of separate "houses" based on age, and the house that the church sponsored consisted of twelve to fourteen year old boys.

A few times a year the Youth Minister would take a group of church kids over to the Ranch and conduct a joint Youth Ministry Program, allowing both groups of kids to intermingle. It allowed the Ranch kids an opportunity to socialize with our church kids. I thought that this was such a cool idea, I had to check it out for myself, so I tagged along.

When it came time to do the closing prayer, the Youth Minister asked the kids to add their own prayer concerns. What surprised me was that the Ranch kids out-prayed the church kids ten to one. The Ranch kids were far more in tune to their prayer needs than our church kids were and were far better at vocalizing them. This was most likely due to the fact that the Ranch kids were used to group counseling and personal therapy, but I knew then that these kids were very special. I was impressed with their faith.

The Youth Minister told me that he went out to the Ranch once a week to lead an hour of Spiritual programming for them and invited me to join him. He was very gracious to share the Ranch Ministry with me, and we developed a tag-team ministry style. By then I had a large repertoire of songs, Christian storytelling and Bible studies geared for them, and together he and I would take turns doing a small portion of the whole hour in rapid succession. We had to keep a fast pace in order to keep their attention. It would only take a few minutes of pre-planning to put the hour together; it wasn't just a disorganized mess, but the style kept the hour moving quickly so that the kids wouldn't mentally wander away. It was very effective, and I was able to learn from him and he from me, and we both grew our resources in youth ministry.

The Ranch was run on a very structured schedule, and I eventually had the opportunity to take two kids at a time off the campus for a few hours. My time was limited but I would find time every other Saturday to give them a little bit of normalcy for a while by taking them to the park to play frisbee or catch with the football, or bike ride through the neighborhood. That gave me a little time to get to know them better, which would allow me to do a better job at providing them with spiritual care.

When the Youth Minister scheduled time with the city soup kitchen for the church kids to serve meals to the homeless, I suggested we also bring along three Ranch kids. Perhaps by getting them out to serve

A PASTOR'S PROFESSION

others, they could see that even as they struggle with their own personal issues, they weren't alone in pain and suffering and personal problems. My Ranch kids did a great job serving meals to the homeless.

At the end of the year I received an excellent report from my M.I.C. Pastor, and as he was approaching retirement, I also was the recipient of a wonderful set of Bible Commentary books, one volume for each book in the Bible. His generosity and thoughtfulness would help me begin my pastoral ministry.

Hillary Clinton once said that "it takes a village to raise a child", but it also takes a village to raise a pastor. Becoming an ordained minister doesn't happen in a vacuum. It takes the work of many people who will shape and form a future pastor. It also takes many different people within the church to give their approval before a pastorate is bestowed upon a candidate for ministry.

######

PREPARING FOR MINISTRY PART II

The second year of seminary was much like the first. In addition to the classroom work there would be a meeting with the Candidacy Committee who wanted to see how I was progressing. There were preaching assignments and I would check in occasionally with my home congregation. They deserved to be brought up on my seminary progress and would appreciate a sermon every now and then. I was still earning a paycheck by servicing the vending machines at the trucking company a few hours a day as well. But on top of it all, I wanted to get out beyond the walls of the seminary and learn by actually doing ministry.

I had been contacted by an old acquaintance from my camp counselling days in Michigan. He was our Camp Director in my second year, who at the time was a church pastor with the summer off. He took the position of Director at Stoney Lake Lutheran Camp and then made a career out of Outdoor Ministries, serving as Director at other Lutheran Church camps before eventually settling down as Director of Camp and Outdoor Ministries in Indiana.

Indiana had three camp and retreat centers in the state, and he ran all three year round. He asked me if I would be interested in helping to run some of the youth retreats in Indiana. So three or four times a year I would head out to Indianapolis, three hours West, meet him at the Synod office and travel together to one of the three camps and run a weekend retreat for Confirmation-aged kids, aged twelve to fourteen. The church groups in Indiana and Kentucky would arrive on Friday night with their students. They would bring their own chaperones to stay with them in the cabins, and he and I would provide the programming. We would host about one hundred to a hundred thirty kids at each of our weekend retreats. I often led the entire weekend, providing the group leadership, Bible studies and break-out sessions where the chaperones would lead small-group discussions.

We would work all day on Saturday and end with a Sunday worship service, preparing the kids to help lead the various parts of worship. The retreats were a big hit with the Lutheran churches in Indiana and Kentucky.

On one trip home from the northern-most camp in Indiana, he and I spent the entire three hours back to Indianapolis brainstorming a new idea. We would put together a high school mini convention camping experience. We would provide a campsite for each church to bring their own tents and food, and we would provide resources and programming for workshops that the high school campers could choose from, a Christian music band, and speakers for all-camp gatherings. We split up the responsibilities to make it happen and it was a huge success and became a yearly tradition in Indiana.

Back in Columbus I was still intrigued with inner-city church ministry. Ever since my Saginaw inner-city experience, I wanted to know more about how the church does ministry in the inner-city. There was a Lutheran church in Columbus that seemed to be doing more than just the basics in the inner city and I wanted to see what that looked like.

I attempted to get placed there for my M.I.C. church but I was instead assigned elsewhere, which turned out to be just fine. It opened the door to ministry that I didn't even know existed. Still, I wanted to learn more about ministry in the inner city. One day Pastor Carol at St. Peter's Lutheran Church put a notice on the seminary bulletin board. She was looking for volunteers to help chaperone a weekly program; inviting the neighborhood children to the Y.M.C.A. It was one of the ways the church was reaching out to the neighborhood of which it served.

GERALD THOMAS

I contacted Pastor Carol to let her know that I would help. Some nights we hosted fifty kids or more and had to make two trips from the church parking lot to the Y.M.C.A. There were two things to do at the "Y", play basketball and swim. Basketball was out of the question as the games were made up of inner-city high schoolers and I was no match for them. I chose the pool and swam with the kids. Perhaps I was just trying to be a camp counselor again; I would toss the children in the water, allowing them to do water flips and the like.

It was a wonderful opportunity for the kids and a great idea to give the neighborhood children an alternative activity on a Friday night, and all I wanted to do was make the kids feel safe, loved, and important. Little did I know, Pastor Carol was already making mental notes to be used against me in the future.

######

ESTABLISHING PASTORAL IDENTITY

By the second half of our second year of seminary, our efforts turned towards internship. Churches applied for the program. Sometimes a church wanted some extra pastoral help because they were too big of a congregation for only one pastor but still not able to support another full-time pastor. Other times, like my M.I.C. church, the church kept two pastors busy, and they were seeking still additional pastoral staffing. The upside for the church was that an intern could fit into the budget. The downside, however, was that the intern was in fact a student of pastoral ministry, who would be learning by doing. The intern would also only be assigned to the congregation for one year. An internship committee would be formed by the church members who would meet with the intern monthly. They would write reports on the intern's progress throughout the year and give feedback to the intern. The program would be highly managed and supervised by the church's pastor.

Interviews began at the seminary to match up the interns with the available churches who were seeking an intern. We went back and forth between what type of church would be right for each of us; a large church with many members, or a small one. Urban, rural, or suburban?

At first I saw myself at a suburban-type church because that was what I was used to. My home congregation was a large suburban church. I had always been a member of large thousand-member churches. Even my M.I.C. church was a two-thousand member church.

The director of internships who was leading the interviews suggested something different. He needed a more mature student to take an internship site at a small rural church in western Virginia. "Think about it," he said, "it would help you establish your own pastoral identity."

A week later we began the second round of interviews. "I thought about what you said to me last week," I told him, "I'll go to the Virginia site."

"Well, that one's been taken," he answered, "but I have a real nice church outside of Cincinnati. It's a large congregation."

"What happened to the pastoral identity stuff you were talking to me about last week? Now you're telling me just the exact opposite." I knew then that this guy was just trying to sell his wares. This process had nothing to do with what was best for me.

"Well, you know, sometimes we have to make adjustments," he backpedaled, and he handed me the church's application from Cincinnati. "Look it over and tell me what you think."

On the third interview a week later, I met with him again. "I looked over the application," I said, "I'm sure it's a good internship site, but you really sold me on that pastoral identity issue and how that would be a good thing for me, and now you've done a complete turn-around on me."

He thought for a moment. "I do have another site, it's a detached site like the one in Virginia which means there is no pastor at the church. Your supervisor will be from another church fifty miles away. It's a smaller congregation, rural, and they had a pastor but they're in a transition between pastors. It's a new site, so I'm not familiar with it, but it would give you a chance to work on pastoral identity. If you want it, I don't see why not."

So instead of going to the internship site in suburban Cincinnati, I decided on something totally outside of my experience. I chose a small church in rural West Texas, and I began corresponding with the congregation.

Eventually, all of the internship assignments were complete, and my classmates and I concentrated on finishing the second year of seminary and the approval from our Candidacy Committees in order to go on internship. I spent the first ten weeks of the summer working on my Clinical Pastoral Education (C.P.E.) at a local hospital.

A PASTOR'S PROFESSION

C.P.E. is a supervised chaplaincy with peer-group support. It's a requirement towards the degree program. The peer group was made-up of five students along with the supervisor. A large part of C.P.E. is verbatims. As we visited with hospital patients throughout the day in a chaplaincy role, the C.P.E. students were required to choose one conversation of some significance, write it down from memory 'verbatim' and share it with the peer group and supervisor for evaluation.

"Why did you say that?" is the primary question the peer group members would ask, which requires an answer. The whole experience is designed to help the C.P.E. student filter out his or her personal issues, biases, experiences, in order to be a better listener and thus a better spiritual counselor. In four hundred hours of supervisory and peer-group evaluation, a C.P.E. student would hone his pastoral skills in counseling by visiting hospital patients.

We would also be responsible for a project and a presentation to the group. I volunteered for the hospital's Residency Drug and Alcohol Rehab Center. It was a wing connected to the hospital. I met with the Rehab Director, introduced myself, and told her I was interested in exploring how the chaplaincy department could be helpful in the Rehab setting. She and I talked about our goals, and she gave me full access to the program. A couple of times a week I sat in on the group sessions and before or after the Rehab Group session, talked with individuals in the Resident Treatment Program. I also had complete access to the medical library at the hospital and did a little research on addictive disorders.

As the ten-week C.P.E. program came to an end I presented my project to the group called, "Drug and Alcoholism as a Disease, an Addictive Disorder and Spiritual Care in Rehab." It ended up being an hour-long presentation and my peer group listened intently. It was a very interesting C.P.E.

It also made for a hectic summer. After putting In my eight hours a day at the hospital, I would drive to the trucking company and fill the vending machines for the vending company. There was very little supervision from the company, and I wanted to make sure that they were always taken care of. The company would never receive a complaint from this account.

Once a week I still went to the Ranch to do the Youth Program. The Youth Director at the M.I.C. church would be on vacation for most of the summer or too busy with other church functions, so I was the Spiritual Director at the Ranch that summer as well. They were such cool kids, and the last week was bittersweet. They had already known that it would be my last time there, and that I would be moving to Texas for my year of internship. After the hour program and saying goodbye, some of the boys came up to greet me personally. One boy had brought me a gift.

"This is for you," he said, and he presented me with a wooden project he had made in his shop class. It was a board of sorts, the wood was smooth and shiny kind of like it had a Formica finish, with two holes drilled out on either end lengthwise, and a border nailed around the edge, and small pegs sticking up out of the surface.

"Oh," I said surprisingly, "What is it?"

A PASTOR'S PROFESSION

"It's a penny-hocky board. You play penny hockey on it. I made it in shop class," as if I should have known this, "and I made it for you!"

"Of course. Thank you!" I said, and I remembered back to that little nine-year-old boy in Mt. Pleasant, Michigan, digging out of his pocket that piece of candy he had kept for me all day long. It was a gift of appreciation as best they knew how.

"How thoughtful of you," I told him with a smile. He smiled back. "I'm going to take it with me to Texas." And I did just that.

######

POUND THE INTERN

The time had come to pack up a truck, secure the car onto the trailer to be pulled behind the truck, and make the three-day trek to West Texas. The seminary had provided travel money which the internship churches had put up based on a flat fee. The money was then divided up among the interns, the most going to the interns going the farthest distance and so on. My internship congregation was expecting me in three days. They had already sent me a little welcome package with things that they thought would be helpful and might help get to know them a little better. They had been without a pastor, and they were just as eager for my arrival as I was in getting there.

I arrived in Wilson, Texas, population 525, on the third day. The church was easy to find because they had provided me with a picture in the welcome packet. The little city was surrounded by cotton fields and there wasn't too much to the town. It was a one-blinker town. Not a traffic light, just a red blinker at the two-lane highway which passed through it.

There was a downtown strip, but it was mostly closed down and boarded up; a sign of better days gone by like much of rural America. At one time this was a thriving community which had built itself up around cotton farming, but that was back when it took a lot more manpower to pull in a cotton crop. Now it only takes a few people to work a thousand acres.

I pulled up next to the church property, which consisted of the church, and education building, and next to it a parsonage. This is where I would stay for the next year. I walked across the street to the closest house and knocked on the door. I introduced myself and the neighbor directed me to a house up the street on the corner who were members of the church. I walked up to the house, knocked on the door and met my first parishioners. Within ten minutes there were twenty church members at the parsonage to help unload the truck.

It was a strange feeling. I didn't know any of these people but at the same time it seemed like I did. They were friendly, warm and eager. Some of the women showed up to greet me and offered to unpack my boxes and put everything away from me. "How considerate of you," I said, "but that's OK, I want to take my time and set up the house, thanks though."

A PASTOR'S PROFESSION

One-by-one, they left me to the task of unpacking and finding a place for my household belongings. The next day I would be busy just acclimating myself to a whole new environment.

On Sunday I met the whole congregation. I had prepared the sermon on the trip down. The gospel text for that Sunday was from Luke, the story about a man who built bigger and bigger barns to house all of his possessions.

"God has a sense of humor," I started my sermon after reading the Gospel lesson. "Here I am, a city boy, sent here to talk to you about barns!" The church was packed with cotton farmers. They broke out in a good laugh. Good sign. They had a sense of humor as I cracked the ice. "But really," I continued, "the Gospel isn't so much about barns as it is about how we accumulate earthly possessions. I'm reminded of it every time I move. I seem to acquire more and more stuff."

After the worship service, I greeted everyone. It would take a little time to get to know everyone. One of the women informed me that later in the afternoon we would have a potluck dinner to officially welcome me to the community and we would have a pounding.

"Pounding?" I asked, "but I just got here."

She laughed. "Don't worry," she said, "it's a good thing."

After a good old-fashioned Lutheran potluck dinner, I found out exactly what a pounding was, and yes, it was a very good thing.

It was an Old West Texas tradition, perhaps it was a tradition in other rural places as well, that when a new pastor arrives all the church members bring something for the pastor's pantry. Canned goods, dried goods, groceries of all kinds. Some members of the church gave gift certificates to the grocery store or even cash meant for groceries. There were some gags too. Some of the canned goods had the labels torn off.

"Is it beans or Alpo?" I asked as I went through the bags of groceries in front of the group. "Only time will tell," I joked. They all laughed. We all had a good time.

Yes, a pounding was a very good thing. It was the congregation's way of saying, "Welcome," and "We're in this together," and "We take care of one another."

As the weeks went by, I would settle in, find out what their expectations of me were. I would preach and lead worship every Sunday, visit the members, especially those who were sick or in the hospital, and be the resident pastor for the year. The congregation also had six young people who were in need of Confirmation instruction. I would create a curriculum and teach the confirmation class once a week for one school year and at the end of the year I would confirm their faith. Lutherans baptize infants because we believe that in baptism, it is God who does the work, and we receive the grace that God bestows upon us. There's nothing that we do to earn God's grace. It is a gift from God alone. But at the baptism of an infant, the congregation and parents of the child make a promise to educate the child in the Christian faith. That's where Confirmation comes in. After one, two or more years of Christian education, the young Christian, usually about fourteen years old, takes

A PASTOR'S PROFESSION

their faith as their own. The congregation had six young people who were of confirmation age, and it would be my job to educate them.

There would be other responsibilities, too. Leading the church council and the day-to-day running of the church, meeting with my supervising pastor in Lubbock, as well as meeting with my internship committee for guidance and feedback, pastors meetings, educational commitments with the seminary and the synod; Baptisms, new-member classes, funerals if and when necessary. It was going to be a busy year, but the first order of business was to learn everybody's name.

######

PASTORING IN THE COUNTRY

It didn't take long to settle into the daily rhythm of pastoring a rural congregation. The community revolved around the cotton crop, the amount of rain received, and the harvest. One hailstorm could ruin a full year's worth of work and over the years often did. What looked like a bumper crop was no crop at all until it was harvested. Even then too good of a crop could ruin market prices if there was too much cotton on the market. There are so many variables to making a living from farming.

The congregation itself had been through seventy-five growing seasons. Some of the older members of the congregation could claim that their daddy helped construct the church. It amazed me that on any given Sunday there were four generations of the same family sitting in the pews. It was a family church stoked in tradition. I had never experienced a church quite like it.

It was also a church in healing. The previous pastor got in trouble for physically assaulting one of the members. That's why the church wasn't quite ready for another pastor. They needed a little breathing space and some time to heal. There had also been some hurt feelings along the way, and I found that part of what I did in visiting those people was to listen to their concerns and try to help them reconnect to their church. Pride can often lead to hurt feelings. My pastoral visits became the bridge for some families to find a way back to their church.

I also began visiting an older woman in the congregation. She had been a pillar of the community and the church. She had taught Sunday school her whole adult life, raised a family here, and now she had brain cancer. She had been such a faithful woman, and the cancer progressively worsened. She became bedridden and I would visit her at her sister's home, where she lay in a hospital bed in the living room. She would always ask for prayer, and I would end our prayer with the Lord's Prayer so that she could pray along. Even when the cancer took her speech away, she still was able to recite the Lord's Prayer with me. Her faith was ingrained in her so deeply. I visited with her twice a week. Her name was Mary Beth.

I had developed a Confirmation curriculum for the year and was meeting weekly with my six Confirmation students in the church basement which was finished with classrooms. I guessed that this was the traditional place to meet with them, even though there was a newer

A PASTOR'S PROFESSION

education building next door, so I didn't question their choice of classrooms. We would spend the year exploring things like the Ten Commandments, the Lord's Prayer, the church's Ministry and the Sacraments.

In the Lutheran tradition, there are two Sacraments in the church. Baptism and Holy Communion. They are sacraments because those are the only two things that Jesus actually commanded us to do. "Go and Baptize. . ." and "Do this in remembrance of me." The words in Greek are actually in the command form of the verb. Spanish also has a command form of a word, English does not.

I also assigned the class to take notes on the sermons and turn them in. I developed a simple form for them to use to tell me a little about what they got out of the sermon. I wanted to train them a little in their listening skills. Finally, I made it a requirement for us to go to church camp.

It was the tradition of this congregation for the Confirmation class to also receive their First Communion on Confirmation Sunday. This is an old tradition not normally practiced in other Lutheran churches. Today communion can be administered at a younger age, but some churches still hold on to the older ways.

I was meeting monthly with my internship committee, getting feedback from them. The committee consisted of five people from the congregation who oversaw my pastoral ministry. I was also meeting once a week with my pastoral supervisor, who pastored a larger congregation in Lubbock. He had been the pastor who filled in since the previous pastor at my church had left until my arrival. He knew the congregation well.

One day I had gone to Lubbock and decided to check out the mall. By chance the mall was hosting an Expo for all of the nonprofit groups in the area to set up a booth. It was a way for the nonprofits to connect with the community and show people who they were and seek volunteers to help in their cause. All of the social service agencies were present and I was, like other mall visitors, going from booth to booth, table to table, and looking, out of curiosity if nothing else.

I came across a booth for a West Texas Boys Ranch, and by chance the director himself was working the booth. I was interested in the Ranch only in comparison to my knowledge of the Buckeye Boys Ranch in Ohio when we started a conversation. I introduced myself, I told him that I was an intern pastor and that I had been involved in Spiritual Care work at the Ranch in Ohio.

He said that this was exactly the kind of thing he wanted to get started at his Texas Ranch and had thought about how to go about implementing a Spiritual Care program. I knew exactly how to do it, and he if he would like, could devote one hour a week to the cause. The director was elated, and I started going out to the Ranch once a week to provide a Spiritual Youth Program for the residents of the West Texas Youth Ranch.

When I showed up at the Ranch for the first time, the Director had put the word out to be expecting me. I told the House Parent my plan to lead a Bible study, and he cringed. I guess he was expecting one of those fire-and-brimstone type of preachers. I didn't really need his approval

A PASTOR'S PROFESSION

because the director had already approved it, but I assured him that it was going to be OK. There would be no shaming. I would use Christian storytelling, music and Bible Studies to convey the message of the Gospel. No Fire and Brimstone preaching. These young people needed to hear the gospel.

The ranch was smaller than the one in Ohio, and the kids were a little older than the ones in Ohio, fifteen and sixteen-year-old boys, who had gotten in trouble with the law. The Courts had placed them here rather than a juvenile lockup facility, perhaps because they saw some hope still in a positive outcome for them. The other big difference between this ranch and the one in Ohio was that this one was an actual working ranch. The residents here actually raised and cared for animals and took the animals to livestock shows. The Ohio Ranch was a ranch in name only. I would provide the spiritual angle to these young men's rehabilitation.

And so the internship began to take form. I prepared and preached a sermon every week, led worship, and presided at Holy Communion, which required special permission from the Bishop. I baptized infants and adults as well. I developed a new member class for two spouses of members, who themselves wanted to be members of the congregation. Little by little, the rhythm of the year came together.

######

GERALD THOMAS

IT'S NOT A NINE TO FIVE JOB

In a meeting with my supervising pastor, he told me that he normally takes his Confirmation Youth on a Fall weekend retreat to Ruidoso, New Mexico. Ruidoso is a beautiful mountainous ski resort town far different from the flat plains of West Texas. There was a church in Ruidoso that opened itself up to visitors for overnight retreats. Since I also had six Confirmation-age youth, perhaps we could both bring our groups together this year.

Then my supervisor gave me my assignment. I would be responsible for leading the retreat. Little did he know that this would be an easy assignment for me; I had led numerous retreats for youth in Indiana in the past two years while at the seminary.

I presented the idea to my students and their parents, and they were all in favor with one condition. Each of them wanted to bring a friend. That could be arranged. My supervisor rented two church vans, one for me and one for him. We could take extra people so long as we didn't go over the fifteen-seat maximum.

There was one additional problem to get worked out. All of my kids were in the marching band, as were their friends. What's more, altogether the group pretty much made up the entire marching band and they were required to play at the Friday Night Football game.

High school football in West Texas is almost as important as church, so we made a compromise. The kids would play to the end of halftime so that they could perform their halftime show. Then they would shut down for the second half of the game. The football team would just have to play the second half of the game without a band. We prepacked the van with sleeping bags and clothing before the game. I drove the van to the game, which happened to be out of town that week, and after the halftime show was over, we headed to Ruidoso, New Mexico. My supervisor's church would already be there waiting for us.

I was ready to lead the retreat for thirty youth and after breakfast the next morning we got started. In the afternoon we took a break and went to the ski mountains for a little hiking. It was off-season and the only snow was in the shade. Then back for dinner and a little more retreat work. I like to devote some time at night to preparing for a Sunday morning worship, where all of the students can participate with the readings, the prayers, and I gave a short message.

On Sunday after breakfast we would have our worship service and then start the journey back home. We stopped along the way, here and there; it would be a more leisurely pace than it was getting there. The weekend youth retreat turned out very well. All thirty kids had a great experience in Ruidoso, New Mexico.

When we finally arrived in Wilson it was already dark and there were some people at the church in the education building. I was helping the kids get unpacked and making sure they had rides back to their homes, looking forward to a little rest from a very high-energy weekend when one of my church members gave me the news. Mary Beth had succumbed to her cancer earlier in the day.

GERALD THOMAS

The rest would have to wait. Nobody ever said that the pastor's job was nine-to-five. So I changed into some more professional clothes and headed out to Mary Beth's son's house to console the family and begin to prepare for a funeral. It would be my first funeral as an intern pastor.

If my church members were concerned about whether or not the intern could handle a funeral, they didn't let on. They could have called my pastoral supervisor in to do the job, but they didn't. But I wasn't about to let them down. I met with Mary Beth's family each day before the funeral talking to them about her 'favorite church hymns, some possible Bible passages we could use and I went ahead and prepared a sermon, never thinking to ask anyone what they thought about having an intern officiate at a funeral. I just assumed that I would be the person to do it.

I would employ the same principle that I used to use at the radio stations. Before you pop open the mic, know exactly what you'll say, know what you'll be doing next, always be prepared for the possible "curveball" that the situation might pitch at you, and most importantly, don't stumble over your tongue. The same principle applied to officiating at a funeral, only the mic would be on for a little longer.

And I practiced. I'd slip into the church at night, locking myself in and I ran through the funeral service, once, twice, I didn't count. I practiced my sermon. I was going to present the best funeral ever. For Mary Beth, for her family, for everyone in attendance.

The church members went into funeral mode, automatically. They knew what they needed to do, and they left me to do what I needed to do. On the day of the funeral the men directed traffic and parking,

A PASTOR'S PROFESSION

ushered, took care of the audio and video. They were flawless. My supervising pastor was sitting in the pews. Perhaps he was there as a safety net, maybe he was there to pay respect to a faithful woman of the congregation. Whichever it was, nobody said.

When the time came, I began the service and officiated my first funeral. The practice paid off; it was flawless. I felt that I had given a service fit for the person we were there to honor. As I see it, a funeral service is first and foremost a worship service. But it also honors the life of the deceased. But the whole experience should always point us back to God.

After the service had ended I was the first person out, then the congregation, about two-hundred people attended, was ushered out one row at a time. It was customary to assemble outside on the sidewalk in front of the church because there was no room to congregate inside the church. Outside people could visit and mingle about.

One of the women in on my internship committee came storming out the front door towards me. A smile on her face from ear to ear.

"You . . . Did . . . Great!" she beamed. "We are so proud of you. It's like you've been doing this for years!"

"Yeah," another said, "I think we found our pastor."

So it was true. They had their doubts as to whether or not I could pull it off, but they trusted me anyway. And I had pulled it off with flying colors. My supervising pastor concurred.

GERALD THOMAS

After the funeral dinner that the women prepared and served in the education building, I took an extra plate of food back to the Parsonage for later, and I slept. It was Wednesday and I had been going strong since the football game on Friday, and I still needed to prepare a sermon for Sunday.

There would be one more funeral that year. I received a phone call at 3:00 AM "John may have had a fatal heart attack," his brother told me. In my fogginess of sleep I wondered which part we were unsure of – the fatal part or the heart attack part.

Instead, I said, "Where are you? . . . I'll be right there," and I headed for the hospital in Lubbock, a thirty-minute drive, not knowing what to expect. Maybe the heart attack wasn't fatal. Or worse, John had died, maybe of a heart attack, maybe something else. Unfortunately, it was the latter of the two. John was full of life the day before, and suddenly, without warning, he had died in his sleep.

The church went into funeral mode again, but this time I learned something about the Ministry of Hospitality which I had never experienced to this degree until now. John was very well known, respected, and well liked throughout the West Texas farming community and people were shocked to learn of his sudden death. People came from far and wide to visit his wife at her home. There was a constant parade of people coming to the house for three days straight.

The women of the church took over the household chores of hosting all the people who passed through. They took shifts running the house, making sure the food was always plentiful, the coffee pot was perking, and the guests were fed. It was an enormous task and the women of the church stepped in so that the new widow needed not to lift finger. It was a tremendous outpouring of love and care. It was the Ministry of Hospitality at its finest.

The men of the church rose to the occasion as well. On the day of the funeral some helped to direct traffic and get cars parked in the limited space we had available. Others ushered, helping to seat people. They anticipated a larger-than-normal number of people who would be attending the funeral, so they borrowed all of the chairs that the Baptist Church next door could lend, and they set up chairs in the church basement as well as the education building with closed circuit monitors for viewing. They set up chairs in the side aisles of the church as well. No empty space would go unused.

So while the women took care of the hospitality, the men handled the physical aspects and logistics of the funeral, and they left me to my task of preparing the funeral service. It was a well-oiled machine, everyone doing their part. Five-hundred people attended the funeral for John. It was by far the largest funeral I had ever seen.

After the funeral service we did an interment service at the cemetery a mile outside of town. I traveled with the funeral director in the lead car, followed by the hearse, then the limousines with the family, followed by the rest of the cars. When I got to the cemetery and walked to the top of the hill, I looked back down the road. From where I stood I saw a mile-long procession of cars all the way back, with cars still turning onto the road from the street that the church was on. It took another twenty minutes for everyone to congregate atop the cemetery hill. When everyone had finally arrived, I concluded the funeral with the interment service.

My internship experience taught me that the church's ministry is a shared responsibility between the congregation and the pastor. We were in it together to the glory of the LORD. Everyone had their part to play in this great drama. A pastor would have a specific part to play, but it wasn't the whole picture . . . not even close!

######

INVITE THEM AND THEY WILL COME

By June I was beginning to wind down my internship year. I had the honor of confirming the faith of my confirmation students. We had worked all year toward Confirmation Sunday, which was in May. The first week of June I took them to church camp, and now the congregation would hold their annual Vacation Bible School.

V.B.S. was a yearly tradition; a perpetual motion. After one year's V.B.S. was completed a committee chairperson would be elected for the following year. The church would get monthly updates from the chairperson throughout the year on how the upcoming year's V.B.S. was progressing. They wouldn't be needing any pastoral leadership to pull this off.

I was sure that I would have my part in it, doing the opening, perhaps leading in some singing with the guitar, and a closing prayer each day.

A PASTOR'S PROFESSION

But I wanted to do more without interfering with the congregation's ability to lead themselves in this traditional undertaking. I decided that I would provide them with more kids than they had ever had in any previous year. I had no doubt in my mind that they could handle it and would even thrive with a large number of participants.

As the week got closer plans began to materialize and I wrote press releases and delivered them to the newspapers in the neighboring communities. Wilson didn't have its own paper, but the residents read the "Wilson Column" in those neighboring newspapers. But that was just a start.

On the weekend before our V.B.S. would begin, I went door-to-door in the community inviting people to send their children to our Vacation Bible School, on Monday through Friday beginning at 6:00 PM.

It paid off. We accommodated one-hundred twenty children on the first day. Registration took a little while, but the congregation handled it like pros. All the church members were there to help pull it off. My newly confirmed members were there too – all six of them – to help with the youngest children. I was so proud of them.

Each night I would look over the attendance roster. If a child was absent, I'd write up a "We Missed You" postcard addressed to them from the assortment of cards we used for Sunday school. I'd walk the cards up to the post office each night and drop them in the "In Town" slot so that the absentees would receive them the very next morning and know that they were missed. We kept the attendance up all week long.

GERALD THOMAS

We were "Cruisin' with Jesus." That was the name of the V.B.S. The church had purchased a V.B.S. in a box from a Christian publishing company. All the components were furnished. The theme was that of a cruise ship and small groups would go to different stations that were set up around the church property.

As I had anticipated, I would be called on to lead the opening, teach a song or two, and then the children would get into their small groups and go through the different stations, each small group starting at a different station. They would all end up together at the ship's "Galley" to make a cruise-themed snack. Then the entire group would go back to the church where I would provide the closing.

On Friday, however, the church members wanted to deviate a little from the curriculum. The congregation loved making ice cream. It seemed like we ate ice cream at every church council meeting. It was just what they did, and they wanted to share their love for the treat by having an ice cream social on the last evening of V.B.S.

Someone brought a rowboat earlier in the day and placed it on the front lawn of the education building. That evening everyone brought freshly made ice cream and jars of different toppings and they put everything in the rowboat. Then after the program, everyone in attendance helped themselves to an ice cream Sundae.

But before our ice cream social got underway, there was still one more part to the "Cruisin' with Jesus" week. Everyone would be in the church for the closing ceremonies. At the last minute they realized that they needed someone to play the part of Jesus.

A PASTOR'S PROFESSION

"Pastor," one of the church members said, "Will you be Jesus?"

Once again, I played the part of Jesus. This time I would play Resurrection Jesus. There were no words, instead it was part of a small drama acted out to a cassette tape which was provided in the V.B.S. program. I stood on a chair in the front of the church, draped with a long white robe. A make-shift curtain was held up between me and the V.B.S. participants, who sat in the church pews. As the music crescendoed and on cue, according to the written script, the curtain would be dropped, they would turn the spotlight on me, and there I would be with my arms extended up to the sky in bright dazzling white in all the glory of the Resurrected Lord.

It was a little over-the-top to say the least, and quite uncomfortable to be portraying the Risen Jesus. Perhaps it was even an unfair emotional tug of the participant's heart strings. But it was what it was – the Resurrection Jesus.

Something about playing the part of Jesus: you can't volunteer for the part. It has to be bestowed upon you. Other people must initiate the action. I had never volunteered to play the part of Jesus, and this was now the fourth time doing so.

My Jesus Resumé was now complete. I had played "Crucifixion Jesus" at camp in July 1983. Then I played "Personal-Appearance Jesus" twice at two different churches. Now I had played "Resurrection Jesus" in June of 1996. Twelve years and eleven months had passed between "Crucifixion" and "Resurrection."

GERALD THOMAS

Vacation Bible School was a great success. My congregation handled the large number of children like pros. I was proud of them and as I suspected they were even energized by the experience. There was one small glitch in the outcome, however, and it pertained to an identity issue of sorts.

A week or two afterwards, I was invited to lunch after church by a couple in the congregation. They were babysitting their three-year old twin grandchildren and we all went to a restaurant in the neighboring community for a casual meal. We parted ways after lunch, and I would be told later what happened later that day.

The children's parents came by to pick them up that afternoon and the children's grandmother wanted to share with their parents about the lunch outing.

"And we went to lunch today, didn't we?" she asked them.

The twins nodded in unison.

"And we had a special guest with us, too, didn't we?"

Again the twins nodded in agreement.

"And who went to lunch with us today?"

They both answered together, "Jesus."

"No, no, no," she laughed, "That wasn't Jesus, that was Pastor."

Oops. I have always told my Jesus handlers to be sure to let the children know that I wasn't really Jesus. I was just pretending to be Jesus. But this time in all of the confusion and spur-of-the-moment way in which I was asked, there was really no way to warn the children otherwise. And now the youngest children at Vacation Bible School got the wrong impression of me. I supposed that they would forget about it eventually.

About three years later another situation came up and the story found its way to me. Apparently some of the church members were discussing Vacation Bible School and remembering back when they hosted over one-hundred children the year I was there. Perhaps it was during a church council meeting or a V.B.S. committee meeting when the conversation came up.

"How come when Pastor Thomas was here, we had so many kids at our V.B.S.?" Someone asked the others in attendance.

"I think he went out door-to-door and invited people," another responded.

"Oh, Maybe we should do that."

It was true. The congregation did thrive at hosting so many children at V.B.S. and it took another three years to realize it. Now they were ready to do it up big once again.

Never underestimate the power of a personal invitation!

######

DON'T DRINK THE TAP WATER

There were only a few weeks left of my internship. Plans were already being made for the move back to Columbus and a return to the classroom for one more year of studies. Another intern had been assigned for the Wilson site. He would begin his internship here on the last week of July.

Everything had gone well, even better than anyone, including me, had expected.

Throughout the year four brothers would visit me and I welcomed them into my home, the parsonage. The boys lived across the railroad tracks with their family; mother, father, and some extended family members. In all, there were fifteen people who lived in a very dilapidated shack behind the house of their grandfather. They were quite poor. Sometimes the two older boys would stop by, age twelve and fourteen, and sometimes the two younger boys would visit, age six and ten. Often all four of them would knock on the front door. I had a large collection of movies and often I would host an impromptu movie-watching party with them in the front room.

I had also taken the two older boys with us on the youth retreat in Ruidoso and all four of them attended the V.B.S. program and sometimes the older ones even attended church and other church-sponsored programs. I even visited the entire family a number of times throughout the year at their meager home, making myself available as a pastor, even though they weren't members of my church.

The older boys weren't very disciplined, especially the twelve-year old, and I had to scold them a few times for their rambunctious behavior or just misbehaving, but for the most part they seem to be pretty good kids.

One evening the older boys were visiting and they wanted a drink of water. The drinking water is kept in the refrigerator because everyone around here knows that you're not supposed to drink the tap water. It was told to me early on that the tap water should not be used for drinking because it will ruin your teeth. That's why people who have lived in this community for a long time had brown teeth. The water tends to eat away the tooth enamel.

To combat this whole situation, grocery stores in the area provide a vending machine outside the store. Put a quarter in the slot, put a gallon jug in the product-dispenser door, and the machine delivers a gallon of filtered water suitable for drinking. The water is filtered in a variety of ways.

So the boys headed to the kitchen and to the refrigerator. Only when they got there they found something other than water. They retrieved instead a pitcher of punch. Before I got to the kitchen, they had drunk some of the punch. The problem was the punch had Tequilla in it. I had made it for myself a few days earlier.

"Noooo," I said, "don't drink that!" Too late.

When I told them that it had alcohol in it, they bolted out the back door. They always acted in that fashion, just ran away when they did something that required a negative reaction from me. It was peculiar behavior, I thought, but that is how they would react to me. I didn't think it was such a big deal, so I didn't think too much more about it.

They stayed away after that incident as though they were afraid of me. I didn't know why; it was not as though I would be physically abusive towards them. I never was. They just seemed to have a peculiar way about dealing with conflict resolution. They would run from it.

Their dad is the person who talked to the deputy sheriff who lived in town. Not over the alcohol, not over any accusation of wrongdoing on my part at all, but just over the fact that the kids had stopped visiting me at the parsonage and he thought that to be strange. It seemed to him that his sons were avoiding me.

According to the deposition transcripts, the deputy sheriff, without a complaint, began his investigation by putting the boys in the back seat of the police cruiser and transporting them to the City Hall, a couple of blocks from their house. He didn't say a word to them as to why or where they were going. The older brother began to cry. He must have thought that he was being arrested. At the City Hall he confessed that he had some alcohol at the preacher's house. Two sips is what he would later say he had consumed.

The next step in the deputy's investigation was to interview me. Yes, it was true, they had gotten into the alcoholic drink. They didn't drink too much before I stopped them. I'm sure that they didn't even realize what they had done until I told them. No one got drunk, not even close. They just went to the refrigerator and instead of retrieving the drinking water, they retrieved the spiked punch.

The deputy interpreted the boy's crying to signify that something more sinister had happened but that wasn't the case. There was never an accusation made. He cried because he was scared that he was in big trouble. No one told him why he was being, or what seemed to him, "arrested." The deputy told me to stay away from the family. Then he called my supervisor.

A PASTOR'S PROFESSION

After meeting with my supervisor, he decided to write a letter to the seminary about what he knew regarding the situation. There was no accusation of real wrongdoing, although the boy's crying made it seem like maybe there was. I was so close to leaving anyway, the seminary could deal with it when I got back to Columbus.

When I arrived back for the fourth year of seminary I had a meeting with the internship coordinator and another professor. They found that there was no real wrongdoing on my part. If there had been, the seminary would have had no regret in tossing me out by my earlobe. But the letter would stay in the file, which would be found by some overzealous lawsuit lawyers eight years later. They would exploit that letter for all they could get out of it!

######

PLANTING SEEDS

I had continued my visits to the Ranch weekly unless something at the church came up that needed immediate attention and the young men residing at the Ranch now looked forward to my visits. Even the House Parent who first cringed at the idea of hosting a preacher had lightened up his attitude towards me. Two weeks prior, I announced that this would be my last visit. They knew from the beginning that I would be there only until the end of July.

GERALD THOMAS

After my last Bible Study with them, the youth presented me with a framed certificate. It was a "Lifetime Membership" to the Ranch. Like a key to the city that doesn't really open any doors, it was a show of appreciation from them for the time I spent with them, sharing the Gospel Story in Christian storytelling, music, and Bible insight.

But the real appreciation reward came from the Ranch's Counselor/Therapist. He came out to greet me. I had never met him before this day because I'd come out to the Ranch in the evenings after the administration people had already left for the day. He thanked me and then told me that these guys were "talking about God-stuff in their sessions for the first time."

I would never have known that. These young men were placed here by the courts to work on their personal issues; to put the pieces of their lives back together, and now they were doing so with God in the picture. Maybe Jesus would be the glue that would hold those pieces together.

The parable of the sower is found in the Gospel of Matthew 13:3-9, Mark 4:3-9, and Luke 8:3-8. In these passages, Jesus tells his listeners that spreading God's word is like sowing seeds. Not all of the seeds that are sown will bear fruit. Some seeds will die even before they have a chance to take root! Luke's Gospel goes a step further to explain the parable. There are many reasons why a seed doesn't grow to maturity. "But as for that in the good soil, these are the ones who, when they hear the words, hold it fast in an honest and good heart, and bear fruit with patience and endurance." (Luke 8:15).

A PASTOR'S PROFESSION

Just like the farmers in the area, a pastor plants the seeds of faith in hopes of a bountiful harvest. It was nice to know that perhaps the seeds I planted here were at least beginning to sprout.

The day had come to make the journey back to Columbus. Church members had stopped by the evening before to help me load up the truck. The church held the traditional potluck luncheon after my last Sunday worship service to say farewell.

I had seen an entire growing season and witnessed how seeds turn into plants, how cotton is harvested and then processed into bales of clean cotton and how those bales get turned into cotton thread and weaved into giant rolls of denim for the manufacturing of blue jeans. Of course I witnessed the last half first, arriving in July in the middle of the growing season, and then I saw the first half of the next harvest, but I could turn it around in my mind easily enough. And I spent a year with the farmers who earned a living doing so.

It was a great year. Internship had helped to put a lot of pieces together for me. It solidified my calling and gave me my pastoral identity. My church members here had taught me so much; we did great ministry together.

With the good-byes already said on Sunday, I got in the truck on Monday morning without any fanfare to begin the three-day trip back to seminary to start my last year of schooling. The congregation would be welcoming a new intern next Sunday.

######

GERALD THOMAS

PUTTING IT ALL TOGETHER

I arrived back in Columbus on the evening of the third day. Some classmates had already returned, others were still yet to arrive. The August humidity in Columbus was stifling. Having been in West Texas for a year, where twenty-percent humidity was considered high, I wasn't used to the Midwest summer air. I spent the next few days settling in and visiting with my classmates as they filtered back from their internships. Everyone had stories to share, and I noticed a change in them. They seemed more pastoral now. Perhaps they noticed the same change in me.

Senior year classes would be a little more advanced now that internship was under our belts. The classes were designed to pull things together for our final year of studies. Not everyone had passed internship for one reason or another, but one of the first things that the seminary did was bring us all together to share with the entire group, including professors, something about each of our internship year. We would each have twenty minutes to give a presentation. How do you get an entire year into a twenty-minute block of time? It wasn't easy, but any more time and we'd be there for three days! The twenty-minute time limit was strictly adhered to and quickly used up.

I needed to secure a job as well. I could have easily called up the vending machine company, but I wanted to find something that was ministry related. The director of the Boy's Ranch promised me a job before I left for internship, but I wanted something that I hadn't done yet;

something to round out my ministry experiences. I called on my supervisor at the hospital where the summer before I completed my C.P.E. requirement. He was now in a different position at the agency. He was currently in charge of providing chaplains to privately owned nursing homes. He was pretty close to signing a contract with a nursing home and he would need someone to fill the contract. He wanted me to stay in touch.

After meeting with the registrar to figure out the classes I needed to take for the year, I was still nine credit-hours short for completion of the degree. I'd have to choose a few more electives. I looked through the catalog and found a very interesting Independent Study. It involved a year-long chaplaincy at the city's domestic violence shelter. There would be a major paper due at the end of the year on a subject of my choosing. I would interview professors in the different areas of study at the seminary for insight. Education, New Testament, Theology, make some kind of presentation to the social workers at the shelter, and provide pastoral and spiritual care to the residents. The class was worth exactly nine credit hours. Sign me up.

It would be about a month before the nursing home contract was signed and classes were well underway for the fall term. If I wanted the chaplain job it was mine for the year. Sixteen hours a week and twelve dollars an hour. It was the first time I made an hourly wage that was higher than the one I earned at the grocery store. I would have to provide sixteen hours of work to the nursing home, but I could decide how to schedule them. Part of the assignment included providing a weekly category service on Sundays.

Because I had waited so long into the fall semester to secure the nursing home chaplaincy, the work-study programs were limited. Work-study is a Federal Financial Aid program for students that provides grant money for working in a field of the student's study. The grant money covers half the pay while the employer provides the other half. There were only two work-study opportunities left to choose from this late into the semester. One was to go downtown to the Synod office and do filing-clerical work for the church. It wasn't very hands-on ministry-wise, but it could be good career-wise. I'd most certainly get to know people at the Synod office who could steer me into a good church when it came time to seek my first full-time ministry call. Taking this work-study program would be a very good political move.

The other opportunity was at St. Peter's in the city. I already knew Pastor Carol from when I helped out at Y.M.C.A. Night. Now she was looking for a seminary student to help at her after school tutoring program. I was still interested in learning more about urban ministries. This would help round out my ministry experiences and I hoped that Pastor Carol could teach me something about how she does ministry in the inner city. Because I wasn't very politically motivated, I didn't take the clerking job at the Synod office. I called Pastor Carol instead. She gave me the job.

The year was taking form. Besides a full load of classes, I was the staff chaplain at a local nursing home. I would also devote two nights a week at the city's Domestic Violence Shelter, and I would provide tutoring services at the inner-city Lutheran Church. It would be a very demanding schedule, but it would provide me with a well-rounded seminary education above and beyond the classroom work.

One of our first classes was Advanced Preaching. The professor started by asking for a show of hands.

"How many of you preached at least twelve times on internship?" he asked. Everyone in the class held a hand up.

"How many of you preached at least twenty times." A few hands went down. I guessed they only preached once a month.

"How many of you preached at least thirty times?" Only half of the class's hands were still raised.

"Forty times?" More hands went down.

"Fifty times?" Now my hand was one of only three left raised.

"Sixty?" He asked inquisitively. The other two lowered their hands. Mine was the last one raised. I had preached more than any of my classmates.

"You preached more than sixty times? Whew!" I had already figured it out. Every week minus the four Sundays I was somewhere else. Every Wednesday in Lent and Advent, Thanksgiving, Christmas Eve and Christmas morning, plus two funerals. Sixty-Five preaching engagements. It was a very special internship. Now I was looking forward to a very special senior year.

######

GERALD THOMAS

PASTORING IN THE CITY

The city's domestic violence shelter was "underground," in that no one was supposed to know where it was located. Only the telephone hotline is published. When a woman is in need of the shelter services, she would call the hotline and one of the residents would meet her at a predetermined public place and then she would be taken to the shelter from there.

I would also be an experiment for them. How would a man be accepted at a woman's shelter? Could a male even be a chaplain at a woman's shelter? But I actually found it helpful because when a man enters a woman's shelter, he sticks out like a sore thumb! Residents would whisper to one another, "Who is that MAN and what is he doing here?" So word spread like wildfire that I was the chaplain, and I was instantly accepted by the residents. I spent two hours twice a week visiting the shelter, talking with the women, sometimes one-on-one counseling on spiritual matters, answering theological questions, sometimes in a group in the living room.

After a while I suggested to the shelter's shift manager that I would like to hold a Bible study. It would be optional, of course, for the women who would be interested. The shift manager cringed at the idea. I'd seen that look before at the Boy's Ranch in West Texas.

"No fire and brimstone preaching," I assured her. "The Bible is full of women. Strong women of faith, especially in the Gospel. I think it could empower your residents." I didn't need her approval, but I wanted her on my side just the same.

A PASTOR'S PROFESSION

One of the things I needed to be aware of, however, was that abusers often used the Bible out of context against the women they abuse to manipulate them. I assured the shift manager that this was not going to happen. So I led a few Bible Studies on Women of Faith in the Bible.

The women helped one another. They had a terrible thing in common. They all were physically and emotionally abused. They had left their living situation with nothing but a few personal belongings, often their children, and found this shelter as a way out of an impossible situation; perhaps this would be a new beginning. Many of the women would show up with broken legs, broken arms, sometimes both. They would have black eyes that often were swollen shut. The agency would help them start a new life away from their former life of abuse. Sharing their stories with one another also empowered them. They were not alone.

The residency was constantly changing. as some residents became ready to leave the shelter, others were just arriving. One woman became a resident halfway into my chaplaincy. She was younger than most of the other women and she brought with her a two-and-a-half year old son. I happened to be standing with her and five other women when she mentioned that her husband never allowed her to discipline her son. She also talked freely of horrible physical and psychological abuse she suffered at the hands of her husband. She left in the middle of the night in fear for her life.

The young boy, like many two-and-a-half year olds, was a little brat and decided to throw an all-out temper tantrum because he couldn't have what he wanted.

"Time-out, time-out," One of the older women instructed, "put him in the highchair for a time-out." They were teaching her the basics of disciplining a two-year old.

The young mother obeyed and picked up her son who was by now kicking and screaming, his face bright red. The rest of us stood in a semi-circle around the highchair, observing. Once the child was secured in the highchair, he continued his tantrum, arms and legs flailing about.

"I kill you, I kill you. Som-bitch. I kill you," yelled the boy to his mother.

Our jaws all dropped in disbelief. No one said a word as we stared at this baby yelling obscenities at his mother. There was really nothing to say, yet we all knew what it meant. This child had witnessed more than any child should have ever seen. It was abuse handed down from father to son.

"Mmm, mm, mm, mm, mm," One of the women standing with us finally uttered breaking the silence.

My only prayer was that this baby would be too young to remember the atrocities he witnessed at the hands of his father. Hopefully time would heal his young mind.

At St. Peter's, I enmeshed myself in urban ministry, which was on one hand as different as night is from day from my rural internship, but on the other hand it was the exact same thing. Caring for the people of

A PASTOR'S PROFESSION

God. Just in different ways. Pastor Carol had begun an outreach ministry in the neighborhood of the church by reaching out to the neighborhood children. She hired two high school girls to be the tutors, a college girl to run the program, and my job was to supervise the play area upstairs after the children had completed their homework. I would also help tutor until some of the kids had finished their school assignments and wandered upstairs. I noticed early on that the high school girls who were tutoring favored the younger children, so I focused my tutoring on the older ones, the fifth and sixth graders. There were only a few of them.

I tried to be as hands-on as I could in the ministry that Pastor Carol had begun. Once a fourth-grade boy invited me to his violin recital. Of course I would go. I remembered my own childhood and all the choir and band concerts that my parents had attended. I guess a child needs to have someone in the audience for him. The violin recital turned out to be an elementary school band/orchestra/choir concert. If it was important to him, then it had to be important to me. I attended a number of school functions for the children throughout the year because I was invited to do so. I was trying to be a pastor in an urban setting, or at least learn how to be one.

One day Pastor Carol asked me to drive over and pick up four children of a single family. They lived in the neighborhood, but on the other side of the school. It would have been a long walk for them to get to the church and they were running late. When I got to their townhouse, I knocked on the front door and was let in by the children's mother. The kids were still upstairs getting ready, so I sat down in one of the chairs in the living room area next to the kitchen table.

While we waited for the children to make their way downstairs, their mother began to tell me about her six-year old son. The school was going to expel him for an incident that had happened earlier in the day. The boy had apparently threatened a classmate with a pair of scissors. An anger management problem at age six!

While she was still talking, the six-year old came down the stairs and realized that we were talking about him. He began to cry. Sob, actually. Uncontrollably. And as he sobbed, he walked across the room to where I was sitting, and he climbed up onto my lap where he continued to cry. These were tears of shame. Perhaps he was even frightened of himself and what he learned about himself today and what he was capable of doing. He sat on my lap, and he cried his young eyes out.

I remembered back when another little boy of four-years darted across the room to sit on my lap when I portrayed Jesus at his Vacation Bible School in Mt. Pleasant, Michigan. But this time, even without the Jesus costume, it was for real. Some Christians say we are the hands of Jesus when we do things for people less fortunate. Some say we are the voice of Jesus when we speak out for the voiceless. I would add that we are the lap of Jesus when we care for and console those who are ridden with guilt and shame. Even at age six. I believe that in that particular place and time, my lap really was the lap of Jesus.

######

A PASTOR'S PROFESSION

PASTORING IN THE CITY, PART II

I learned a lesson quickly enough at the nursing home. When leading a worship service for the elderly residents, keep things brief and simple. They loved to sing the old classic Christian hymns, however, and I found the guitar chords for classics like, "What A Friend We Have in Jesus," "Amazing Grace," and others. Many of my "congregation" had various levels of dementia. One woman was pretty certain that her son was the President of the United States. During the week I visited with each of them, either by walking the hallways room-to-room, or in some of the public spaces like the t.v. lounges.

One day it was called to my attention by one of the staff's social workers that I might like to visit a resident who was expected to pass away very soon. I knew who he was, and I entered his room to visit him. He had no other visitors to be with him. He quickly told me in no uncertain terms to, "Get Out!" After telling me this for the third time, I considered myself thrown out and I retreated back to the hallway. He was scared to die.

I went back about an hour later. I knew he knew who I was, but he was still unwilling to allow me in to visit. "Get Out!" he yelled. Still a third time I attempted to visit him, but it seemed like I was causing him more grief than comfort.

He died alone. It was unfortunate but that was how he chose to pass away. Sometimes a non-believer confuses the chaplain with the Grim

Reaper or sees the chaplain as some vulture hovering overhead waiting for the moment of death. It's unfortunate, but we must allow a person to choose the way in which they want to leave this world, even if it means dying alone.

The nursing home can be a despairing place. The fact is the residents' stay is less than two years and they come here for the very last part of their lives. The best we can do is honor them in the winter years of their lives and provide them with a humane existence. We owe them that much.

One day one of the social workers came to me with an idea. She wanted to sponsor a Service of Remembrance and invite back all of the families of those residents who had passed away over the last six months. She wondered if I could put together a Service for them. It was a wonderful idea. It was a way to honor those residents and their families and remind them that their loved ones were not forgotten, and neither were they. Families often formed a community here. Many family members got to know each other and supported each other and even became friends through their shared experience of visiting here.

The response to our Service of Remembrance was tremendous. I was honored to provide a brief worship service, concluding with the naming of each resident who had passed away in the previous six months. Our social workers then provided some light luncheon food, coffee and punch, and an opportunity for the families to congregate and visit with one another. They were all happy to see one another.

A PASTOR'S PROFESSION

At the domestic violence shelter, I started to tune in on what my final project would be about. Some of the residents were simply mad at God for being in this horrible situation. How could God, if God is a loving and caring God, allow such misery and suffering?

Others had what I would call a "Sunday School Faith." They held on to some basic Bible stories that they had learned in Sunday School as children, but other than that, there wasn't much more to their relationship with Jesus. But clinging to those Bible stories seemed to sustain them through their adversity.

Still others possessed a more mature faith, at differing levels, which seemed to suggest that they had a deeper understanding of faith as a continuing relationship with their Lord and Creator. A chaplain, in order to be effective here, must be able to minister to people at all of these different levels of faith. This awareness would form the basis of my year-long project.

######

THE INSTINCTS OF A BUTTERFLY AND THE COURAGE OF A LION

The Shelter participated in a national program called "The Clothesline Project." Each participating shelter nationwide would give their residents an opportunity to decorate a tee-shirt with artwork that expressed their thoughts on domestic violence. The shirts would be hung on a "clothesline" in a public place, like a shopping mall, to publicize and educate the public about domestic violence. I once saw a "clothesline" at the Saginaw Mall.

I happened to be at the shelter on the night that our residents painted their shirts, and I had the privilege of visiting with each of the women as they painted their statements for the world to see. One artist's work surprised me. On her shirt-canvas, she had painted a big, colorful butterfly. It covered the entire front of the shirt.

A butterfly doesn't begin life as a butterfly. It starts as a lowly caterpillar. But a caterpillar instinctively knows that it's not just a caterpillar but is instead a butterfly-in-waiting. The caterpillar instinctively knows that wiggling around on the ground is merely temporary; God has intended for the caterpillar to be something much greater. So, at the right time the caterpillar cocoons itself. God has put into the caterpillar's DNA an instinct that will transform it into a totally new creature, one that will no longer crawl – but instead will fly.

She had been that caterpillar. She had now woven herself into this shelter, a cocoon. Now she waited patiently to burst out as a new creation, a beautiful butterfly, in the way that God had intended for her to be. Her instincts told her that God had meant more for her than a life of abuse. She was created to spread her wings and fly.

But before her butterfly instincts could kick in, she needed the courage of a lion. It would take courage to make the change, to go from the familiar into the unknown. It would require a leap of faith to leave, when even the unknown was better than continuing in the familiar. But a lion is fearless. So in the middle of the night, she found the courage she needed to make the change. She gathered her two children, a few items that could be carried, and fled into the unknown.

Now, the butterfly-in- waiting instincts could kick in. She could now become what God had intended her to be and she waited patiently for the day when she would emerge from this cocoon, spread her wings and fly.

As I observed this artist express herself in her artwork, I was inspired, and I would use this image in my sermon for my preaching class. I wanted to share this inspiration with my classmates.

######

WHAT DID I DO WRONG?

At St. Peter's the two high-school girls worked best with the young children, first through fourth graders. There was only one fifth and one sixth grader and these two older children seemed to be getting ignored so I devoted my time to them. One day, seemingly out of the blue, Pastor Carol gave me a directive. She no longer wanted me to tutor at all. She wanted me to just go upstairs and wait for the children to finish their homework. My job was to simply supervise the play area, and nothing more. That seemed odd, but it was her church, her program and she was my supervisor, so I complied. I felt like a scolded puppy, only I didn't know why I was being scolded.

A few days later the sixth grade boy came upstairs, and he asked me, "Would you help me with my math?"

"Ask the tutors downstairs," I told him.

"I did." He said. "They told me not to worry about it." Just as I had suspected. The high school girls didn't know Sixth Grade Math.

My hands were tied. I hated that I couldn't help this boy. He was a good kid, had ADD and just needed a little extra one-on-one help to be able to understand his homework.

One day not too long after that, I was told that I had a phone call in the church office. "Who would be calling me here?" I thought. "It must be Carol." I had noticed that she was absent that day. But it wasn't Carol. It was the Sixth-Grader's mother. He was also absent that day.

"My son brought home his progress reports today," she said after introducing herself. "He's failing everything! I don't know what to do. I sent him to the after-school tutoring program," she continued, "he's not happy I'm telling you this, but I just don't know what to do."

I didn't either, as Pastor Carol had taken away any possibility for me to be of any help and the high school tutors didn't seem to know Sixth-grade math.

"Is there any way you could give him extra time, like more one-on-one tutoring?" she asked.

"Yes," I said, "I'll take him on outside of the program."

I informed Pastor Carol of the phone call I received, and my plans to tutor this boy. He was a great kid and I wanted to help him pass the Sixth grade. I didn't want to lose him to the streets.

I made time for him at his house, teaching him math. It was fun to see something that he was working on to finally click-in.

A PASTOR'S PROFESSION

"I get it! I get it!" He would say, "I'm going to the board tomorrow. I get it!" His enthusiasm was contagious. Eventually I took him to the university library to teach him how to find magazine articles for his class report and I took him to the computer lab so that he could write up his report. I helped him memorize the state capitals, a typical sixth-grade project. I took him under my wing and helped him turn his grades around. By the end of the school year he would pass the Sixth grade.

The school year at seminary continued smoothly enough. Busy, but smooth. My classmates and I would have our last interviews with our Candidacy Committees and be approved for the pastoral ministry of Word and Sacrament, provided that we passed our final classes that last semester.

Then came The Draft. The Bishops of all sixty-five synods throughout the country would get together and divvy up the new candidates based on the need for pastors in their synods. I was chosen to go back to Northern Texas, the synod of my internship. From there we would interview at churches within the synod that we were drafted to at churches in need of a pastor.

I had also interviewed my professors for insight on the Domestic Violence Shelter study. I would end up researching the idea I had about Faith levels in people. There actually had been a great deal of research on this subject so books and articles were plentiful. I would prepare a major paper on the subject and base a presentation on it for the Shelter's Social Workers.

But I wanted to do something more. I was still taken by that surprise artwork – the butterfly. A new beginning. So I decided that I would provide the shelter with a case of brand new Bibles, to be given out upon request to the residents because women often leave an abusive situation with nothing more than the clothes that they're wearing. Perhaps a new Bible could be part of their new beginning. I found a Bible publisher with an easy-to-read translation. The Bibles wouldn't be family heirlooms, they were full-sized paperbacks, but they would do the job nicely. A case of fifty would cost a little over two hundred dollars.

I learned that the seminary collects a fee from each student at registration which goes to the class to be used for class parties and other miscellaneous social expenses. The full amount is rarely used and anything leftover simply reverts back to the seminary. Perhaps a case of Bibles could be my class's gift to the Shelter.

I approached the Student Council with the idea of providing the funding. They all knew of my involvement at the Shelter by now, and they approved my purchase. We were practically finished with our seminary careers so the money I had asked for was left over and would revert to the seminary automatically. We were never going to see that money again. With the Student Council's approval I went ahead and ordered the case of Bibles and proudly presented the Bibles to the Shelter as a gift from my class. They were thrilled with the gift.

I didn't know how controversial that act would be! Many of my classmates approached me to tell me that I had no right to use class funds for purchasing Bibles. "That was our money for our use," one classmate told me. "Why didn't you just ask for donations of old Bibles? I've got two or three I could have donated."

But they missed the point. The whole idea was to give them new Bibles. My classmates didn't understand the significance of the butterfly. My classmates were talking behind my back like I had committed a crime.

Three weeks before the end of the school year, Pastor Carol desired a meeting with me, and she wanted an audience with the Director of Contextual Education. Apparently she had had enough of me.

"He was tossing the children around in the pool!" She told the director.

"Well, yeah, two years ago I did get in the pool with the children, and yeah, I helped them do flips in the water," I retorted.

"And now, he's tutoring a boy on the side," she complained.

"That's true," I said, "but I told her what that was all about. What's the problem? I think that Carol has some personal issues that is making her suspicious of everything I do," I told them. "I haven't done anything wrong, and no one has said that I have."

After a twenty-minute meeting of Carol dumping two years of her suspicions out on me, the director left the decision up to me as to whether or not I could continue working with Pastor Carol and up to her as to whether or not she wanted to have me working with her. There was only three weeks left before the year was over.

Pastor Carol left me and the director in the office. He told me that this all made him highly uncomfortable. Then he asked me a startling question.

"Why do you spend so much of your time with the underprivileged and disadvantaged?"

I was somewhat shocked at the question. I knew he was a pastor. He knew the Bible. "Because the Bible tells us to proclaim the Gospel," I said, "especially to people who are in need of it."

"I hear what you're saying," he said, "but that won't be very popular in the churches."

It seemed that my Confirmation Students in West Texas understood Church Mission better than the seminary's Contextual Ministries Director. Halfway through my internship year, the six of them approached me as a group. They all ran up to me outside and stopped in front of me. That was usually how they would get my attention. Then one of them spoke for the group.

"Pastor, we want to do the sack-lunch program."

"Oh yeah?" I said. I hadn't made it a requirement for them to do a church project or an outreach project for Confirmation. "I'm sure the women's group would let you take over." The women had been doing this outreach ministry for years.

The sack-lunch program had been a tradition at the church. When the social-service agency in Lubbock ran low on sack lunches, they would call us, and the church members purchased enough food items to make 200 more lunches. The meal consisted of items with a long shelf-life: a package of crackers, cheese and lunch meats, a fruit roll-up, a box of juice, and a bag of some healthy chips. Then the women would make up the lunches and someone would deliver them to the agency. My Confirmation Class took it upon themselves to request if they could do the work of assembling the lunches. I was so proud of those kids!

I called the agency to arrange a field trip for the kids to visit the agency so they could appreciate how the lunches they made would be used. I wanted them to see how this Christian outreach ministry that they wanted to be a part of helped the agency serve their clients. The next time the agency called for more lunches, the Confirmation Class showed up to assemble them.

Now I was being called on the carpet by the Director of Christian Contextual Education for essentially doing Christian outreach ministry.

If a church congregation merely ministers to itself, it's not a church. It's a Country Club. A Christian Church proclaims the gospel of Jesus Christ, the love of God, in every way it knows how. A Christian Church finds ways in its unique setting and location to reach out to the world around it with the message of God's love and grace. If this is not "popular" in the church, then it is because no one is leading and challenging the congregation to do it. A church without Christian mission is a dead church.

Pastor Carol left a message on my answering machine. She didn't want me to come back. I could have fought her decision; I had done nothing wrong. But with only three weeks left in the school year and major papers due and tests to study for, I simply left the situation alone. Another letter would be placed in my student file, and it would stay there until the lawsuit lawyers uncovered it. They would exploit it for all they could get out of it.

######

ORDINATION

With three weeks of seminary to go, I developed a severe case of bronchitis. Perhaps I had spread myself out too thin, perhaps the stress of major papers and tests due, or even Pastor Carol's bombshell, I would be out-of-service for a full week. My first thought, that I could stay home and catch up on studying and writing, was unrealistic. The medication made me sleep all day. I got absolutely nothing more accomplished than healing. My professors were generous by allowing me extra time to hand in my final projects and papers. My advisor even stopped by with a casserole. What a nice, caring gesture.

I had also interviewed with the congregation in Texas and had already flown down for a weekend visit. They had expressed a desire to extend a pastoral call to me once I graduated seminary. The church was as far East in Texas as my internship was West. Everything was coming together.

I finished my final papers and projects, albeit a week or two late. My professors hadn't finished grading everything yet, so my papers just went to the bottom of the stack, I presumed. After four years of seminary I had passed and then graduated. The seminary bestowed upon me the degree

A PASTOR'S PROFESSION

of Master of Divinity, M. Div. for short. I was now qualified to pastor a church.

The church in East Texas extended a call to me to become their pastor a few weeks after graduation. They had never had a pastor straight out of a seminary, so I was an experiment for them. On one hand the financial burden would be less demanding on the church's budget. But on the other hand, a pastor right out of seminary won't have the experience like a more seasoned pastor.

The congregation had just gone through a crisis and the previous pastor left on bad terms. Along with the pastor, many church members also left the congregation because of the way the situation was handled. Money was tight so the congregation was willing to trade inexperience for a smaller salary. They were willing to try something new; a pastor right out of seminary. So, with my new degree in one hand and an intention for call in the other, there was only one element left. Ordination.

The Rite of Ordination is performed at one's home congregation. They had been watching my progress from afar and now they were in charge with the laying on of hands and sending forth into the world their "son" of the congregation, the fourth man who had been raised here, attended seminary, ordained, and sent out into the world to proclaim and preach the gospel message in Word and Sacrament ministry.

The church ordination service was well attended for a Sunday afternoon. Most of these people had known me since I was a kid attending Sunday school and catechism, and now they were proud to be a part of my ordination. Family and neighbors I had grown up with were there as well. It's not every day that a neighborhood kid becomes a minister. The pastor, who had been in attendance for the three previous ordinations whispered to me that this was by far the best attended Ordination Service to date.

The pastor of my youth, now retired, would preach. The Bishop of the Synod would bestow upon me the Office of the Ministry of Word and Sacrament. A woman who I had grown up with, who had a marvelous singing voice insisted on singing a beautiful hymn. Then I would preside at the altar over Holy Communion.

It was a time to celebrate. A time to send out into the world a son of the congregation. A time to be proud. The women of the church all pitched in after the service to provide one of those wonderful potluck luncheons. Nobody would go away hungry. They would see to that.

It was also customary that the home congregation would purchase and present their new son with the pastoral stole. It would be a red stole signifying the church season of Pentecost, where the Holy Spirit moves over the people. The church goes through many seasons, and each is represented by a different color. Pentecost is the season after Easter and is associated with the work of the Holy Spirit working and moving to change people's hearts, leading them to the Lord. It is appropriate for ordination when the congregation officially sends one of its own into the world to preach and teach the gospel.

A PASTOR'S PROFESSION

My first pastoral duty would be the following Sunday when I would baptize my own nephew at the congregation of my sister and brother-in-law. Although I had baptized a number of people at my internship congregation, this would be the first baptism as a pastor. But we weren't in the season of Pentecost. The color of the season was green. I would have to go out and purchase a green stole immediately.

My parents were supportive and proud. They were at the graduation and took the whole family out for a very nice celebratory dinner. Now they would host a party after the ordination. Extended family and close friends attended, and they provided a grilled steak dinner. Family members I didn't know too well were there. They were all proud of the first minister in the family. Mom and Dad insisted on being the ones who would purchase my alb, the robe a minister wears at worship. Others provided many gifts that I would utilize through my public ministry.

Having now graduated, accepting a call to be a minister in Texas, Ordination, and now armed with my pastoral alb, a red stole and a green one, the backing of family and friends in the church, I was ready to begin my public ministry.

######

GERALD THOMAS

CHAPTER THREE

PUBLIC MINISTRY OF WORD AND SACRAMENT

THE NEW PASTORATE

I arrived in Marshall, Texas, in August of 1997. Marshall is in the Piney Woods of East Texas and is one of the oldest settlements in the state. It is rich in history and in many ways resembles the Deep South. Although six flags flew over Texas, a seventh flag flew over Marshall. During the Civil War, Missouri relocated its state capital here. The building is no longer standing, but a state historical marker marks the spot. I was told that I should never ask someone who was from here what their granddaddy did for a living because the answer would probably be that he was an outlaw. Back at the time this area was settled East Texas was an outlaw haven. I made a mental note of it.

Marshall's population was twenty-five thousand, a small city, and the people in power intended to keep it that way. As far as most were concerned, the community was too big as it was and there would be little or no major development. It was a prime location and major corporations eyed it, but like the national brewery who wanted to locate here, they went elsewhere. While some communities around Marshall grew, Marshall stayed stagnant in population growth.

The church was built in the mid-1960's, and the congregation was made-up of people who were not from this area. Unlike Saginaw, Michigan, and Columbus, Ohio, and parts of West Texas, Marshall was mostly Baptist and Methodist. The membership of Good Shepherd Lutheran Church was made-up of Lutherans from other parts of the country whose career brought them to East Texas. In many ways the church was a revolving door, hosting those Lutherans who found themselves in Marshall until their career took them elsewhere. To native Marshallites the Lutheran Church would always be viewed as "that new church down the road," even after thirty years of being there. They didn't like outsiders but needed outsiders in order to function. We would always be an outsider in a closed community on the fringe of Lutheran civilization.

The first task of a pastor is to get to know the people who make up the congregation and I got started by visiting the families at their homes and workplaces when possible. Our membership was small, about one-hundred twenty people, and they lived as far away as thirty miles in every direction. After visiting all of our families I started visiting with those people who had left the church following the previous pastor's departure. They didn't have roots in the community, and they certainly didn't have roots in the congregation and when they decided to leave, they had left for good.

As some church members left the area due to their careers, others arrived to make up for the loss but in order to survive, I knew we needed more people. I went to the city's Water Works Department every other week. When someone moves into the area an account is created in their name at their new address. That account is a public record and is public information, accessible to anyone who asks for it. This provided me with some leads for finding people who were new to the area. These are the people who might be seeking a new church home. But my efforts never amounted to even one family visiting us for Sunday worship.

Meanwhile, though, I also was busy with the ministry of the congregation, visiting members who were hospitalized, in a nursing home, or shut-ins – those who couldn't get out of their house very easily. There was the occasional funeral, and since I was ordained I could facilitate weddings, which I did a number of times mostly for young people who had grown up in the congregation and had moved away but want to be married back home. I led Bible studies, taught Confirmation Class, I attended the church council meetings and started a mid-week education program for all ages of children.

We made a lot of improvements to our property. A new road sign with a letterboard so I could put messages on it, new landscaping, new lighting in the sanctuary, a new sound system. Many other improvements to make our church a beautiful place to worship.

We were also involved in some outreach-type ministries. We took our turn at the church-sponsored food bank for two or three weeks each year. I got involved with the Ministerial Alliance, a group of area ministers who met monthly for a luncheon to look for ways to minister to the community as a whole. I took turns with other ministers to provide chaplaincy services to the hospital and nursing homes and would always be looking for opportunities to get our congregation into the mix of community-wide ministries. With my seminary experiences, there was nowhere I wasn't willing to go to provide spiritual care and counseling or worship opportunities.

No doubt about it, I made plenty of mistakes as a new pastor fresh out of seminary and I quickly learned that everything a pastor says and does is highly scrutinized. There was a critic for everything.

"What's wrong with the old sign?" One person questioned after money was donated to fund a new one.

"It's so small that no one can see it and they don't know we're here."

"I can't believe the new eternity candle is electric. Why don't we use real candles." Another said when someone purchased the candle as a memorial.

"So that the church doesn't burn down when no one is around."

"Why are the television commercials on in the middle of the night?" Someone asked.

"Because that's when they're free."

"I think the new windows are ugly!"

"I'm sorry."

And so we marched on together doing the ministry of the church and even when occasionally a family showed up only when they needed the services of the church, we did OK. Any mistakes or missteps I made seemed to be forgiven because I had a pastor's heart, I would hear. I genuinely cared for God's people, and it showed.

######

GERALD THOMAS

HITTING A WALL

Over time I found it useful to utilize a file for sermon illustrations. Whenever I came across a story that might be a good sermon illustration, I'd put it in the file. Then at a later date, if I needed an illustration for a particular sermon topic, I'd have plenty of material available to choose from. It became a helpful tool for me so that my week to week sermons stayed fresh and relevant. While preparing for one particular sermon, I pulled a story out of the file that fit very well into the sermon topic for that Sunday.

I was unaware that Bill and his entire family would be in attendance that same Sunday. Bill had developed brain cancer and he had been in and out of the hospital because of it. His cancer was different than Mary Beth's had been. While Mary Beth's brain cancer progressively lessened her physical abilities, Bill seemed just fine – until he wasn't. Then, he'd be his old self again – until he wasn't. Bill's brain cancer took him up and down like a wild roller coaster ride.

Bill and his wife had two young adult children who had very young children of their own. Earlier in the year I baptized one of Bill's grandsons. I had visited the family at their home, and I had visited them at the hospital every time Bill's cancer took a turn for the worse but by the time I was told about his hospitalization, he had bounced back again. The family did not regularly attend church, but this particular Sunday they surprised me by all being in church together.

Although I don't remember the sermon topic, I remember the sermon illustration I used that Sunday very well: Two men were sharing a hospital room. The man furthest from the outside window was blind. Every afternoon the man whose bed was closest to the window would narrate to his blind roommate the scene at the park from their 4th floor window.

"What do you see?" The blind man would ask.

"Oh, it's a beautiful day at the park. I see a couple having a picnic. I see people walking on the pathways enjoying the flowers. The sky is clear, and the sun is shining."

The next day was the same. "Tell me what you see outside today," the blind man said with enthusiasm.

"Oh, it's a beautiful day at the park. The sun is shining. I see a man walking his dog. I see children playing at the playground. I see a man and a boy playing catch with a football."

And so it went for an entire week. The blind man would ask about the scene at the park outside their window and the man nearest the window would narrate the beautiful scene at the park.

Until one night the man by the window died.

The next day the blind man had a new roommate. "Excuse me, Sir," the blind man began, "I don't mean to be a burden, but would you please tell me what's happening outside at the park?"

The new roommate was caught by surprise. "What are you talking about?" he asked the blind man.

"Well, my last roommate would tell me about what was happening outside at the park. Just look out the window, you'll see it."

"I'm sorry to tell you," the new roommate said, "but I can't see anything out of this window. No one can. This window has been filled in with bricks. It's a brick wall. They filled it in years ago when they added on the new wing."

By Tuesday Bill had fallen ill again and I went to the hospital to visit him. I had never actually seen Bill ill, and by the time I arrived on Tuesday, he seemed like he was back to his old self again. When I entered his room, Bill was alert as ever, sitting on the edge of his bed.

"Hello, Bill," I said.

"Pastor," Bill quickly responded with a grin from one ear to the other, "look out the window." He had been waiting for me.

I turned my head to the right and I couldn't believe my eyes. It was a brick wall. The window wasn't actually bricked in, but the effect was the same. The view from the window in Bill's room was that of a brick wall from the other wing of the hospital. Perhaps at one time he would have had a room with a view, but since the addition of another hospital wing, the view from this window consisted only of the brick wall of the newer wing. My jaw dropped to the floor.

With my mouth and eyes still wide open I turned my head back towards Bill, who was still sitting on the edge of his bed grinning from ear to ear.

"Well, what do you think about that?" I asked him.

"I guess it's what you make of it," he said.

I would love to say that we had an incredible theological conversation about the meaning of the story and what the wall represented, but I

A PASTOR'S PROFESSION

cannot. I just didn't know how sick Bill was and I expected him to bounce back as he always did. Later that week Bill slipped into a coma and the next time I visited him he was in the ICU. He would not bounce back this time. The brick wall would be a special story that we shared. I by telling it and he by living it.

I officiated over the funeral, which was held at the funeral home. The main funeral home in Marshall had invested in large, church-like chapels complete with pews, just like a church. It was roomy and could accommodate hundreds of people and every funeral I officiated was held at the funeral home rather than at the church. One of the hymns that Bill's family chose to sing was "Amazing Grace," one of Bill's favorite church hymns.

"We'll sing verses one and four," the funeral home's organist told me.

"No," I said, "we'll sing one, two, three and four."

"But that will take too long, we'll be here all day!" she retorted.

"We'll sing all four verses. It was Bill's favorite hymn." I insisted.

With a huff any snit, the organist turned away. I dealt with that all the time. We were on someone else's turf, and they wanted to get through the service as quickly as possible. I would have to remind them that this was a worship service, and I was running it.

I got my four verses of Amazing Grace, but I wasn't too popular with the funeral home people.

The funeral ended at the cemetery. Bill was a Vietnam veteran, and the Color Guard performed their ceremony ending in a twenty-one-gun salute followed by the presentation of the flag to his widow. It was an impressive scene. One that Bill would have been proud of.

######

THE WINE PARTY

I received a phone call late one afternoon from a daughter of Stan. "Pastor," she said, "Daddy's in a coma and has been for four days. It seems like he just doesn't want to let go. We've called everyone we can think of to visit him, maybe give him some closure, but he's still just hanging on. We thought that maybe you could stop by and talk to him."

"I'll be there at 7:00 tonight?" I asked.

Stan and Wilma had been married for over seventy years. Wilma had been an active member of the congregation. She had died the previous year. She had been our Altar Guild, preparing the Communion wine, pouring the wine into the little individual glasses each week. She meticulously took care of all of the altar tasks, changing out the different colored altar paraments, preparing the Paton, the plate that the communion wafers are placed on. She would even be sure that I had a glass of water on the pulpit for when I preached. It was through Wilma's final ordeal that I had met their four grown daughters who were now calling me to the bedside of their father.

Stan didn't get around too much in his advanced years and while I was pastor he hadn't attended church at all. But I got to know him at their home and he and I had a lot in common. Back when radio was just getting

A PASTOR'S PROFESSION

started, he owned and operated a bootleg radio station. They called it a "Bootleg Station" because it was on the air unauthorized by the FCC. This was back in the early 1930's.

"We made a lot of money on that radio station, bringing in live music and selling ads," he told me, "until the FCC ordered me to shut it down." He was pretty sure that the newspaper people had turned him in because he was taking away their ad revenue. A legitimate radio license became available, and he went to his uncle, who was a successful businessman in the community. Stan needed five-hundred dollars to purchase the license, which was a great deal of money back then. But his uncle couldn't see wasting so much money on a "passing fad." So the radio license went to another community.

He was also into photography, and I had toured his photo lab in the workshop next to the house. This was another interest we had in common. Stan and I got along just fine and now he was at the end of a long and interesting life.

I entered the bedroom where he laid, seemingly asleep but he was in a coma. All of his four daughters were in the other room, and they had asked me to talk to him one-on-one. Through my past experiences I knew that people in comas can often hear everything that is happening around them. Someone who had been in a coma and came out of it told me that she heard everything and even recognized people's voices. She just didn't understand what was happening, or why, and couldn't communicate back. With that in mind I always assumed that a comatose person is aware of their surroundings and is listening, even if this is not true in every case.

"Stan," I started, "it's me, Pastor. You know, you've done a good job. You've raised a fine family, lived an interesting life. Everything is going to be alright."

I didn't get too much more into my conversation with Stan when one of his daughters showed up at the doorway with a bottle of wine and two wine glasses. "Pastor, would you care for a glass of wine?" She asked me.

"No thank you, I'm fine," I answered politely.

"Oh no, you don't understand," she said, "me and daddy shared a glass of wine every night before bed."

"Oh, well, if that's the case, then sure. Let's have a glass of wine." I agreed.

She poured two glasses of wine, one for me and one for herself and as we sipped and talked, Stan breathed his last breath and passed into the Lord's presence.

It is truly a holy experience to be with someone when they pass from this life. It is an honor to be invited into the closest circle of family and friends at a time of the most intimate point of Human-meets-Creator. It is a time of reverence and peace in the context of pain and sorrow. Reverence and peace for the one who has passed on; Pain and sorrow for those left behind to mourn their loss. I had been present when Wilma had passed away at the hospital, and now I was present for Stan's heavenly homecoming.

A PASTOR'S PROFESSION

######

PEACEKEEPER AWARD or BREAKING THE RULES

I was elected President of the Ministerial Alliance, which meant that I led our monthly meetings and made the reservations for our monthly luncheons, and I would be the spokesperson for the area ministers if necessary. One of our biggest projects was the annual Christian Unity Service held in January on Martin Luther King, Jr. Day. It had been pointed out that Sunday Worship is the most segregated time of the week. Our service of Christian Unity was an attempt to bridge the gap in at least some small way. Attendance was good at about five hundred people each year.

The activities of the alliance-sponsored programs, including the Christian Unity Service, brought in some money through offerings which the Alliance could use for projects we decided to do in the community. It wasn't much, but it would help us do some community-wide ministry and outreach.

At one of our monthly meetings the suggestion was made that we should use some of our offering money to sponsor a scholarship. We'd give two five hundred dollar cash scholarships to graduating high school seniors, one male and one female, and we'd call it the Peacekeeper Award. Senior Scholarship Night was a big deal in the community. One night a year nearing graduation, the seniors and their families would gather together and celebrate all of the scholarships earned by the students. Not only the usual scholarships given by universities and colleges, but those that the local business community kicked in as well. And the local businesses rallied behind their senior graduates by providing thousands of additional dollars in scholarships every year.

The ministers at the monthly meeting considered the idea and favored it. But first we would have to figure out a few things. What's a Peacekeeper? And what criteria would we use to decide who gets the award? These would be things that the Alliance would have to hash out, but everyone was in agreement that the Ministerial Alliance would sponsor the First-Annual Peacekeeper Scholarship.

Because no one minister in the community knew all of the graduating seniors, we decided to ask high school teachers to vote for who they considered to be a Peacekeeper. We would have to seek permission from the Superintendent of Schools and the Principal for that. Once we had their preliminary approval, we then had to figure out what criteria would be used for voting. What exactly is a Peacekeeper? That was the question we had to answer and like any group of church people, we assigned the task to a subcommittee to report back next month.

The subcommittee consisted of me, the pastor whose idea it was, and a third pastor from a more fundamental-type church. The three of us met a couple of weeks later to work out some type of road map that teachers could use in suggesting a recipient.

"I think a Peacekeeper," started the fundamentalist preacher, "is someone who obeys all the rules."

A PASTOR'S PROFESSION

"No, I don't think that's it," I answered. "A Peacekeeper is not necessarily someone who follows all the rules." I knew where he was coming from, though. His predecessor was fired by the congregation for failing to disclose that he had been divorced. Their Christianity was rule-driven.

"Sometimes, a Peacekeeper might have to actually break the rules." I continued, "No, I don't think we're looking for Yes-Sir Yes-Ma'am type of kids. Besides, Jesus broke the rules."

"Well, the Jewish rules," he retorted.

"Jesus was Jewish, so of course the Jewish rules." I wasn't going to give in to the Peacekeeper Award going to someone who was afraid to break a rule or two for the sake of peacekeeping, whatever the definition we placed on it.

The pastor whose idea it was chimed in, supporting my position. We weren't going down that road. Somehow, we were able to come to an agreement as to a definition for Peacekeeper, and some criteria to provide the teachers at the high school so that they could cast their votes.

The teachers provided us with a clear winner, a young man and a young woman graduate who we would bestow upon the title of Peacekeeper. They would each receive a five hundred dollar scholarship and a plaque from the Ministerial Alliance. Being President, I had the honor of presenting the award and proudly did so.

######

GERALD THOMAS

MENTORING ON THE FRINGE

Sometime during my first year of pastoring the Marshall church I received a phone call from the school counselor at the junior high asking me if I would join their mentoring program. The counselor had a number of seventh and eighth graders who could benefit from having a mentor; an adult who could give a kid a little extra time, a listening ear perhaps, be a role model. I agreed to take on the role. The first two years went well enough. The third year though, the school counselor bumped things up a notch by giving me two of the more challenging students in the school.

By the time I met Mark, a seventh grader, he was already in trouble with the law. He was very impressionable and was running with some kids who were not acting in his best interest. Although he seemed like he was calm, cool, and collected on the outside, on the inside he was in turmoil.

"I can never do anything right," he would tell me. When I prompted him to elaborate, he would give examples of a home life of constant belittling. He was a twelve-year-old with very low self-esteem, and he was easily led astray. I was his mentor through his seventh grade and into the eighth.

I started visiting Mark at the school. By the next school year, however, I ended up visiting him at the juvenile detention center. He and his friends had vandalized a vacant house. They had broken in and did extensive damage to the inside of the house and now Mark was facing serious juvenile charges.

A PASTOR'S PROFESSION

Mark, already on probation for an earlier incident, was sentenced to the Boot-Camp Program for Juvenile Offenders. The program was a military-type physical endurance program that was thought to shape kids into obedience by marching them around in formation and having them do push-ups and other physical exercises in a military boot-camp style. It was also designed to simply wear the participants out.

In October of the eighth grade, Mark was required to report to the high school parking lot at 0500 hours, 5:00 a.m., Monday through Friday for a morning boot-camp session. From there he would be transported to the junior high school for a full day of classes and then be transported back to the high school parking lot for another session of boot-camp which would last until 1800 hours, or 6:00 p.m.

The problem was, he lived at his grandmother's home with his father and brother, fifteen miles outside of the city limits and they had no meaningful mode of transportation. I lived just a few blocks from the high school. So it seemed logical that I volunteer to help.

I would pick Mark up on Sunday evenings, I had a guest room that he decorated with a few of his personal belongings. This would be his bedroom during the week. I would wake him up at 4:30 a.m. each day, take him to the high school parking lot by 5:00 and then pick him up at 6:00 p.m. at the end of the day. He'd be pretty worn out by then having barely enough energy to eat, do homework, and then go to bed. On Friday I would pick him up at the high school parking lot at 6:00 p.m. and take him back to his grandmother's house for the weekend. This went on for six weeks, until December First.

I had made the third bedroom at my house into an office and in November my computer was on the fritz. It was four years old and a Sunday newspaper advertisement showed off the newest computers on the market. Faster, more memory, less expensive and I could obtain one with no money down and no interest payments. I was soon the proud owner of the newest, fastest computer on the market. I didn't realize that when I purchased it, but when I unpacked the components back at the house, I learned that the new computer came with a camera that could take pictures and videos right onto the computer. I didn't anticipate the trouble it would cause.

Mark graduated from his boot-camp and I let him keep the spare room as his own, and allowed him to stay there when he wanted to. He hated staying at his grandmother's house, as negative as it was, and he rarely stayed there. He was more apt to stay at his friends homes and when he stayed with me, I knew that he would at least stay out of trouble. I had bought some computer games if he needed something to do and we both downloaded music on the new computer before Napster shareware was found to be illegal.

It was the second week of December, a Friday evening when Mark asked if he could stay the weekend, or at least part of it, at my house. He was playing on the computer when I received a phone call from a woman who was a member of my church. She was in a local nursing home and having a difficult time adjusting to her new situation. She was crying. I

A PASTOR'S PROFESSION

told Mark from the other room that I would need to step out for a little bit, that an emergency had come up that I needed to deal with. I would be gone for about thirty minutes to an hour, but I'd be right back as soon as I could.

He responded, "OK, I'll see you later." I left him alone in the house and returned about forty-five minutes later. I didn't know it then, but Mark had been on the computer camera program when I left. His response was recorded on the video program. While I was away, he made a series of very explicit videos.

The next morning Mark asked if he could have a friend over. I knew who he was referring to; I had been the one to encourage their friendship. While Mark had self-esteem issues, Shawn was just the opposite and I thought that they could be helpful to one another. I had some errands to do that Saturday, but they could tag along. One of the errands I had planned was to buy a Christmas tree and decorate it for Christmas. We could make a day of it. My goal to steer Mark into a different group of friends and his request to have Shawn come over played right into that goal.

Shawn brought along his little brother, who was eight years old. While I entertained the youngest of the three by watching a movie video with him in the living room, I left Mark and Shawn to their own amusement on the computer. They had computer games to play, music to download and I checked in on them from time to time to make sure that they were behaving themselves. The little brother and I watched a comedy, which he loved.

When I returned to look in on the older ones, I found that they were not behaving themselves at all. I caught them exposing themselves on the computer camera. I explicitly told them that their behavior was absolutely inappropriate, and they would have to get off the computer altogether. Besides, it was already noon and we had some errands to run. It was time to redirect them into a more constructive activity.

I took them with me to buy a Christmas tree, to run a couple of other errands, and eat lunch. Then we returned to my house and I had them help me decorate the Christmas tree. By then it was getting time that I should drive them all back to their own homes. I went into my bedroom to get some presents that I planned on putting under the tree when I noticed that someone had gone through the dresser drawers. All of the dresser drawers had been left open about one-half inch. So I did a quick inventory and realized that a roll of quarters was missing.

That's when it hit me. Mark had brought with him on Friday an empty duffel bag. At first I thought that he needed the bag to take his personal belongings that he left from when he was staying here for his boot-camp. On a hunch, I went into the guest room where the duffel bag lay on the floor and I opened it. Just as I had suspected. The roll of quarters was inside it along with five dollars in loose change. I couldn't let this slide.

At first he denied it, even causing a big scene like he was offended for me to even think such a thing, but being that he was basically caught red-handed, he finally admitted to stealing the money.

A PASTOR'S PROFESSION

"How could you?" I asked, "after everything I've done for you."

"I needed some money to buy some Christmas gifts," he replied.

"I would have taken you out to buy gifts if you wanted to. You just finished boot-camp. Have you not learned anything?" I said sternly.

"Please don't tell. I'll get in trouble again," he pleaded.

"You're already in trouble again. You did it to yourself." I answered. "Here I am, looking out for you and you're sneaking around behind my back and robbing me blind!"

I didn't tell on him. I took him straight home with instructions that he would not be allowed back into my home, indefinitely. I would only visit him at the school from now on.

When I got back to my house I got on the computer and I deleted the pictures and videos that the two teenagers had made and I found the videos that Mark had made the night before and I deleted them as well. What I didn't know was that they really didn't delete altogether, rather the file simply moved to the "Trash Bin" file and that's where they stayed until January, after I came back from my Christmas vacation.

I came back to Marshall after the first of the year to a wintery mess. An ice storm had knocked the power out and the whole area was in the dark for nearly a week. Luke, a fifteen-year old whom I also mentored, lived across the street from the church with his grandmother. Their house was hit hard by the ice storm when a tree limb fell across the electric line, separating it from the house. When the electric line broke away from the utility box, it fried all of the electronics in the house, including his computer. The house was without electricity for two additional weeks after the ice storm. So when Luke asked me if he could use my computer to do some homework, I naturally wanted to help him out.

He obviously knew computers better than I did and when he accessed my computer he found the video clips and pictures that Mark and Shawn had made in the Trash Bin of the computer. He downloaded the clips onto a CD and smuggled the CD out of my house. The next day I received the phone call. He and his friends were now demanding that I pay them five thousand dollars.

It was absurd of course. I wasn't involved in any of the clips or the pictures at all. But some people would be embarrassed if this ever got out. The five thousand dollar blackmail demand turned into buying him a new truck. That's where I could stall him. He was only fifteen. He couldn't own a truck yet. That would give me some time to get that CD back and destroy it.

Besides, I was already interviewing for a pastorate at another church. It wouldn't be long before I would be leaving Marshall anyway.

######

ARRESTED

It was the first Friday in May 2001. A beautiful spring day. I had danced with the blackmailer and his friends since January, all of us acting as though nothing was wrong. I had been interviewing at other churches since November – before any of this happened. The church in Marshall wasn't going to grow and attendance was in a downward trend. Too many members were moving out of the area and not enough Lutherans were moving in. In addition to that there were some deaths of some key people and I read the proverbial writing on the wall. This congregation couldn't sustain a full-time pastoral ministry.

I had already accepted a call to a larger, more stable congregation. This church was more like my internship site, an older multi-generational family church that was not as susceptible to people moving in and out to sustain the ministry. Just a few more days and I wouldn't be here anymore. I could just fade into the sunset.

I usually took Fridays off, my Sabbath, but there were a couple of things I needed to do to prepare for Sunday. I needed to put in a couple of hours in the office, then I'd have the rest of the day off. When I pulled into the church parking lot at 9:00 that morning, Luke the blackmailer and one of his friends came running out of Luke's grandmother's house from across the street and greeted me in the parking lot.

"Why aren't you in school?" I questioned them.

"Senior Skip Day," Luke answered.

"But you're not a Senior. You're both just Sophomores."

"Everyone's doing it," he said.

"I hardly doubt that. You both need to go to school!"

"We want to go over to your house," he said.

"No way. You're skipping school and you're not going to my house. Besides, I've got some work to do." I knew that they weren't going to go to school, but I wasn't going to condone their truancy. I went into the church. They stayed in the parking lot and played basketball.

By Eleven O'clock, I was done for the day. Everything was now ready for Sunday Worship service – my last one in Marshall. The boys were still on the basketball court.

"Come on, I'll buy you guys some tacos. Then you need to go to school." I told them. The truth was, all I had in my wallet was three dollars. Tacos were cheap. On the way back I pointed to the high school parking lot. "Look," I said, "everyone is not skipping school today." I directed their attention to the student parking lot. There were plenty of cars parked in the lot. "I want you to get there for your afternoon classes." I dropped them off in the church parking lot, which was next door to the high school. Then I went back to my house for the rest of my day off. "Go to school," I told them one last time.

At Two O'clock I decided to get out of the house. I stopped at the ATM machine, withdrew twenty dollars and ate a late lunch at the fast-food burger joint. Then I decided to make a visit to Mark's grandmother's house. Mark had gotten in trouble again with the law and since January he had been incarcerated in the Texas Youth Commission. TYC was usually the end of the line for young criminals. It was prison for kids. The Youth Judge had concluded that the Boot Camp Program hadn't made an impact on him, so this time Mark was sentenced to a year in Youth Prison. He was thirteen years old. He would turn fourteen in July.

A PASTOR'S PROFESSION

I was interested in visiting with his grandmother, but I also wanted to get an update on Mark's progress. I told her to let him know that I was asking about him and that I hoped this would bring an end to his troubles with the law. This was when I learned that Mark would be locked up until December. By the time I got back to my house it was Five O'clock.

It wasn't but ten minutes later that there was a rap on the kitchen window, where I was standing over the sink. I didn't see them pull up, but two plain-clothed men were standing on the other side of the window flashing their badges. The badge identified one of the men as FBI. The other man was a detective from the Marshall Police Department. The FBI Agent told me to come out of the house. I complied and was promptly handcuffed, my hands in front of me rather than behind, and I was placed into the back of a police cruiser and then transported to a holding cell at the city jail.

The FBI Agent would testify that they had received a phone call stating that a preacher in Marshall was being blackmailed. The agent replied that they needed a little more than that to go on. The caller called back a second time with more information and exactly which preacher in Marshall was the subject of the blackmail. With that information, that FBI agent and the local police detective had been working all day on the case. They had gone to the high school to interview Luke, but of course Luke had skipped school that day. They finally caught up with him and he told them where they could retrieve the CD.

The FBI Agent then applied for an arrest warrant and a search warrant which he promptly executed on me. While I was in the holding cell at the city jail, police were searching my house for evidence. Evidence of what, I had no clue.

It was about Eight O'clock when they came back and retrieved me from the holding cell and they took me to the detective's office at the police station. Maybe by now they had realized their mistake, that I had committed no crime. I signed a paper recognizing that I understood my rights – the right to remain silent and the right to have an attorney present. I wanted to hear what they had to say and the only way to do that was to sign the paper.

Then the questioning began. I answered their questions about the day, including taking the two teenagers to buy some tacos before telling them to go to school. I told them about the other teens having made pictures and videos and about me kicking them off of the computer for doing so, I told them that I erased the files they made but I didn't know at the time that those files merely went to the Trash Bin. I told them that Luke had found them, downloaded them onto a CD, smuggled the CD out of my house and proceeded to blackmail me for a truck, which I had no intention of purchasing for him.

Then the Agent asked me, "where did you go for lunch?"

"I went to Burger King," I answered.

They looked at me as though they had just caught me in the lie of the century. "Now I know you're lying," the Agent said, "you went to Taco Bell."

A PASTOR'S PROFESSION

"No . . . well, I told you I went to Taco Bell to get the kids some tacos, but later I went to Burger King for lunch."

"You're a terrible liar," snapped the Agent.

"Why don't you stop lying and tell the truth," the detective said.

"Everything I'm telling you is the truth," I said. But then I realized that they weren't interested in the truth at all. They were just going to twist everything I said around to suit their own agenda. They were just trying to trip me up on my own words. So at that point I just shut my mouth. They could talk all they wanted but I would say nothing in return. Maybe I shouldn't have been so willing to talk at all. But I had nothing to hide. But then again, they didn't seem to care what the truth was.

#####

MAKING BOND

I spent the night in the city jail and at 6:00 a.m. I was transported to the County Jail and booked in. I still didn't know what the charge was. I was put in the holding cell with all the arrestees from the past twenty-four hours. Every day at 8:00 a.m., all the new arrivals would see a Magistrate Judge via closed circuit-television who would officially arraign everyone, inform the arrestees of their charges and their rights, and set a bond.

One by one we made our way to the front of the line and stood facing the camera. I had been charged with one count of sexual performance of a child and bond was set at fifty thousand dollars. After everyone saw the Magistrate Judge, we were put back in the holding cell to work on making bail. A Bail Bonding Company was willing to bond me for a ten-percent fee. I would have to come up with five thousand dollars cash. I had three thousand dollars in the bank. I would need another two.

I would have to make the most difficult phone call of my life. First I called my sister, then my parents.

"What?" they said in disbelief when I told them where I was.

"I'm in jail," I repeated. "I can't talk too much about it right now, but I need two thousand dollars to get out." They put together the money and I assured the bondsman that I would have the money as soon as I could get to the bank, which closed at noon. It was Saturday.

The bondsman made my bond and was waiting for me in the visitor's area when I was released at eleven-thirty. Thirty minutes left before the bank closed. The bondsman would drive me back to my house so that I could get my car and then follow me to the bank so that I could pay him. Plenty of time.

But a (not so) funny thing happened on the way to my house. As we waited to turn left into my driveway because of oncoming traffic, we got rear-ended by an SUV. The seat belts work well. The car, however, was totaled. The same officer who had transported me to the county jail earlier that morning was now in front of my house writing a police report.

"What was your name, again?" he asked me. Now I was a witness to an accident.

Needless to say, we miss the bank's noon closing. "Just stop by and pay me on Monday," the bail bondsman told me.

A PASTOR'S PROFESSION

It was a foregone conclusion that I would be fired from the church, so I didn't show up on Sunday, which would have been my last day anyway. So much for "innocent until proven guilty." The story had already been all over the news, even though there wasn't all that much to say. The detective and the FBI Agent worked together but hadn't even investigated yet; they wouldn't interview anyone for another week.

On Sunday the Bishop would be at the church, a vote would be taken to remove me from the pastoral office, I knew that much. After Sunday's church service, I waited at my house for the Bishop of our Synod and the President of the congregation to visit. They didn't show up, but I knew that my public ministry was over.

######

GERALD THOMAS

PART TWO

A PROFESSION OF INNOCENCE

A PASTOR'S PROFESSION

CHAPTER FOUR
PRE-TRIAL

SENSATIONALISM IN JOURNALISM

On Monday the television reporters were out in full force, reporting an arrest that hadn't even been investigated yet. Journalism is sensational when a news story is focused on things other than the facts, designed to press the emotional buttons of the audience. Local TV reporters love sensationalism because it gets them ratings. The television reporter from Texarkana decided to do an on-the-street interview with parents picking up their children at the closest elementary school. The school was in the next neighborhood over, across one of the busy main streets, at least half a mile away from my house. I would have had no reason to even go by that school.

"How do you feel," the reporter would ask parents picking their children up from school, "that he's living down the street?"

"Oh, it's just terrible," a parent would respond.

"How do you feel that he's out?" Came a question to another, "he has a right to make bond."

"What about our rights?" Came the response.

Sensationalism at its finest. I wasn't ever accused of trying to lure little children from the elementary school. But the TV reporter made it seem like I was.

The uncle of the blackmailer happened to be one of the reporters. He took every opportunity to sensationalize the story, even driving all the way across the state to interview people in West Texas. Whenever a sexual abuse story came up in East Texas, he would report, "and it may be related to the Thomas case."

There was never a relation to anything else, but using certain words in reporting gets the reporter off the hook. Words like, "maybe," "could be," "helps to," are not stating actual facts. So using these types of words means that a fact "might" be true. This is also known as poisoning the jury pool. Not once did the TV reporter add a disclaimer statement, "Oh, and by the way, the blackmailer is my nephew and I have a personal interest in the outcome of this story." He would go on pretending that he was presenting a fair and unbiased account of a news story.

I spent the week shopping for an attorney and found one who I thought was capable. To pay the twenty thousand dollar fee, I cashed out my retirement account. I was still short but family members helped by pitching in the rest.

Throughout the week some of the clergy in the community stopped by to visit, which was very helpful. My Bishop, the so-called "Pastor to the Pastors" kept away. Some members of my church were also supportive. I was grateful for them as well.

######

A PASTOR'S PROFESSION

ARRESTED, AGAIN?

The news media kept the story at the top of the broadcast, or on the front page of the newspapers throughout the week, speculating, sensationalizing on the content of the case. That Friday, one week after my original arrest, the Agent and the Detective went to Waco to interview Mark where he was incarcerated in Youth Prison. They also interviewed the other teenager on the videos. I wouldn't see the police reports for another two months.

I received a phone call around Eleven O'clock on Friday from a pastor in the community who I knew. He asked me to meet him for lunch. I was headed out the door to meet him at a local restaurant when the police arrived. I wouldn't make the lunch engagement. Instead I was arrested again. Without any words, the officer took me back to the county jail and booked me in.

"There must be some sort of mistake," I thought, "I did this already."

Once again I waited in the holding tank with all of the new arrestees until the following morning and then waited my turn in line to see the Magistrate Judge via closed-circuit television. The charge was the same as the first, "Sexual Performance of a Child."

"There must be a mistake," I told the Magistrate Judge, "I was just charged with this one week ago."

"This is a new charge," he answered, "and it says here that there are charges pending in another county."

"That's a lie," I said, "there are no charges in any other county."

"Your bond is set at fifty thousand dollars."

It was a lie. There were no charges in any other county. The FBI Agent and the Detective lied to the Magistrate Judge in order to get him to set a higher bond. It worked. This time I wasn't going to be able to make bond.

On Monday I received a visit from my newly-hired attorney. She advised me just to stay put for now. "If you bond out," she said, "they'll just make up a new charge and arrest you again. You'll just be wasting your money. Wait until you're indicted by the Grand Jury. Then we'll get a bond set and they won't be able to rearrest you and we'll know what we're dealing with."

It was getting to the middle of the month. The rent on the house was paid up until June First. Something would need to be done about that. A few church members visited me at the jail and they became my life-line. My parents took a week off from their lives and came down to Texas. They stayed at the house and began the process of packing up the household belongings. They received special permission from the Sheriff to visit me every day that they were in town. Then, with the help of a lot of men from the church, they put everything I owned in the storage unit.

I settled in as best I could at the county jail, where I would remain for the rest of the summer.

######

A PASTOR'S PROFESSION

FEDERAL HEARING

The first indictment came from the Federal Grand Jury. Two counts of Inducing to Engage in Sexual Conduct of a Child, two counts of Producing a Performance that included Sexual Conduct, and one count of Possession of Child Pornography. The first step now was to have a hearing on whether or not the court would grant me pre-trial release. In the Federal Court System, there is no bond or bail, rather a decision to either hold or release a pre-trial detainee. That decision rests on the court alone. A Federal pre-trial officer came to the jail to conduct an interview. He would put together a very thorough report and recommendation which the Federal Magistrate Judge would rely on.

A few weeks later I was taken to Federal Court, a ninety-mile trip, for my pretrial release hearing. I was taken there by the FBI Agent and the Detective. "Where's your car?" The FBI Agent asked me.

That was definitely outside the realm of investigation. "Don't worry about my car," I said, "It's in a safe place." We had already made arrangements with the auto finance company and deferred two payments. That bought me a little time. Now the FBI Agent has made it his personal mission to find and repo my car!

We pulled up to the side entrance of the courthouse. The television cameras were stationed outside and were rolling. The cameras weren't allowed inside the courthouse. My attorney was already inside waiting for me and she had a copy of the report and recommendation from the Pre-trial Release Officer.

"I'm afraid I have some bad news," she said, "the Recommendation is to not allow you out for pre-trial release." I couldn't understand why. The interview had gone very well. My attorney couldn't understand it either. "But," she went on, "the prosecutor is on vacation this week. They're going to reschedule the hearing for next week."

Once I was back downstairs in the holding cell, my attorney let me read the police report based on the interview they had conducted with Mark where he was incarcerated in Waco and my heart sank even further. The police report stated that Mark told them that I had forced him to take those illicit videos! I couldn't believe my eyes. He stated that I told him to "do it right" or he'd have to go back to his grandmother's house and he didn't want to go home so he had better do it right. It's exactly what a kid with low self-esteem might say. I was devastated. It was absolutely untrue. But now I knew what I was dealing with, a chronic liar. They took me back to the jail depressed and totally devastated.

Exactly one week had passed and this time the Sheriff's Deputies took me to the courthouse. My attorney had scolded the FBI Agent and Detective for transporting me. They weren't supposed to do that. The cameras were rolling again as we pulled up to the side entrance of the courthouse. My attorney was already waiting for me inside.

"I've got some good news for you," she said calmly, "since last week they've changed their recommendation."

"What?" I asked, not believing what I had just heard. After a week in the dumps, it wasn't registering.

A PASTOR'S PROFESSION

"Yes. They are now recommending pre-trial release. I think the main guy was on vacation and when he got back, he didn't agree with it and well, they changed it."

"Wow!" That's all I could think to say.

She continued, "but they still want to argue to keep you in, I don't know why, the judge is going to put a lot of weight on the recommendation, but the judge never saw the first report, so I'm ready."

"Well, great," I said, not believing this new turn of events.

The Federal Prosecutor put the FBI Agent on the witness stand for questioning. His main reason for wanting me to be denied pre-trial release was his fear that I would contact the government's witnesses. Of course I had no intention to do that. Then it was my attorney's turn to cross examine the Agent.

"Why did you re-arrest him one week after his original arrest?" My attorney started out.

"We were afraid that he would take off," the Agent answered.

"But when you re-arrested him, he was where he was supposed to be?"

"Yes, he was."

"Did you have a reason to stop by his house earlier in the week?"

"Yes, we did."

"And why was that?"

"We had taken pictures of the interior of the house, the different rooms and the like, and we forgot the camera, so we went by on Monday to retrieve it."

"So you knocked on the door, Mr. Thomas was at home, and you asked him for the camera you forgot?"

"Yes we did."

"Did he give you the camera?"

"Yes, he did."

"So, Mr. Thomas was cooperative?"

"Yes, he was."

"And he was where he was supposed to be?"

"Yes, he was."

I sat there, thinking that finally, someone is defending me, and doing a fine job of it. Then my attorney changed the subject.

"Now, you say that you're afraid that Mr. Thomas is going to contact the witnesses. Since after you told him not to contact anyone involved in the investigation, do you know if he has?"

"Not that I am aware of."

"Now, isn't it true that Shawn has left the area and moved to Dallas?"

"That is correct."

"And Mr. Thomas wouldn't know where to locate him?"

"That's correct."

"And isn't it true that Mark is locked up at T.Y.C. in Waco?"

"Uh. . . I think he's out."

A PASTOR'S PROFESSION

My jaw dropped. Here it is June and he was supposed to be locked up until December. They gave him a deal. Either directly or indirectly, Mark got paid for his statement. I was certain of it. Over a year later I would stumble on the 'smoking gun.' It was a letter from the Youth Judge stating, "if I would have known about this I would have never sent Mark to the youth prison." Mark, at all of fourteen-years old, had figured out that he now had a get-out-of-jail free card.

After the hearing was over, the Magistrate Judge made her decision. The Federal Court would grant me pre-trial release. We already had a plan in place. I would be allowed to go to Florida and stay with my sister and brother-in-law. My sister would put me to work at her pizza restaurant and I would return to Texas if I was needed for court.

But there was still one more hurdle before I could go to Florida. I would have to wait for the State Grand Jury to indict me. So back to the county jail I went until the Grand Jury convened in August.

On the trip back to the county jail, the Sheriff Deputies commented to me that my lawyer really did a great job. I was beaming from ear to ear, so happy that finally, for the first time, I had been defended.

######

THE STATE BOND HEARING

The weeks rolled by in the county jail. Some of the older members of my church stopped by to provide me with the support that I had once provided them. The Grand Jury met once every ninety days and in the first week of August they handed down their own indictment. It was identical to the Federal indictment. Two counts of inducing sexual conduct, two counts of producing a performance that included sexual conduct, and one count of possession of child pornography, all based on the blackmailer CD. The next step was the bond hearing in State Court.

It was the first day of August, ninety days after my initial arrest when I went before the District Judge, the Honorable Bonnie Leggat, in order to decide my bond. I stood in front of the judge's bench, my attorney behind me to the left. On the rights stood the District Attorney and the Assistant District Attorney. No one else was in the courtroom. The State argued that under no circumstances should I be let out on bond. I would be a danger to society and besides, I had no real connection to the community. Who's to say that I wouldn't just take off altogether?

"Show me some evidence of that," the judge told the D.A., "besides I have this Federal Court Order here in front of me saying that he can go to Florida."

"But that's just too far," the D.A. argued, "and it's too easy to leave the country from Florida."

The judge wasn't buying their argument. "He doesn't have a passport, does he?"

"No, your Honor," replied my attorney.

"And besides, he'd of had to have surrendered it to the Federal Marshals." Then, the judge turned to me.

"Mr. Thomas, you're not going to swim to Cuba, are you?"

A PASTOR'S PROFESSION

I smiled. "No, Your Honor." This was going my way.

"And you don't own a white Bronco, do you?" She asked in reference to the O.J. Simpson chase-scene that was still fresh in everyone's mind.

"No, I don't, Your Honor." It was definitely going in my direction.

Then she turned to the D.A. and his assistant. "Unless you can show me some kind of evidence, I see no reason to deny a bond in this matter." They looked back at the judge with blank stares.

There was no evidence and the D.A. knew he had lost the argument. So he went to Plan B, to make the bond as high as possible. Judge Leggat wasn't buying that approach either.

"We never do this piece meal bond, fifty thousand for this one, twenty for that one, fifty more for another one." The D.A. was losing Plan B as well.

"One hundred thousand for everything," she finally determined. "If he can't make bond, he can reapply at a later date for a reduction." The hearing was over.

The first call I made was to my Bonding Agent – the one who originally bonded me in May only to get his car totaled in a rear-end collision while taking me to get the money. "I'll write the bond for six thousand," he said. I told him of my intentions of going to Florida and staying with my sister, coming back to court as needed. "No problem," he said, "I'm not worried about you."

And he didn't have anything to worry about. I was in no way considering absconding from the law. The only way through this was to go directly through it. I was a religious leader in this community. I would go forward with as high a degree of dignity and certainty in faith as I could possibly muster. To do anything otherwise would be to go against everything I stood for and all of my preaching these past five years would then have been in vain. No, he had nothing to worry about from me. I would march head-on, straight into the fires of hell if necessary, God be with me!

The second call I made was to a dear friend in the congregation who would go down to the Bonding Agent's office and put up the money for the bond. I was almost there.

Now it was nearing Five O'clock on Friday. It had been three hours since my friend paid the Bondsman. Something was not right, so I called the Bonding Agent and my agent answered.

"What's going on?" I said, "Why am I still in jail?"

"We're working on it. Things just got a little complicated. You'll probably have to stay the weekend. But don't worry. We're going to get you out. We're working on it right now."

"Alright." What else could I say? I had absolutely nowhere else I could go, and I wouldn't be getting out today.

Monday morning at Ten O'clock came the announcement over the speaker. "Thomas, pack up. You made bail." They wouldn't have to tell me twice. I was ready. They processed me out, handed me my personal possessions – watch, wallet, clothes, and I headed to the front lobby where my bondsman was waiting for me.

A PASTOR'S PROFESSION

He took me to his office which was in walking distance from the jail. When I entered the front door of the small office, there were six Bond Agents sitting around the office, all of them looking at me, as if to say, "so this is the guy, huh?" They had been working all weekend to pry me out of that jail. It seems as though the Sheriff made it difficult and balked at the idea that I was going to Florida. Even with two court orders, one Federal, one State, the Sheriff wouldn't sign off on the bond. I'm only assuming that the Bonding Company used a different location in another county to get the necessary signatures. I'm really not sure exactly how the details played out.

Then I was introduced to an older white-haired gentleman who had come in all the way from Dallas to help work out my bond. He was the owner of this and a number of other bonding companies throughout East Texas.

One of the other agents spoke. "When Mr. Salvador tells us to get you out, we're going to get you out."

"Wow," I thought. I had become somewhat of a trophy. A prize fought over between the Sheriff and Mr. Salvador and his staff of bonding agents. But I was out and very grateful for that.

"And by the way," Mr. Salvador said, "before you leave for Florida, be sure to pay us another four thousand dollars."

"O.K." I answered, even though I figured that Mr. Salvador didn't realize that you can't get blood out of a turnip. And right now I was indeed in the turnip category as I was fresh out of money. Apparently, one of the Sheriff's sticking points was that I hadn't posted the entire ten percent of the bond. Somehow I would have to raise another four thousand dollars. Half came from my parents and the other half came from another friend, the pastor from a neighboring church who had been supportive. Bless their hearts for coming through for me!

I called another friend from the church to come pick me up and take me to my car. The tires were low on air and it needed a jump start because it had been sitting idle since May, a solid ninety days. But we got it going and I spent some time visiting a few of my church members, those who had shown some support for me throughout the past three months.

I had also called my attorney to let her know that I was out. We would meet for lunch the next day. "I'd pay," I told her, "but my credit cards probably don't work anymore." She laughed. I gladly let her pay for lunch. She gave me a few hundred dollars which was our original agreement when I signed my retirement check over to her. I needed to purchase auto insurance and gas and food for the trip to Florida.

"This will get you to Florida," she said, "after that you're your sister's problem." My sister already had plans of hiring me as soon as I got there. I'd have some cash in my pocket from tips starting on the first day of work.

I purchased the car insurance and still had over one hundred dollars for the trip. I gassed up the car, got the oil changed, and then I headed east towards the Sunshine State.

######

A PASTOR'S PROFESSION

ATTACKING THE WARRANTS

It felt good to be in a new place, one where nobody knew what was going on in my life back in Texas. Like she had promised, my sister put me to work right away. It also felt good to start making some money again, being productive in some way. Of course, it was somewhat of a façade because what was going on in Texas wasn't going away simply because I was one thousand miles from it. Even so, it was a nice break from it all.

I was instructed to phone in once a week to my bonding agent, just to let him know that I was still where I was supposed to be. He had also told me that if I needed to go out of town, just let him know in advance so that if anyone asked him, he could tell them that he knew where I was. I would also be required to phone in once a week to my Pre-Trial Release Officer for the Federal Court. I was transferred to the Orlando Office for that purpose. In all, these tasks would take me less than five minutes a week to complete.

My attorney was working on a legal brief on my behalf back in Texas. She was arguing that the whole search warrant was baseless from the very start, an unconstitutional search and seizure of my property and person. When a law enforcement officer wants to arrest someone and search a person's home for evidence, they have to provide an affidavit to a judge or magistrate judge who will then determine whether probable cause exists to support the warrants. Only after the warrants are signed by a judge or magistrate can the police act on the warrant.

GERALD THOMAS

Most affidavits for an arrest or search warrant are two or three pages long, detailing the officers investigation. The FBI Agent's affidavit for my arrest was one paragraph consisting of three sentences. My attorney would argue that it was so 'bare-bone' that it could not be relied upon by police who executed the warrant. Added to that was the fact that the FBI Agent went to a state court to get the necessary signatures from the judge. Knowing that his bare-bone affidavit wouldn't cut it in Federal Court, he took it to state court because a Federal Agent will pretty much get anything he wants walking into a state court. Now we would challenge the warrant in Federal Court. If it doesn't stick on review, the whole case would go away.

My attorney wrote a twelve-page brief and submitted it to the Federal Court. The prosecutor would have sixty days to write a response, which he did. The Magistrate Judge wasn't quite satisfied so she ordered oral arguments. She wouldn't let us know exactly what she was looking for from the oral arguments, so both the federal prosecutor and my attorney were kept in the dark, but they would both have the chance to present their arguments face-to-face in front of the Magistrate Judge.

A court date was set and I would make the thousand-mile trip back to Texas in order to be present. This time I would be dressed in a suit and tie rather than a jail jumpsuit and I walked in through the front doors. No television news cameras this time. This court appearance was off the public radar.

I walked through the metal detector inside the front door and as I put my keys back into my pocket and my watch back on my wrist, the U.S.

A PASTOR'S PROFESSION

Marshal who was working the metal detector asked me, "Who are you representing?" He apparently thought I was an attorney.

"Well, actually," I said, "I'm being represented."

"Oh, O.K." He answered, "go right in."

My attorney was already in the courtroom. The FBI Agent was also there to defend his arrest warrant. He sat at the table with the prosecutor and I sat at the table with my attorney. They both presented their arguments in front of the Magistrate Judge in turn with vigor. My attorney then confronted the FBI Agent for cross-examination.

We had met before the hearing began and my attorney showed me pictures of all the things that were taken during the execution of the warrant. This was the first time I saw all that they had taken. Mark had apparently left a pair of underwear in the dresser drawer of the guest bedroom. They had taken that. They also took photos of my brother's and sister's children. They took three bottles of alcohol and twenty business cards from the foreign exchange students from when I helped chaperone the foreign-exchange student trip out West. Each business card had the student's personal contact information to where they lived in a foreign country. Everything they took had a logical, innocent explanation.

"Why did you take these items?" My attorney asked the Agent.

"Uhm. . . " He paused to think of the right answer. "We thought there might be more victims." He answered.

Just as I had suspected. This was a witch-hunt right from day one. He hadn't even done an investigation until a week after my arrest. It was a fishing expedition which turned up nothing. Besides, there were no 'victims.'

I would go back to Florida and await the Magistrate's decision which was handed down a few weeks later. "Granted in part, Denied in part" was the decision to our Motion to Dismiss based on an illegal search and seizure. Even though the affidavit was 'bare-bones' there was at least minimum probable cause to support the warrant. But everything taken besides the computers would be thrown out as being outside the scope of the warrant. The bottles of alcohol, family photos and everything else could not be used against me at trial, except for the computers.

We had won, but at the same time we had lost. The case would march on.

######

TRYING TO PROVE INNOCENCE

It was now February of the next year, a full nine months after my original arrest. The Marshall Police detective continued investigating the case, going back to requestion Mark and Shawn and others on a monthly basis. Now, nine months later, there were no accusations of any sexual misconduct from anyone. The worst statement against me was from Mark who claimed that I directed him through the use of threats to make those illicit videos. It was a lie, of course, I wasn't even in the house at the time.

"Let's send a private investigator out to talk with them," my attorney suggested, "maybe a P.I. can get to the bottom of this."

"Great idea," I said, and the next time I came to Texas I met the Private Investigator hired by my attorney.

"Look at his statement, I told the investigator, "'Do it right or I'm going to take you home.' That's just silly. This is a statement from a kid who has very low self-esteem, who feels that he can never do anything right. And any ways," I continue, "how do you do it wrong?"

The P.I. chuckled. "Yeah, I see what you mean."

I continued, "The police are using Mark's self-esteem issue to lead him down the path they want him to go on. "The investigator assured me that he would do what he could.

The investigator first went to Dallas to talk with Shawn. He was now living with his mother there. Shawn had never said anything negative about me. But his mother politely told my investigator that Shawn would not be speaking to an investigator about the matter.

Then the P.I. went to visit Mark who, now out of youth prison, lived with his grandmother. The investigator was permitted to take Mark outside to talk, away from the rest of the family. But just when the investigator felt that he had gained a rapport and was ready to move into the real issues of the interview, Mark's grandmother stormed out of her house with a telephone in her hand. She handed the phone to the P.I.

"Under no circumstances will my client be talking with you today," the voice on the phone declared. "If you want an interview it will be with all of my clients at one time, and I'll be present with them." It was the lawsuit lawyer, another force now working the case behind the scene. The P.I. wrote in his report that he was pretty sure that Mark was about to tell the truth, but he was shuttered by the lawsuit attorney. The whole investigation was a bust, except for learning that there was now a lawsuit already in the works.

It was now March and I had to show up in State Court for an appearance. It ended up being just a docket call where there were no new developments and the case was pushed back again. I really didn't even have to be there and had made the thousand mile trip for nothing. I might as well check in with my attorney.

"Would it help if I took a polygraph test?" I asked her.

"Don't take a polygraph test if you can't pass it," she warned me.

"Oh, I can pass it. All I have to do is tell the truth. I had nothing to do with directing or making those videos in any way," I exclaimed. "I didn't even know about them until days later."

"Okay," she said, "I'll set one up."

I met with the polygrapher on a Saturday morning. We first went through the questions to be asked. He would ask a total of ten questions with three of them being the 'hot' questions, or questions involving the issue to be tested. The other seven questions are 'factual' questions like "Is your last name Thomas?" He would ask the ten questions three different times, each time in a different order. Then he would measure the difference in my breathing and heart rate and compare those physical responses of the hot questions against the factual questions in order to determine whether or not I was telling the truth on the hot questions.

The three hot questions revolved around my knowledge of Mark making illicit videos. Mark told the FBI Agent that I had directed him to make the video clips. Question: "Were you in the room when Mark made the videos?" Answer: "No." Question: "Did you direct Mark to make videos?" Answer: "No." Question: "Did Mark make the videos for your pleasure?" Answer: "No."

The polygrapher wrapped a cord around my chest to measure my breathing. He attached some wires to me to measure my pulse rate. And he attached a device to my finger to measure perspiration. Then he asked the ten questions, three times in a different order and watched the computer screen for the results after each of my answers.

When it was all over, the polygrapher asked me, "So, how do you think you did?"

"I passed," I told him, "and if I didn't pass there is something wrong with your machine."

"You passed," he finally admitted, "I'll write up a report and give it to your attorney."

"Thank you," I said. I knew I would pass, but now I had something concrete to back me up. I called my attorney. "I'm done," I told her, "and just for the record, I passed. He'll be sending you a report."

"Oh, you don't know how happy I am," she said.

"Yeah, me too." With that accomplished, I headed back to Florida.

######

THE OTHER INVESTIGATION

It wasn't long after my return to Florida when FedEx delivered to me a copy of the first lawsuit. There would be other revisions to come in the following months. Two lawyers were busy working on their own investigation. Now they were ready to begin the process of suing. They weren't just suing me, far from it. They were suing every entity of the church that they could think of!

They had identified nine teenagers who knew me, even though none of them had ever made a complaint about me. Apparently, whether they had a sexual-abuse claim against me was a trivial matter. The nine teenage boys would be the plaintiffs in the suit; Luke the Blackmailer and two of his friends, Luke rarely visited me alone; he would always bring one or both of his friends with him. Then there was Shawn and Mark and Shawn's eight-year old brother, followed by the two brothers in West Texas and the newest mentor kid that the school assigned to me after Mark was incarcerated, whom I had only met twice at the school for a half-hour session each time.

The first order of business was to have all nine of them interviewed and examined by a psychiatrist in Dallas. The psychiatrist's report would be the foundation for the lawsuit, which was paid for by the lawsuit lawyers. The psychiatrist determined that each of his subjects, except for the eight-year old, was either suicidal, or highly suicidal and would require a lifetime of therapy at a cost of hundreds of thousands of dollars and in some cases, millions.

"Really?" I thought. "And no one has ever claimed to have been sexually abused by me, not even after a year since my original arrest. Incredible!" I couldn't see them pulling this off. The usual way this worked was that after a case of sexual assault went to court, then the lawsuit would begin. This was backwards. It was the tail wagging the dog.

I watched the interview video. They all denied that anything had happened. The older brother from West Texas admitted that he had "two sips" of alcohol. Nothing more. It was a total sham, but this would get the lawyers the depositions they needed in order to hone the lawsuit. There would be three more editions of the lawsuit, each one redacted further from the previous one.

I, too, would be called back to Texas for a deposition. Six hours of questioning by the head lawsuit lawyer. I chose to plead the Fifth on advice from my attorney, who was not invited to the deposition. The Fifth Amendment of the Constitution declares that an accused has the right to remain silent. With charges still pending, nothing good could come from answering these questions. I had already seen how the FBI Agent and the Detective took the truth and then twisted it around to use against me. I wasn't going to fall into that trap again.

GERALD THOMAS

There were ten lawyers also present, each one representing a different entity of the church being sued, there to defend their unique position. I had no lawyer. Those ten lawyers were not there to defend my interests.

The lawsuit lawyer asked a lot of questions designed to get under my skin; to rile me up. But if I answered even one of those stupid questions, I would be legally obligated to answer them all. I sat there for six hours and had to take everything he was dishing out. "I declined to answer any questions under the Fifth Amendment of the United States Constitution." I would repeat it after each and every question throughout the entire six hour deposition.

Then each church lawyer wanted to ask questions as it pertained to their individual clients. They went around the entire table, and one by one I told them that I declined to answer their questions, each time citing the Fifth Amendment.

######

COPPING A PLEA

The Federal trial was scheduled for June. My attorney had shared the polygraph report that I had passed with the Federal Prosecutor. He was now willing to drop all of the charges if I would plead guilty to one count of Possession of Child Pornography based on the blackmailer's CD. If the images were on the computer hard drive, then according to the law at the time, I was technically in possession of those images. The Federal Prosecutor would also cap the sentence at sixty months in prison, rather than the one hundred twenty months if I were found guilty by a jury. I would do forty-four months because in the Federal system a prisoner does eighty-five percent of the sentence. With "good-time" credit, in other words behave in prison, the earned good-time would make up the other fifteen-percent of the sentence. Then there would be three years of "supervised release," kind of like parole.

"Did you talk to the State Prosecutor?" I asked my attorney.

"Yes I did," she answered. "The State is also willing to drop all of the charges if you plead guilty to Possession, and they'll run it together with the Federal time. You'll do it all in Federal."

This was something to consider, especially if the State and Feds were on the same page. It could be an easy end to this mess. My public ministry career was ruined even if I were found to be not guilty. No church would ever consider me. Now, after a year of investigating me, requestioning all parties involved over and over, nothing else had surface, and rightfully so, because I had never sexually abused, assaulted or molested any kid. The State and the Feds seemed satisfied now that there was nothing more to come from this investigation.

######

THE FIRST BOMBSHELL

Over a year since my initial arrest, one of the mentor kids decided that he was harboring a secret all this time. Through the lawsuit lawyers 'investigation', he would say that he was sexually assaulted by me. The

State would add a second-degree charge onto the list of charges. The details were sketchy, he couldn't remember when it happened, just that it happened sometime while he was at least fourteen years old.

I decided that I would not veer off course. I would meet this new charge head-on. So I went back to Texas to turn myself in. By now I knew the routine at the jail. If I got myself arrested by 7:00 a.m., I could see the Magistrate Judge at the 8:00 round-up, post bail and be back on my way by 10:00 at the latest.

I walked into the Warrant Officer's office at the Sheriff's Department. In Marshall, the Sheriff's Office, jail and courthouse are in the same building, making it a convenient one-stop-shop. It was about 6:30 a.m. when I arrived, and I introduced myself to the Warrants Officer on duty, telling him of the outstanding arrest warrant. He looked it up on the computer. "I'm not showing a warrant for you," he said.

"Yes, there is a warrant," I said, "and I want to take care of it."

He made a couple of calls and in a few minutes the detective handling my case arrived. The detective confirmed that in fact there was a warrant but he would have to look for it somewhere in the building.

"Do you want a cup of coffee?" the Warrant Officer offered.

"Sure," I answered.

So while the detective and his staff scoured the building in search of the warrant, I shared a cup of coffee with the Warrant Officer. Finally at close to 7:15, the detective came back with the arrest warrant. With the warrant in hand the detective walked me over to the jail. No handcuffs, I was the one trying to get myself arrested. Unfortunately, I missed the cut-off time to see the magistrate over closed-circuit. I would have to wait another twenty-four hours and be arraigned with all of the day's new arrestees tomorrow.

The next morning I was arraigned on one count of sexual assault of a minor under the age of seventeen, a second-degree felony. I made bond and was processed out by 10:00.

It was an election year and the District Attorney would make it a point to be visible at every turn of my case. The next day the newspaper ran a short article. It was spun in the D.A.'s favor. "District Attorney Rick Barry asked Thomas to come in and he was arrested without incident."

The paper made it sound as though there was a shoot-out. Not even close. The D.A. did not request my presence and I had a heck of a time getting myself arrested at all.

"Someone at the local paper was trying to help get the D.A. re-elected," My attorney would tell me when I read the article to her.

######

WRAPPING UP THE FEDERAL CASE

I told my attorney that I didn't think it was fair that I could be guilty of possession of images that were just floating around on the hard drive. I had deleted them. "It's like going through someone's garbage and saying, 'aha, look what we found?' If it's in the garbage, how can I possess it?" I asked.

"Interesting," she said, "but they could give you 10 years for each one."

"I just don't think it's right."

It was the first week of June and the Federal trial was looming. A Federal jury pool was on standby and I had a major decision to make. Take the deal or go to trial. I looked over a catalogue of all the federal prisons in the country. I would be considered a low-security prisoner. The possession offense was a non-violent crime. And there was a low-security federal prison outside of Detroit, back home. The low-security prison in Milan, Michigan was one of the older prisons in the country, but it catered to non-violent, white-collar type prisoners.

"Can I request a particular prison?" I asked my attorney.

"You can," she said, "it's not guaranteed, but they try to put you close to home." She knew the federal system, having been a federal prosecutor before becoming a defense attorney.

So the plan was, if I took the plea deal, I would go to a low-security federal prison and then the State would come and get me, take me back to Texas where I would make that same deal and then the State would take me back to the federal prison in Michigan, or wherever I was, to serve my sentence.

"You can do this, Jerry," she said, "but if you want to go to trial, I'm ready. It's your decision."

There's a reason why ninety-seven percent of federal defendants take a deal. The prosecutor comes at you really hard so that you're looking at a lot of prison time. Then they have some room to work with on cutting a deal.

I thought it over and then called my attorney a few days later. I would take the deal. A court date was set for Tuesday when I would appear in Federal court to enter a plea of "guilty" to one count of possession of child pornography.

Except there was one problem. The judge had changed my court date to Monday at the last minute. The television cameras were there. The FBI Agent was there. Even the District Attorney was there, all standing out on the sidewalk in front of the courthouse. The D.A. had made the sixty-mile trip so that he could get his face in front of the television cameras. There was no other reason for him to be there. This was a federal matter. Except it was an election year.

But no one told me that the date had been changed. I wasn't there. They made the trip for nothing.

My attorney ran over to the courthouse to make the case. "Your Honor, no one bothered to tell us that you changed the date from Tuesday to Monday. Mr. Thomas is here in town, but he's under the impression that his court appearance is tomorrow. I called him, but he's not there." I was out visiting some church people for lunch. I had no idea that the judge had changed the court date.

After my lunch and visit I came back to the motel where I was staying. The front desk people were excited, but not in a good way. "There was a detective out here looking for you," they told me.

"Now what?" I said, "What did he say?"

"He wouldn't say." They responded, their eyes widened with curiosity.

I called my attorney and found out what had happened. "It's not like you were prohibited from leaving your motel room," she said. "It's all taken care of, though, the judge changed the court date back to tomorrow."

An hour later there was a knock at my motel room door. It was the detective. "Just wanted to remind you about your court date tomorrow," he said.

"I know," I said sharply. "Why do you think I'm here?"

"Just relaying a message." He replied. It was a message from the FBI Agent. I think his middle name was "Overkill." Dramatic Overkill.

The next day, Tuesday, I went to my court date and pled guilty to the charge. The prosecutor would still be required to tell the judge what the evidence would be had they gone to trial. First, he had to prove "Interstate-transport." This is what gives the federal court jurisdiction over a case, and it is usually misunderstood by people unfamiliar with the law. The computer was assembled in Texas using parts made in other states and other parts of the world. The software came from Washington State where Microsoft Inc. is headquartered. The computer was then purchased by Best Buy Inc., warehoused in Oklahoma before it was shipped to a store in Texas where I purchased it. That satisfies the Interstate Transport Act. It has nothing to do with committing a crime across state lines, although this too could satisfy the Act.

A PASTOR'S PROFESSION

The prosecutor then laid out the blackmail scheme, how the CD had been confiscated from Luke, and why the arrest was made. He followed that up with computer forensic evidence proving that a particular computer, registered to me, stored the images found on the CD on the hard drive of said computer. It was enough for the judge to concur with my guilty plea and he then pronounced me "guilty." I would come back to court in about thirty days for a sentencing hearing.

The television reporters were all there waiting to get a camera shot. They were on the steps of the main front door. But they miscalculated which front door my attorney and I would be using. Consequently the shot of my entrance into the building would be from far away. The cameras were not allowed past the front door, but the reporters were in the courtroom taking notes. Then they were waiting again for my departure on the front steps with their cameras rolling. This time we would have to walk right through them.

They can surround you as you walk on the sidewalk. They just cannot hinder your movement. They surrounded us, asking questions to rile me into saying something. It riled my attorney enough. She barked at them to back off. I had nothing to say to them. I walked calmly to the car with my attorney, my head held high. I owed them nothing.

It was the top story on the evening news. One reporter said that I was guilty of interstate transport. He obviously didn't understand the concept. Another reporter began his story with my attorney telling them to back off. The Blackmailer's uncle had gotten a shot of me walking through the parking lot. He was two hundred yards away and zoomed in for what appeared to be a close-up. His narrative was that I was running from the camera. None of them reported about the blackmailing scheme, instead reporting that the young man gave the video clips on a CD to the police.

I sat in my motel room, watching the news reports on the three television stations at 6:00, thinking, "Were you not all in the same courtroom that I was in?" Sensationalism at its finest.

The next morning I went back to Florida.

######

THE SENTENCING HEARING

A month later, the first week of July, I traveled back to Texas for the sentencing hearing. A Pre-Sentencing Investigation had been conducted, a very detailed biography that the judge would use for sentencing. My sentence though, was predetermined at sixty-months.

I rode with my attorney for the ninety-mile drive to Texarkana. The Court used different courthouses for different parts of the process. My plea bargain was made in Tyler. I had a seminary friend, a classmate of mine who joined us at the last minute. He followed us in his own vehicle. He had come to lend some moral support.

When we got close to the courthouse, we saw that the television reporters were already set up on the steps of the old courthouse awaiting our arrival. Both of us had already had enough of these guys. She pulled into a parking lot and made a phone call.

She was talking to someone in the U.S. Marshal's Office, located inside the building. "Would you do me a big favor," she said to someone on the other end of the phone, "we're trying to avoid those reporters and cameras at the front door. Would you please meet us at the side door? I'll drop Mr. Thomas off there if you'll be kind enough to open the door for him. We're just a minute away."

The Marshal was kind enough to meet me at the side door, the door I had used when I was transported here while in jail. My attorney and my friend parked in the lot across the street from the courthouse and walked in through the front door, separate from one another.

"Where's your client?" the reporter sneered.

"Oh, he's already inside," she retorted. The reporters missed their first shot at getting me on camera.

Once inside I sat in the courtroom with my attorney, waiting for my name to be called. I wasn't the only one with court business that day. The lawsuit lawyer was also present and so were some of his clients. They had no business to attend to, he was just trying to acclimate them to the inside workings of the court. My friend was roaming around on his own. I pointed out to my attorney who some of the plaintiffs were. She had seen their names only on paper. Now, here they were – some of them – live and in person, watching and listening to the court proceedings.

When my name was called, my attorney and I took our places in front of the judges bench. We stood there as he thumbed through and read the paperwork. "Is there any conditions to this plea?" he asked us.

"Yes, Your Honor," my attorney spoke up, "it's conditional on the State giving the same thing."

A little more reading and the judge pronounced the sentence. Sixty months in prison with three-years of supervised release.

"Your Honor," My attorney spoke again, "could Mr. Thomas have thirty days before commencement of sentence to get his affairs in order?"

The prosecutor said that he had no objection to that request. In fact, he added, it would be about forty-five days because they were backlogged.

"We'll send you a letter when the time comes telling you when and where to report," the judge said, and with that the hearing was over.

Then my friend met up with us. He had something to report. "I wasn't trying to overhear them," he told us, "but I couldn't help but hear them. It's not like he was telling a secret, and he didn't know who I was. They're planning a little ambush when you go outside. They're going to get you out there, surround the car and block you in and then stage a protest for the cameras."

"Really?!" I said.

"We need an exit strategy and I've got an idea on how to do it," he said, I was all ears.

"I'm parked across the street. If you go out the front door and look to the right you can't miss me. I'll be standing there. I'm parked in the first row, facing the courthouse." Then my attorney would go out and drive around the front of the courthouse from the West end to the East end. The camera crews stationed at the front door would assume that she was going around to the other side of the building to pick me up on the east-end door and then they would follow her around. This should open up the front door for a clean exit.

"I like it," I said.

No sooner than we had our plan of escape figured out, the lawsuit lawyer approached us. "I've got some papers for Mr. Thomas to sign," he started, "I don't want to do it in the courthouse, wouldn't be appropriate to sign them in the building. We can sign them outside. OK with y'all?"

So this was the set-up for their little ambush. He wants me to sign some papers outside, in front of the cameras. Cameras that couldn't be brought into the courthouse. He had no idea that we already knew everything about his plan.

My attorney played her part perfectly. "Can I sign them? I'm his lawyer." Of course she could, he would have to agree to this request. But that got me off the hook entirely.

It came time for us to execute our plan, a counter-attack to their staged demonstration. My friend went out first and took his place next to his truck. I stood at the window on the second floor hallway. The window overlooked the front steps of the courthouse where the television cameras were stationed. To my right was a staircase that would take me right to the small lobby downstairs next to the front door. When I saw my attorney drive around the front from the right to the left, I would dash down the staircase, out the front door and into my friend's waiting truck parked across the street. I'd be out of the area before they knew they'd been had.

I watched intently from the second-story window for my cue. There was no other traffic around this century-old courthouse, not another car in sight. They'll see her and then think they had figured out where I was going to exit the building and then follow her around to the opposite end.

There she was, driving around from right to left, never once looking at the camera crew, just looking straight ahead, as if she was attempting to sneak by, right in front of them.

"There she is!" I heard one of the reporters shout. They took the bait and rushed to meet her at the East end of the building. I raced down the staircase and checked the front door. The coast was clear and I calmly walked out. I immediately saw my friend to the right, leaning against the front of his truck, arms folded, watching his plan unfold.

One of the camera operators decided to go to the opposite way and positioned his camera on the West-end door, the door I had went into that morning and each time I went to this courthouse while in custody. I passed within twenty feet of him but he was too busy watching the door that he thought I might come out of; he missed me completely. No one covered the front door. Our little counter-attack and exit strategy had worked flawlessly. I walked across the street without being seen to my get-away vehicle.

Parked next to my friend's truck was the FBI Agent and the Detective who had made the trip together. They were also standing in front of their vehicle. They had seen the whole plan go down and they were now laughing wildly.

"Boy, you really know how to dodge them," the Agent said to me between laughs.

"Yeah," I said, "I'm getting pretty good at it." I got into my friend's truck and we drove off.

My attorney met up with us in the lobby of the hotel where I was staying and the three of us took a booth in the far corner. She handed me the newest version of the lawsuit that she had signed for and I looked it over. "Total trash," I said, "How can he say these things? None of it is true."

"The thing about writing a lawsuit," my attorney said, "you don't have to prove any of it."

"Look!" I said to my friend, who was also my seminary classmate, "he's suing each and every one of our seminary professors!" and I started reading off the names that my friend would recognize. "Incredible! Maybe I should sue his law-school professors." That brought a smile to all of us.

That evening I watched the three newscasts on television. I wondered how they would pull it off without having a clip of me walking in or out of the courthouse. That's what they get for trying a stunt like that, creating a story that was staged for the cameras.

The news story didn't make much sense without me there. The uncle of the blackmailer reported, "Thomas managed to elude our cameras but we caught up with his attorney." A shot of my attorney signing some papers atop the hood of her car. A shot of her walking away, sunglasses over her eyes, refusing to make a comment. I could imagine their news directors asking them, "how could you not get the subject on camera?" I smiled at the thought. It was a good day. We had thwarted a staged demonstration, leaving them with little to talk about. Their plan to sensationalize the story had failed.

######

THE SECOND BOMBSHELL

One of the lawsuit lawyer's clients was absent from the courtroom that day, Mark – the one who had lied about my involvement in making his illicit video clips. It's not like he needed to learn the inner workings of the courtroom, he had already been through the court system plenty of times in his young life. Now he was in the County Juvenile Facility again, this time he was caught with some of his friends stealing CD players out of cars. His fate was sealed. He knew he was headed back to Texas Youth Prison. He had gotten his first sentence commuted when he was able to come up with a lie – one that the FBI Agent and the Detective readily accepted, even though the evidence didn't support it. This time, he knew they would throw the book at him, giving him an even longer sentence than the first. He did not want to go back to Youth Prison.

It was now July, fourteen months after my original arrest. The detective had investigated thoroughly. The lawsuit lawyers had been talking to him regularly as well. Mark knew he had a way out of his dilemma – a get-out-of-jail-free card. He would tell them exactly what they wanted to hear. He would make himself out to be the victim by playing into the hand he was dealt.

In doing so I would become the villain and he would be set free; he wouldn't have to pay for his crime. But in order for his plan to work a second time, the story would have to go way over the top.

According to the police report, the lawsuit lawyer visited Mark in the County Juvenile Lock-up. Mark told him that he had a secret, one that he hadn't told anyone before now. He told the lawsuit lawyer that he had been raped by me on three separate occasions back when he was thirteen years old.

The lawsuit lawyer had finally gotten the story he was looking for in order to push the lawsuit forward. It was a win-win situation for both of them and a losing proposition for me. By making himself out to be the innocent victim, he would be forgiven for his crimes and I would be looked upon with disdain, contempt, and even hatred.

The lawsuit lawyer called the district attorney with his great discovery. The D.A. in turn called the detective who went to the Juvenile Detention Center and wrote down the story. Was it Mark's idea or was it the lawsuit lawyers idea?

I received a call in Florida from my attorney regarding the three new first-degree charges that would be added to the list. She told me that the D.A.'s Office had told her that they were not going to arrest me again, instead we could take care of the matter the next time I was in Texas. So

I went about my routine in Florida. Five weeks from now I would be starting my Federal sentence. The letter I was waiting for was still four weeks away.

But a week later there was a knock on the front door. It was the Florida County Sheriff's Deputy and he had come for the sole purpose of arresting me for the new charges in Texas. The deputy was kind enough to allow me to call my attorney. She called the D.A.'s Office and then called me back. They had lied. Apparently it didn't look good when someone who was accused of a hideous crime turns himself in. They wanted to show the community that they go after their criminals and haul them into jail to await the delivery of justice no matter how far away they had to travel.

The Marshall Texas Detective and a co-worker made the thousand mile trip to Florida to retrieve me from the county jail. I learned later that the Sheriff refused to make the trip. "If you want him, you go get him," he told the D.A.

Heading back to Texas in the back of the police cruiser, I told the detective, "I didn't do this."

"It's best you don't talk about your case right now," he answered.

"But you're the detective working this case, right?" I asked.

"Yes, I am," he said matter of factly.

"Well then, here's my statement," I replied, "I didn't do this."

He shrugged his shoulders as if to say, "the truth is merely a trivial matter." Then he sped back to Texas in record time.

A PASTOR'S PROFESSION

"This is it," I thought, "with three weeks left it would make no sense to bond out." I was put in an isolation cell. I had already been convicted in Federal Court and they wouldn't allow me to mingle with the pre-trial detainees.

But one day, just after the jail personnel had passed out lunch, a Bologna sandwich and a peanut butter sandwich, the door to my single-man ten by ten concrete cell opened and the jail Sergeant stood in the doorway holding a piece of paper.

"The judge is giving you a P.R. Bond," she said.

I was taken by surprise. "What?"

"You can go. It's a personal recognizance bond. It means you don't have to make bond." She explained.

"Really!?" I was still shocked. Such a turn of events. She handed me the bond paperwork.

"It's not signed yet. It'll be signed this afternoon." She said.

I flushed my sandwiches down the toilet and headed with the Sergeant to the front door. Once again, I was free.

I walked down the street to my Bonding Agent's office. He was just as surprised as I was on this turn of events. "The judge P.R.ed me," I told him, and I handed him the P.R. bond.

"I wish it were signed," he said.

"They told me that it would be signed this afternoon. I wasn't about to argue with them about it."

He seemed to understand. He made a copy for his file and returned the paper to me.

But now I had another immediate problem. When I was arrested in Florida I had twenty dollars in my wallet. The Florida jail charged me ten dollars for a "booking fee" and one dollar a day to stay there, another ten dollars. They had taken all of my money. Now I was penniless, I was hungry, and in Marshall, Texas, I was homeless. Maybe I should have eaten those sandwiches!

I had a good mind to march right down to the police station and demand that the detective take me back to Florida. Instead, I called one of my pastor friends, the same good friend that had helped me with the extra bond money that Mr. Salvador demanded. He picked me up at the bonding office, took me to eat, bought me some clothes and a bus ticket back to Florida. I was blessed with great people on my side who I could rely on. Praise God for good friends!

######

THE LONGEST RIDE

Two weeks after I returned to Florida I received the letter from the Federal Court. I was to report to Milan, Michigan Federal Correctional Institution on the following Monday by 4:00 p.m. I purchased a bus ticket to Indianapolis where I would visit my other sister. My brother would take me the rest of the way the following day.

On my last day of freedom, I watched my nephew, the one who I had baptized five years earlier, leave for his first day of kindergarten. I would

A PASTOR'S PROFESSION

be starting my first day of prison later that same day. It was a four-hour drive from there. My brother and I stopped for one last free-world meal, a good burger and fries, before we walked through the front door of Milan F.C.I. one minute to four. Once inside, we walked up to the counter.

"Cutting it pretty close, there huh?" The guard of the counter remarked.

"Why give them any more time than they've got coming?" I responded.

"I can't argue with that," he said. "Now go have a seat in the waiting room. And don't go anywhere."

I laughed.

######

A NEW CAREER

I settled into my new residence. The facility is old, one of the oldest prisons still in existence, but a newer addition had been built, two new resident buildings and a rec yard outside the original structure. The rec yard was huge. It included a half-mile paved track which surrounded two baseball diamonds, a soccer/football field, covered picnic tables and other recreation activities like weights, horseshoes, and an arts and crafts shop. The prison also housed a factory which produced metal-fabricated filing cabinets which are utilized in federal offices world-wide.

The factory worked three shifts making filing cabinets of all types and the prisoners were paid for their labor. Not like real-world pay, but adequate enough to buy whatever you wanted at the prison commissary, pay for phone calls, and still save something for when you are released. My job was in the chow-hall dish room. It's a start.

It was a low-security prison. The prisoners here had been convicted of non-violent white-collar offenses. One young man I met passed a counterfeit twenty-dollar bill. He had copied a twenty onto his computer, and when he sent the computer in for repairs, the copied bill was found on the hard drive and matched to a list of counterfeits that had been circulated. Another prisoner had been convicted of making and selling unauthorized passports. There were some bank robbers who had used a note to rob a bank with, not a gun, so it was considered a non-violent robbery, and there were plenty of people with a variety of drug convictions.

One day as I was making my way to the rec yard, a prisoner who I had never met stopped me. "How'd you do it?" Is all he said.

"Excuse me?" I replied.

"I know who you are. You're the C.E.O. that's been on the news, embezzling all that money. I just want to know, how'd you do it?"

I smiled and walked away. I guess I could be an embezzling C.E.O. It's a lot easier to be that than a minister who was wrongfully accused of sexual assault. Since they have me figured out as being an embezzling C.E.O., I guess I could play that part.

A PASTOR'S PROFESSION

I was at the Milan Federal Prison for one month, taking in everything that was my new surroundings when the Texas Sheriff deputies made the trip to Michigan to pick me up and take me back to Texas for my appearance in court. I was going back for the sole purpose of signing some papers and making the deal formal.

######

A NEW D.A. IN TOWN

A few days after being back in the county jail, having been booked in for the fifth time, I was appointed an attorney. I could no longer afford to retain my own, but it was for the purpose of making this deal formal.

"I got a guy off a murder charge back in 1984," my newly appointed attorney boasted. That was nearly 20 years ago, I thought. What have you done lately? But this case wasn't so difficult. Just sign some papers for the plea deal that was pre-arranged.

By October I had a court date set. My name was called out to go to court. My new attorney was there to greet me and we quickly made our way to the courtroom and took our seats.

The Assistant D.A. stood to speak. "Your Honor, the State Is offering a plea deal. If Mr. Thomas will accept one count of possession of child pornography the State will drop all the other charges, but reserve the right to prosecute on the sexual assault charges. The state further agrees that the charge would run concurrently with the Federal charge that he is currently serving."

GERALD THOMAS

"There will be no deal on this case," the judge said, "Mr. Thomas will go to trial on all counts. I don't know why we're here. We already discussed this." They had. The lawyers had already figured this out before I came into the courtroom.

My lawyer spoke up. "I want it on the record, Judge, that you won't honor this deal."

The judge said, "Well, I want it on the record that I didn't know about the deal."

"I need time to prepare, Judge," my lawyer responded. "I thought we were just going to sign some papers on this case. Now you want me to go to trial."

"We'll reconvene next month and go from there," the judge said.

It was an election year and in November the people cast their votes. For as much publicity the District Attorney had gotten surrounding my case over the past year-and-a-half, he should have been a shoe-in for re-election. Instead he lost to a hometown candidate who had been raised here, left to get a law degree, some experience as an Assistant D.A. elsewhere, and was now ready to come back home and make a career in the courthouse of his youth.

When I went back to court in early December, after the elections but before the new D.A. took office, the exiting D.A. didn't show up. He would give the new D.A. the task of trying my case. The new D.A. would take office on January First, 2003. My case would be at the top of his to-do list.

A PASTOR'S PROFESSION

While I waited for my new attorney to familiarize himself with the case, I wrote a letter to my previous attorney. I had written many pages of notes that could now help in building a defense. I asked her to send my new attorney all of those notes and especially wanted a copy of that polygraph report. Perhaps by showing this new D.A. that I had passed the first round of lies against me, I could get another polygraph test on the new set of lies, the ones that hadn't been made-up yet when I took the first test.

By January, my new attorney possessed the papers from my previous attorney, including the polygraph report, which I expected would give me some credibility. I asked my new attorney to share the report with the new D.A.

He did so and reported to me the D.A.'s answer. "We don't need a polygraph test to convict you." I didn't get another test and couldn't afford to pay for another. The new D.A. had his own agenda. The voting public would expect him to win his first case on the docket. He was looking for a conviction at all cost. The trial was now scheduled for February 4, 2003, twenty-one months after my initial arrest.

######

DISCOVERY

My attorney met with me three times before the looming trial date to go over the evidence and discuss how best to present a defense. He gave me a box of papers that he received from the D.A., the exact same papers he had to work with. I spent the next week familiarizing myself with the contents. The next time we met I would have my chance to explain myself and show him what I had uncovered.

"Look at this," I told him. It was a computer generated timesheet that showed the exact time that the boys made each of the video clips. They were one and two minutes apart, varying in length, about ten of them in all. With the time-sheet in hand we watched the videos. I wanted to match the times to each video.

"Look at the last one they made," I continued, "it's the one where I walked in on them and saw what they were doing. While I'm still talking, it's cut off, right before I told them that they had to get off the computer for misbehaving. It's cut off! You have to tell the jury this. Because according to this time sheet, it's the last one they made. It proves that I told them to quit doing that on my computer. I kicked them off the computer but that part is cut off. This has been tampered with. The proof is edited out." I hoped that my attorney would be able to show them this little detail that my innocence hinged on.

"Look at this," I told him, "the ones that Mark has said that I'm in there directing him, clearly I'm not. Look at this," I said. You hear me talking way in the background, but you can't hear the words of what I'm saying. That's because I'm not in the room. This is where I had to go on an emergency run to the nursing home. But, you can hear his response. He shouts, 'OK, I'll see you later.' That proves I'm not there. Anyone can see that, can't they?" I asked my lawyer. He looked back at me with a blank stare. Wasn't he getting this? "Besides, I passed the polygraph test on this."

Then I read through the police reports. It seemed clear to me what was driving this whole mess. "The police report is clear about how the accusations were made," I said, "This is actually written well. It says," and I read it, "'the victim told his lawsuit lawyer, who then contacted the D.A.'s office who then called me to go to the Juvenile Lock-up facility to take the report.'

"Clearly, the lawsuit lawyers are in the middle of this. Isn't this obstruction of justice or something?" I asked, again to the blank stare of my attorney. "It shows that Mark has an ulterior motive for making up these accusations. He's afraid he's going to back to Youth Prison." I was starting to feel good about my case, after I uncovered all these little details for my attorney's defense.

"You're gonna be convicted," he said matter-of-factly.

"No. Just show the jury these things. Explain to them what this is really about." I pleaded.

"These kids will be highly coached. They'll have an answer for everything," he explained. "Besides, I have my reputation to think about."

"What? Your reputation? You're my attorney. Just tell them. Explain to the jury what's really going on."

"You really should take a deal," he said.

"There is no deal. Remember? The deal fell through. The judge wouldn't accept it. Besides, I know the truth. I didn't do it. If they get on the witness stand and lie, well there's nothing I can do about that. I'm not taking a deal against a bunch of lies."

"I can't blame you," he answered, "I think I'd do the same thing."

######

A PASTOR'S PROFESSION

CHAPTER FIVE

THE TRIAL

THE FIRST DAY

On the morning of the trial, I was taken to the property room of the jail. My sister in Florida had sent me some clothing, a suit and some ties, shirts and dress shoes. It is a cardinal rule that the jury cannot see a defendant in jail clothing or handcuffs. It's too prejudicial to the defendant. I dressed into my suit and tie and was taken to the courtroom. There were two trials scheduled for the week and we had chosen a jury the previous week. It was five minutes before the start of the trial.

Before we got into the courtroom, the District Attorney met us halfway down the long corridor and had me whisked into the D.A.'s office and into a conference room. My attorney and his assistant were already there, sitting at one of the long tables. The D.A. sat me at the other table.

"This is your one and only chance to make a deal," he barked. "The State is willing to drop all charges against you if you choose to plead guilty to two of them. One of the charges must be a second-degree. They'll be maxed and stacked, meaning a ten-year and a twenty-year sentence ran consecutively. When you finish one sentence, the other will begin."

I was facing third-degree, second-degree and most recently, three first-degree charges. But thirty years? I can't see it. Besides, the judge already has made it clear that she would not accept any deals. But now, here is a second D.A. willing to deal. I knew that they didn't have much of a case against me. The jury would certainly see what this is really all about, wouldn't they?

"Hurry up and decide. The jury is waiting!" The new D.A. demanded.

My attorney and his assistant sat quietly at the other table. I couldn't believe this guy wanted me to make this decision under the gun like this, five minutes before trial.

"I've done these kind of cases before and I've never lost one," he said. I didn't know what to do. On one hand, if I took the deal, I wouldn't be open to three life sentences, but on the other hand, I'm innocent. And this guy wants me to decide right this second. I wanted to talk to my attorney. He was sitting this one out, on the sidelines, without giving me any legal advice. What should I do? Thirty years and I'll be seventy years old. No, this isn't right.

"Hurry up and decide, the jury's waiting," he barked again. My attorney had already warned me about this guy. "He is an arrogant S.O.B." He told me. "I know. I've worked with him before." Now this D.A. was back home, having just won an election in his hometown. I was an out-of-towner to him.

I hate a bully and I despise arrogance. And then I made my final decision. "Let's go to trial."

A PASTOR'S PROFESSION

I was marched out of the office as quickly as I was marched in, down to the courtroom and through the side entrance. I took my seat farthest from the jury box. Next to me was my attorney's assistant, then my attorney. At the table closest to the jury box sat the new District Attorney and his assistant.

Once we took our seats, the bailiff announced the judge's entrance. "All rise, Court is now in session, the Honorable Bonnie Leggat presiding."

"You may be seated," the judge said as she took her seat at the bench. "Are there any matters that need to be taken up before we bring in the jury?"

"Yes, Your Honor, the defendant has informed me that he is not going to take a plea that the state has offered. The state has offered to accept a guilty plea of ten-years on a third-degree charge and twenty-years on a second-degree charge, which the defendant has refused," The D.A. announced. I thought to myself that the judge wouldn't accept it anyway. She had already said so.

"Anything so that these kids won't have to testify," the D.A. told the judge sounding sympathetic. "And I would ask the court that when they are called to testify, that the courtroom would be cleared."

"Can I do that?" The judge questioned. "I don't think I can do that. Mr. Thomas, do you have a problem with that?" she asked me directly.

"Yes I do, Your Honor," I said, thinking that if they're going to lie, they'll have to do it in front of a full courtroom. Let's not make it easier on them to lie.

"Your request is denied," she told him. "Anything else before we get started?"

"Judge, we ask for a Motion in Limine concerning the use of juvenile history of these kids. Juvenile history and adjudication is not admissible for impeachment purposes under the law," the D.A. said, "We would also ask for a Motion in Limine before going into allegations involving a civil suit pending as a result of this case. To show relevance before he goes into that."

A Motion in Limine is a type of motion made by either party that the other party cannot go into a particular subject matter freely without first asking permission from the judge and showing that the matter is relevant. It's a type of objection before the issue even comes up. The prosecutor did not want the issue of the lawsuit to come up at trial and this was his attempt to keep that evidence out, away from the jury.

"You mean I need to approach the bench before I bring that in?" My lawyer asked.

"Oh great," I thought, "this is the most important point. It's the lawsuit lawyers who are behind this whole thing. We must be able to talk about that." I sighed.

"I will grant both of the State's motions," the judge responded. "Bring in the jury."

A PASTOR'S PROFESSION

One by one, the jury came out of the jury room and took their seats in the jury box. My lawyer had already warned me about behavior in front of the jury. "Don't make any facial gestures, sounds, comments," he said, "juries don't like that. Don't show any emotions. Just sit there and act respectfully."

After some instructions to the jury on how the process worked, admonishing them to talk to no one about the case during the trial and some other house-keeping rules, the State was asked, "Is the State ready?"

"The State is ready, Your Honor," the D.A. announced.

"Is the defendant ready?"

"Defendant is ready, Your Honor," my lawyer answered. I only hoped it was true. Then the indictment was read. All eleven charges. Count one and two, that I exposed myself to the two boys who made the video clips. Not on the clips, but according to them, some other time throughout the time they knew me. It wasn't true. I never did such a thing. Counts three through seven revolved around the video clips that the teens made. Three and four, that I induced the two to engage in a sexual act, depicted on the video clips, and count five and six, that I promoted the performance of their acts, and count seven, that I possessed said performances that were on the computer hard drive that matched the performances on the CD that the blackmailer held.

Count eight was that I engaged in a sexual act of another teenager, one of the other mentor kids not associated with the video clips and was at least fourteen years of age. And then counts nine, ten and eleven, that I actually raped Mark on three separate occasions. All of it simply not true.

I sat there hoping that this jury could see through all of it. I knew it would be challenging and now with the motions limiting my lawyer from bringing up the issues of the pending lawsuits, my chances of an acquittal became even more doubtful.

Then came time to enter my plea on each count. My lawyer leaned over and whispered something in my ear. "Plead guilty to something. You've got to give them something," he said.

Well, since I had already pled guilty to the possession charge in federal court, I supposed it would only make sense to plead guilty to it here in state court. They said it was on the computer hard drive, so I'll take responsibility for it. The judge asked me to stand and I did so with my lawyer also standing and the judge asked me how I pled, one count at a time. I plead not guilty to each count except count seven, and to that I pled 'guilty.'

After asking the jury to step into the jury room, the judge admonished me on the guilty plea, making sure that I understood the consequences of this third-degree sentence, punishable by a two to ten-year prison sentence. Once satisfied that I understood what I was doing, the judge accepted my guilty plea. It was now time to begin the trial.

"Bring the jury back in," the judge instructed the bailiff.

#####

A PASTOR'S PROFESSION

THE EVIDENCE

After opening comments from both the prosecutor and my attorney, the State began its case against me by calling its first witness. It was Luke, the one who had downloaded the video clips from the "trash bin" of my computer and then used a CD of the clips to blackmail me for first, five thousand dollars, then a used pickup truck.

Being sworn in is kind of a misnomer. The first thing a witness has to do is raise their hand and swear to tell the truth, the whole truth, and nothing but the truth. Any God-fearing jury member will believe that in taking an oath to tell the truth, that witness will in fact tell the truth. But a witness who is not God-fearing will not necessarily tell the truth. In actuality, the oath is merely a legal formality that must accompany any 'sworn testimony.' It is only a way to go back at a later date to prove that a witness lied. Without an oath, an opposing party cannot later go back to prove perjury. The oath does not necessarily mean that a witness is going to tell the truth.

I remembered an old television program from the 1960's, called, "Perry Mason." Perry Mason was a criminal defense attorney played by Raymond Burr. The show always ended in the courtroom, Perry Mason cross-examining a state's witness. Mason would intensely cross-examine, and in every episode, the witness would admit to committing the crime. The prosecutor would once again accuse the wrong person of the crime, but Perry Mason always got to the truth of the matter.

It doesn't happen like that in real life. The average person thinks that they can spot a lie, but even some teenagers are very good at lying. Often it takes years to get to the truth in a criminal case, if it happens at all.

It wasn't long into Luke's testimony that the lies began. Luke never drank freely or smoked freely in my house as he stated. I knew that he smoked, but no one would ever be allowed to smoke in my house. The only kind of drinks I made was fruit smoothies, without alcohol, although I had some alcohol for my own personal consumption.

Then he went into how he obtained the CD. He told the court how he "started rummaging and going through the CD's and stuff." But the reality is that he found the clips the boys had made in the "trash bin" which I thought was entirely deleted. Then he downloaded them onto a CD and carried the CD out under his belt.

The prosecutor took him into the blackmail scheme. "Well, one of the first things that happened," he told the jury, "is we called him asking for five hundred dollars, or something like that." It was five thousand dollars, but a minor detail. Later it was a truck.

Next the prosecutor led him through the contents of the CD, introducing it to the jury for the first time. "Now at some point did you meet with the FBI Agent?"

"They searched my room and found it," he answered.

"You didn't tell them at first?"

"No."

"Why not?"

A PASTOR'S PROFESSION

"Because I didn't know what it was about. I didn't think it was about that. They just came into my house." I thought to myself, what else could it have been about?

Then it was my lawyer's turn to ask questions on cross examination. One of the first questions he asked was, "Do you have a lawyer that represents you?"

"I believe so. Yes, sir," was his answer.

"Believe so?" I though, No, you know so. You were at the Federal Courthouse that day when your lawyer was planning an ambush for the t.v. cameras. Surely you remember that!

"You have talked to him about this case?" My lawyer asked.

"Yes, sir."

"How many times?"

"A few."

"Well, a few is relative. Could it be twenty times or thirty?"

"Most likely less than that."

"Okay, ten times?"

"Around that, probably."

Good job, counselor. You got him to finally admit that he's been talking to a lawyer, frequently.

Then my lawyer changed the subject. "Did Mr. Thomas ever try anything with you?"

"No, sir."

"Ever say anything out of the way to you?"

"No, sir."

"Did you ever see him out of the way with anyone else?"

"No, sir."

"And you said you were there a hundred or so times all during this period and you never saw any of this type of activity, did you?"

"No, sir."

"And whose idea was it to ask for five hundred dollars?"

"I'm not sure."

You're sure, I thought, you were the one to put the idea together from the start. That's why you downloaded those clips in the first place.

"That had to be your idea, wasn't it?" My lawyer followed up.

"To take the CD?"

"Yeah."

"That's what I said." Luke said in a sassy tone.

"And you know that was against the law?"

"Yes, sir."

Then, my lawyer went into the blackmailing scheme. "How did you first contact him? When you first talked to him?"

"Pay phone. I didn't do it. My friend talked to him on the pay phone."

"So you don't know what your friend said?"

"Something about five hundred dollars. May have been five thousand dollars. I don't know. I just know it was for money." He knew, I thought, it was his idea.

Another point for the defense. My lawyer finally got him to admit it was five thousand and not five hundred dollars.

A PASTOR'S PROFESSION

My lawyer then passed the witness and the prosecutor went into a movie I had rented for us to watch, a day when he brought over his two friends who were also plaintiffs in the lawsuit. The prosecutor made a big deal about a brief scene of a topless woman, but on cross examination, my lawyer, after a series of questions, got him to admit that "it wasn't really an X-rated movie, just an R-rated movie."

I thought my lawyer got some things accomplished with this first witness; the defense scored some points. First, we established that he had been conferring with an attorney, even though the lawsuit itself was not mentioned. Then, we established that the prosecutor was blowing things out of proportion, the movie, drinking, smoking, wasn't really happening like they wanted to portray it. All in all, I was feeling good about the way things were going. But we were just getting started.

After brief testimony by Luke's grandmother, who owned the house that Luke lived in, which didn't amount to much for or against either side, the next witness called by the prosecutor was the FBI Agent. He would be the only law enforcement witness at trial. Although he originally arrested me, along with the local police, his knowledge of the more serious charges was very limited. In fact, the three first-degree charges didn't even come into being until after I was already sentenced in Federal Court. They were not his charges, rather they were only State charges. The Agent could talk about the part of the investigation that overlapped with the State's investigation, but once the lawsuit lawyers became involved, the FBI Agent was out of the picture. The lawsuit lawyers worked directly with the local police and the prosecutor.

The State's detective would not be called to testify at all. Only after studying law would I understand why. The prosecutor didn't want to 'open the door' to how the detective obtained the police report. If the local detective were to be put on the witness stand, he would be subject to cross-examination by my lawyer and it would surely come out that the lawsuit lawyers were behind the first-degree accusations, a fact that the prosecutor wanted to stay hidden from the jury. In that regard, using only the FBI Agent as the sole law enforcement witness was a kind of bait-and-switch tactic. The jury would never question it.

The FBI Agent took the witness stand. After discussing how he became involved with the case and how he obtained the CD from Luke's bedroom, he then was questioned by the prosecutor about the contents of the videos and pictures.

"There appeared to primarily be two young men. One was black and one was white. That were – in some of them they were just clowning around. In some there appeared to be sexual activity." He told the jury.

"And what did you obtain an arrest warrant for?"

"It was a state offense, Sexual Performance of a Child. We had viewed the CD and had witnessed the two boys. They were – I will use the term, 'monkeying around.' They were talking just – talking sexual things but in a playful kind of goofing off kind of manner."

A PASTOR'S PROFESSION

I wanted to jump up right then and there and tell the jury, "Did you hear that? This is the FBI Agent saying this people, it's just two teenagers goofing around." But I could only hope that they were paying attention.

On cross-examination, the FBI Agent admitted to my lawyer that over time their stories changed. Then, he admitted something that I had told my lawyer before trial.

"Could you tell how long Mr. Thomas had been in the room when you heard his voice?"

"A substantial portion of that Mr. Thomas was not – or his voice was not in it. And then shortly after I hear his voice, it stopped. The video clip stopped."

My attorney had found a way in and continued. "Would that indicate to you that maybe he came in and caught them doing this and stopped it?"

The prosecutor objected to this line of questioning, but the judge overruled him. The prosecutor didn't want us to ask this question. Then the Agent responded, "I would not describe what was going on in the video clip as sexual acts. It was more just juvenile behavior. Filming themselves and they were in their underwear and they were putting the camera in their pants. They were just saying juvenile things. Okay, 'Locker room' talk for a lack of a better description."

Once again, I wanted to stand up and ask, "Why are we here? Why was I even arrested?" But I sat quietly in my chair.

GERALD THOMAS

The FBI Agent continued, "Almost immediately after I heard Mr. Thomas's voice, it turned off almost immediately, but I do not know how it turned off or who might have turned it off."

I thought, we're almost there. It got cut off as I told them to get off the computer. I had kicked them off the computer at that point. The timesheet shows that and proves that it was the last one they made. We were close to settling the issue, but not quite close enough. There was a reason why my voice was cut off at that point. The blackmailer didn't want my scolding them and my kicking them off the computer to be known. The evidence had been edited.

My lawyer was wrapping it up now. "You didn't hear Mr. Thomas encourage anyone to do it, did you?"

"I didn't hear him encourage anyone to keep doing it."

"You are not testifying that he told those two boys to do that on TV?"

"No, sir."

"Could it be just as easily explained that he had walked in there and caught them doing something that they shouldn't do and made a comment and then reached over and turned it off?"

And that's as close as we got to uncovering the mystery of the cut-off tape. I wished my lawyer would have gotten that computer-generated time sheet to prove that this was the last one in the sequence of video clips, which would prove I told them to stop, because they did stop at that point. But I would have to settle for this. It wasn't bad. The FBI Agent was actually helpful to my defense in some ways. And of course, he had no knowledge of the police investigation into the sexual assault allegations, so the jury would never know how those accusations actually came to be.

The last witness for the day was a computer forensic expert for the FBI. After running through his credentials and how he had obtained my three computers, a chain-of-custody of the evidence, and the techniques he used to see what is on the hard drive of a particular computer, he went into the specifics of the case.

The prosecutor went to State's Exhibit Fifteen. The one that shows the order that the clips were made. The same time-sheet that I had shown my attorney to show that I kicked them off the computer. The same time-sheet that proves that the last one they made is the one that my voice is cut short, while I was talking.

"That would be the creation dates of the files," the computer expert testified. We were getting close to unraveling this. But six minutes before my entering the room to tell them to get off the computer, my voice is heard talking from the other room. I wasn't in the room but in the background my voice is heard, and the prosecutor used this to try and prove that I'm in the same room. I'm not, but the computer seems to have a sensitive microphone that picks up background noise. Can't understand what I said, but the prosecutor has just flipped my evidence against me before I could use it to my advantage.

Then on cross-examination, my lawyer asked him, "Of the three computers in evidence here, which of these machines were these video clips made on?"

I was astonished at the answer. "I do not know. I can't tell you if they were even made on those computers."

By now, my jaw was to the ground. I had pled guilty to possession of this material because I was led to believe that the video clips that the boys made were floating around on the computer hard drive somewhere.

"So, you never went into these to see how much of that stuff was in there?" My attorney went a little deeper.

"Yes, I did," the expert responded.

"What did you find?"

"I did not find any link between the CD and the three computers."

I felt like I had just been bamboozled. I pled guilty to Possession of Child Pornography and I wasn't even in possession of it. There was no trace of the video clips on the computers and I wasn't the one in possession of the CD.

Finally, the prosecutor had a chance to ask the questions on re-cross examination. "When you push delete on a file in your computer, does that actually physically wipe out all the data that constitutes that file?"

"No, Sir. It does not," the expert answered.

"Does it in fact, simply take the first digit of the name of that file and place it with some other thing like an underline, so that the computer doesn't recognize that file as being there any longer?"

"That's correct."

"Deleted files can get totally wiped out by other files being written over?"

"That's correct."

A PASTOR'S PROFESSION

I learned a lot about computers on the first day of my trial. I learned that anything and everything that has ever been looked at on the Internet is retrievable with forensic software. Just because something is deleted doesn't mean that it's not there anymore. But, when the computer needs more space to save files, it can delete files that were no longer saved.

Years after my trial the Fifth Circuit would make a ruling on these types of files, only accessible with forensic software. They ruled that files that are essentially "saved" only by the computer, and by how the computer operates, it is not necessarily grounds for a charge of Possession of Child Pornography. As one Federal Judge puts it, even simply viewing something is not the same as possessing it. A prosecutor would now have to prove that the computer user didn't just have care, custody, and control of the computer, but also have access to those files. An average computer user, without sophisticated software, would not have access to the computer hard drive.

The first day of trial was over. I felt OK about how the trial progressed. The defense won some points, the prosecutor tried to flip some things around, prove things that were not the reality. After the judge dismissed the jury, I was led back to the jail to change back into jail clothes, eat a jail dinner, and wait for the next day.

######

GERALD THOMAS

THE SECOND DAY

The second day of trial began with the state calling on one of my mentor kids. He was my third one in the three years while I was involved with the program. The police and the lawsuit lawyers had worked with him for over a year before something seemed to jog his memory about an occasion where a sexual act supposedly took place. The prosecutor spun the 'delayed outcry' to be in his favor.

"Just so we understand, and this jury understands," the prosecutor began," you never came forward and told your parents, did you?"

"No."

"You never came forward and told the police until they actually came and contacted you, did you?"

"Yes." The prosecutor wasn't going to ask about the role that the lawsuit lawyers played in coming forward with the story or how many times the police contacted him.

My attorney attempted to minimize the story. "So out of all these times you were there, there was never any sexual conduct other than that one time?"

"Yes, sir."

"What have y'all been doing before that?"

"We were just watching movies and playing on the computer."

"What kind of movies were you watching?"

"I don't know. They were just everyday movies. Nothing bad."

"He never did offer you a drink, did he?"

"No, sir."

A PASTOR'S PROFESSION

"You were smoking before you knew Mr. Thomas?"

"Yes, sir."

"Did he ever talk to you about stopping?"

"No, sir." That wasn't true. I often told him he shouldn't smoke, and he wasn't allowed to smoke around me.

"Did your mother know that you were smoking?"

"No, sir."

Then my attorney changed the subject. "Now when you use the computer over at his place, was Mr. Thomas in there with you?"

"Sometimes, but most of the time he was usually in the kitchen."

"Was there a camera on his new computer?"

"I don't know. I don't remember."

"Did you ever remember taking any pictures or any videos?"

"No, sir."

"Now, I want to talk to you a little bit involving sexual behavior of this defendant; correct?"

"Yes, sir."

"You remember that pretty well?"

"No, sir, I don't remember any of it that well."

I wanted to stand up and ask, "Why are we even here? This young man doesn't remember, except what he was told to say by the lawsuit lawyers. He either has a terrible memory, a selective memory, or he was coached to not get too detailed into something that was a lie to begin with.

After my mentor kid, now eighteen years old, finished, the prosecutor called a second computer expert to testify. Not satisfied with the first one, they took the computers to another computer forensic expert for a second opinion.

After running through his credentials, he went into the process he used to investigate the hard drive of a computer. "We actually read every, single physical sector on the hard drive . . . we actually have some very specialized software that we can actually read that drive the same as if it were the files on the regular hard drive."

"Are you able to identify or review files that are still remaining on the hard drive?" the prosecutor prompted him.

"We can look at any deleted files, Internet history files, pictures, both present and the ones that have been deleted. We can do a lot of things that people are not used to seeing happen."

This is precisely what the Fifth Circuit Federal Appeals Court determined to be not legal; a fishing expedition into a hard drive with sophisticated software when the user does not have access to its contents. Unfortunately, my trial was years ahead of this important decision.

Then the computer expert told us what his assignment was. "We were asked to do a full forensic examination of the computers, looking for any kind of information relating to graphics, emails, and things of that nature." "In other words", I thought, a fishing expedition into my computers.

"I actually found almost every image on the CD was on the hard drive at one time," he testified, "but I wasn't able to review them. They had been deleted. Not only deleted, they had been overwritten by newer data." In other words, all of the video images no longer existed on the computer.

He continued, "Most users believe when you hit the key or put something in the recycle bin in the Windows system, that it is deleted." That's exactly what I had believed. "It is not. The file name is deleted from the computer. It would be similar to going to the library to check out a book, and most of us remember the old card catalogues they had in the front of the library. If you go to that card catalog, remove that card catalog file for that book, then you have done the exact same thing as delete a file off your computer. However, the book that is on the shelf still resides there. The same applies to the file on the hard drive. Just deleting it does not make it go away."

"Now, did you find that there were any videos that matched the hard drive?" The prosecutor continued.

"No, sir. We looked for the videos. They were not there. All that we found was a link, a pointer. Those videos are not there. They have been overwritten with newer data."

Are you hearing this, Jury? I thought. I am not in possession of those videos. The second computer guy agrees with the first. They don't exist on my computer.

"You viewed the video clips didn't you, off the CD from the blackmailer?" My attorney cross-examined.

"That is correct."

"Now there are four video snippets where Mark is engaged in a sexual act. You recall?"

"Yes, I do."

"In those videos, is Mark alone or is someone else in there with him?"

"As far as I can tell, he's alone on those."

His testimony matched the FBI Agent's testimony that Mark is alone when he made four sexually explicit video clips on my computer, contrary to what Mark said in the very first police interview and the reason I was originally arrested. It was definitive proof that Mark had lied in his original statement.

The next witness for the State was Shawn. He lived in one of the two neighborhoods around the church that I had 'adopted.' I wanted the neighbors to know that there was a church right around the corner. I wanted to be a good neighbor. I met Shawn when some of the kids were playing football in the street and I joined them as the quarterback for both teams. I often picked up some of the children and took them to our church's mid-week Sunday school.

Shawn is the boy that I had introduced to Mark, by design. While Mark had very low self-esteem, Shawn had an over abundant level of esteem. He was as sure of himself as Mark was unsure of himself. I thought they would be a good pairing. Shawn was an easy-going, fun, good-hearted teenager.

Then, they made those videos and now the prosecutor and the lawsuit lawyer were blaming me for it. The police interviewed Shawn many times, once a month for ten months after I was originally arrested. Shawn never wavered until the lawsuit lawyers got involved.

And now, a lot of the good things I did were twisted into evil things by the prosecutor. It was true, I bought Shawn and his little brother baseball gloves for their birthday. I felt bad for them for having to borrow one from their teammates every time they took to the field. Extravagant? I didn't thinks so. Yes, I was the one who told his football coach that Shawn needed to go to the hospital immediately. It was clear to me that he had broken his foot. No one else seemed to care. But now, the prosecutor made it seem sinister.

It was true that I got some food for them when they were hungry and there was no food in the house. Now, the prosecutor made it all seem as it was part of a sinister plan.

Then there were the lies. Yes, I did tell Shawn and Mark to turn the computer off, but he said that I did not. That part of the video is mysteriously missing. He told the jury that I had exposed myself. Didn't happen.

My lawyer tried to clean it up on cross-examination. "Nobody told you to put your pictures on the computer, did they?"

"No, sir."

"He didn't ask you to do it, did he?"

"No, sir."

"What kind of movies would you all watch?"

"Movies that he already had like 'Titanic' and stuff like that."

"Did you ever ask him to buy or get an X-rated movie?"

"Yes, sir."

"What did he tell you?"

"He told me no. And then I went over there one time and he had one over there." It wasn't X-rated, it's the same one Luke had already testified to being an R-rated movie.

"He never offered you any alcohol, did he?"

"No, sir."

"Did he tell you all anything at all whenever he first come in that you all shouldn't do that or anything like that?" My lawyer asked referring to the video incident.

"No, sir." Shawn answered. Either he didn't remember or he was coached by the lawsuit lawyers. I definitely kicked them off of the computer. But now I couldn't prove it because that part was edited out.

"Shawn, did Mr. Thomas ever do anything to you?"

"No, sir."

"Never tried?"

"No, sir."

"You weren't afraid of Mr. Thomas, were you?"

"No, sir."

"Did Mark look like he was afraid of him?"

"No, sir."

"Did you ever see Mr. Thomas do anything that you thought was improper with your younger half-brother?"

"No, sir."

A PASTOR'S PROFESSION

#######

THE STATE'S STAR WITNESS

If there was anyone who ever knew how to lie, this kid, who was now nearly sixteen-years old, was it. While others made small lies or omissions, or maybe didn't remember things quite right, Mark laid it on thick and heavy, going out of his way to not just embellish, but literally make things up entirely.

He started out with how he came to know me. "Through the counselor at school when I was in the seventh grade because I was having problems with going to a new school," he testified.

"Now, at some point in time, did things change in the relationship?" the prosecutor asked him.

"Yes."

"What happened?"

"I got put in boot camp and I had to go and live at his place for transportation."

"What did you get in trouble for?"

"Assault on another student."

"And why did you go and live with this defendant at that time?"

"Because I had no way of getting to the boot camp before I went to school." He answered. This was where the truth ended and the lies began.

"Now, Mark, at some point in time, did the defendant ever talk to you about doing some kind of sexual behavior?"

"He would talk about stuff like that."

"Like what?" the prosecutor probed.

"Like animals." What?? Where is this coming from? I thought.

"Did he ever ask you to perform any kind of sexual act for him?"

"Yes." Liar, I thought, I was only like a loving parent or caretaker.

"What did he ask you to do for him?"

"Show him my private parts on the computer screen."

"Did he ask you to masturbate in front of him?"

"Yes."

"More than once?"

"I think."

I just couldn't believe that someone who I took great care of, someone who never experienced abuse from me, someone who I had gone out of my way to help, could get on the witness stand and downright lie about being mistreated in any way by me. It hurt deeply to listen to these things, but he was just getting started.

"Mark," the prosecutor asked, "how did it make you feel when he would make you do these kinds of things?"

"It made me feel like he only wanted me for his own pleasure." Oh, that's rich, I thought, just feed into it. Just feed into the questioning.

He continued thick and heavy. "He would just walk out of the shower naked and he knew we were there." What? No one else said this. What is he talking about? Then the prosecutor went into the videos that he and Shawn had made.

"And did you show some of your private parts on the computer?"

A PASTOR'S PROFESSION

"Yes."

"At some point in time, did someone else come into the room?"

"Yes."

"Who was that?"

"Gerald." He never called me 'Gerald,' this fact was obviously fed to him.

"Do you remember, did he say anything to you?"

"He never did."

"I want to talk to you specifically about the video concerning when you are by yourself, okay?"

"Yes."

"Do you remember at the start of the video, you make the statement, 'I'll see you later', what's going on at that point in time?"

"He was going to the bathroom." I made a note to show my attorney. Really? Who shouts 'I'll see you later' when someone is merely going to the bathroom? We already got the FBI Agent and the computer expert to admit that I'm not there, but Mark wants to hold onto the lie that I was there directing him. This could be the point that proves Mark is a liar, if we can make this point to the jury.

Mark continued, "He tells me to do things for him."

"What hand do you hold the camera in?"

"My left."

"Who else is in that room with you?"

"Gerald."

"And where is he at when that is going on?"

"On the other side of the computer. He is sitting beside the computer desk." I thought, how is that even possible? Look at the pictures of the room. Then, he got into the really terrible, ugly lies. The prosecutor prompted him.

"Now, Mark, when you lived with him during the time you were in boot camp, something else that happened to you when you lived with him?"

"Yes." Then, prompted by the prosecutor, Mark went into graphic detail of a rape. He had the jury eating out of the palm of his hand. Many of the jurors were crying. I was crying, but for a whole different reason, I was crushed beyond description that this kid could go on with such horrid lies about me. It was more than I could handle.

"How many times did that occur, Mark?"

"Three times." Wow, what an imagination. Not just once, but three times!

"In fact, when the police came and first talked to you, you didn't want to tell them, did you?" Of course not, I thought, it wasn't made-up yet, not until he got himself into another legal mess and needed something to offer to get himself out of trouble.

"No." Mark answered.

"Can you tell this jury what you didn't?"

"Because I was - - I was - - " then he broke down and stormed off the witness stand. Oh, that's just great! A stellar performance. Just enough belligerence to make the jury feel sorry for you. I wondered if it was planned or if he really was having trouble lying like that.

The Court took a five-minute recess and then the prosecutor wrapped it up. "Why couldn't you tell the police everything when they first came to talk to you, Mark?"

"I was afraid of what people might think of me." With that, the prosecutor passed the witness. What a mess my lawyer had to clean up, I thought.

He started right off with the 'I'll see you later' comment, that I believe was the key to Mark's dishonest testimony. "You didn't say one word to anybody after that comment did you?" My attorney asked him.

"No."

"Now, you told this jury here that Mr. Thomas was there all the time during that?"

"Yes." Mark just wasn't going to admit that I left the house.

"Do you remember him telling you he had to go to a nursing home to see someone?"

"Objection, judge," the prosecutor rose, "what the defendant said is hearsay." Well, if Mark said that I was going to the bathroom, isn't that hearsay, too? My attorney was just trying to correct a lie.

"Sustained. You can't bring in hearsay," the judge scolded.

"Tell the jury exactly what he said on that tape that you recorded between 7:30 and 7:48." My attorney demanded.

"He told me that he was going to the restroom."

The problem was we could hear me talking in the background on the recording, but the words are not discernible. He could say anything and I couldn't prove him wrong. All that is clear is that he shouts back, 'O.K., I'll see you later.'

Then my lawyer tried to pin down when these sexual assaults allegedly happened. It took a while and a lot of questioning until Mark finally admitted, "I remember that the time that I was penetrated by him was after the videos were taken."

"That would have to have been after the Fifteenth, Sixteenth, and Seventeenth, because that's what the computer says is when you made those videos."

"Yes." Mark answered.

Another smoking gun, I thought, because it was that same day I caught him stealing the roll of quarters, and he never came back to my house. Shortly after that, Mark was arrested. If I can just establish that he never was in my house again after that date, we would prove that these assaults could never have happened. I wrote a note to my lawyer, but he already figured that out and went into his next line of questioning.

"Didn't you make a decision not to go back over there after he caught you stealing some money from his house?"

"I never stole money from his house." Mark answered.

"Didn't Mr. Thomas accuse you of taking some quarters?"

"No. He said that he was going to tell my parents that I stole money from him. That was one of his threats." Oh man, I thought, this kid has an answer for everything.

A PASTOR'S PROFESSION

"And did you admit to him later on that night?"

"No."

"Are you saying you never told him or Shawn, while Shawn was in his car, that you had taken the quarters, the roll of quarters?"

"No." Let's get Shawn back on the witness stand, I thought, perhaps he'll testify that Mark admitted to it in the car. Let's get Mark's grandmother, whom I told that Mark could no longer come to my house. But my attorney simply left the matter alone and then went into a different line of questioning.

"You are the only person that is seen on that television after that?" My lawyer always calls the computer monitor a television. After a while, people just knew what he was referring to.

"Yes." Mark answered.

"The next day it starts off at 10:41. You and Shawn."

"We were just playing around being immature. We were only showing ourselves on there." Same as what the FBI Agent said.

"Mr. Thomas wasn't even in there, was he?"

"Actually, he was."

"Most of that just showed just you and Shawn - -"

"You are a lawyer, figure it out, man," Mark interrupted. "God!" And with that, Mark stormed off the witness stand again. It sounded like an invitation, but every time we got close and put him in a tight spot, he would walk away. He simply wouldn't break from the lies and tell the truth.

During the five-minute break, my attorney turned to me and said, "that kid is a lying S.O.B.!"

"I know," I responded. "You know it too. We just have to tell the jury that."

After Mark came back composed, we went back into the 'I'll see you later' comment. I had written a question and my lawyer read it out loud for Mark to respond to.

"Do you normally tell people when they are going to their own bathroom in his house, 'I will see you later'?"

"I was being sarcastic. Sometimes, yes." He answered. Wow! I thought, this kid won't budge even when it makes no sense. My lawyer went back and forth between the videos and the accusations of sexual assaults, getting Mark to once again say that the assaults happened after he made the video clips, which I knew proved they couldn't have happened, but how to get the jury to see it was another story.

"Now, when he told you - - when had he threatened you? What did he say exactly?" My lawyer was trying to show how crazy Mark's story was.

"He told me, he said, if you don't do this, I will either tell your parents how you stole money from me—" He was starting to get emotional again. "Or I am going to tie bricks around your neck and drop you off a bridge." Oh, that's rich, I thought. Then he said, "I don't want to talk about it," and stormed off the witness stand for the third time.

When he came back composed, my lawyer continued. "Did you tell the police - - change your story and tell the police later that he had placed a gun to your head?" Again, he was trying to show the jury how ludicrous his story had become.

"He did that, the same night." That is what he originally told the police, which is in the police report. The problem was, I don't even own a gun. I have never owned a gun. This clearly came from his own imagination.

Then my lawyer went into where Mark was when the police first came to talk to him. "When I was in T. Y. C. (Texas Youth Commission, a prison for kids.)

"Now, when is the second time they came to see you?"

"I was in Juvenile." Yeah, I thought, looking to go back to T.Y.C. for another crime you committed. Actually, the police went to talk to him about a dozen times over the course of a year-and-a-half.

"Do you recall when that was? What month?"

"I don't remember." Mark answered. "It should be in your notes." Beautiful. A little more belligerence. Icing on the cake.

"And did they come to see you a third time?"

"Yes."

"Is the third time when you told the police about the things that he had done?"

"I can't remember when I told them."

"Did you have a lawyer at that time?"

"Objection," the prosecutor stood up. We were getting too close to the truth again.

"You have a Limine on it," the judge replied referring to the pre-trial motion keeping us from going into the lawsuit. My lawyer got up and approached the bench and the prosecutor followed him. They had a discussion among themselves. Then, the two lawyers went back to their seats.

My attorney continued. "Have you talked with the District Attorney about this case?"

"No."

"Did you talk to anybody else?" He was trying to go into the subject from another angle.

"No." But that was a lie and we all knew it. The lawsuit was already in full swing. So he did talk to someone else; his name was on the lawsuit as a plaintiff.

"Did you mention the sexual assaults to anyone?"

"No. I never told anyone before the police came to me. I was scared." We knew that was another lie. The police report stated that Mark first told the lawsuit lawyer, who contacted the District Attorney, who in turn called the police detective himself. Mark simply would not admit that the lawsuit lawyer was the first person he told this story to.

Frustrated, my lawyer finally announced, "We have nothing further." The prosecutor had one more brief question.

"Mark, as a result of what happened, how many times did you try to commit suicide?"

"Three times."

"Once by drinking bleach?"

A PASTOR'S PROFESSION

"Yes."

"Once by taking pills?"

"Yes."

"And how about the third time?"

"I tried to cut my wrist – make myself bleed to death." Perhaps he had a conscience after all, I thought, but this wasn't because of anything I had done. I sent him a private investigator to try and get him out of this mess of lies, but the lawsuit lawyer wouldn't allow it. Mark saw no other way out. It was a terrible thing to hear, but it wasn't due to anything I ever did to him. I knew, and so did Mark, and I think my lawyer also knew that I never did any of this or anything remotely questionable. But the jury members were the ones who mattered. Could they see through all of the lies? I could only hope so.

With that, the witness was excused. The police detective who investigated the case for the state was never called to testify, so the jury was left in the dark about the facts surrounding who was really behind the scenes, pulling the strings.

######

A LITTLE ICING ON THE CAKE

Next up for the State was Pastor Carol. Now retired, she came down from Minnesota to testify against me. "How is this even legal?" I thought. "I never did anything wrong." No one ever said that I did; there was never any police involvement, just a suspicious-oriented older woman who peeked around corners, watching my every movement. I went to her to learn how she was doing ministry in the city, but instead she took the good things that I did and turned them into evil intentions.

Now, the prosecutor would use her suspicious nature to solidify Mark's lies. This did not come from a police investigation, so it could only come from one place – the lawsuit lawyers who had subpoenaed the seminary's records and files, found a report of Pastor Carol's meeting with the Contextual Education Director and brought it to the District Attorney. This can't be proper, I thought, but my lawyer didn't attempt to object, so I did what I was told to do, sit there quietly without showing emotion.

"I posted in the seminary notice that I would like volunteers on Friday for the neighborhood children to go to the YMCA," she began, "and Jerry Thomas was one of the volunteers for that program." True, I thought, I had hoped it would be an opportunity to learn about ministry in the city.

"Basically, to be there and play with them and be involved with the children," she continued, "Jerry always was involved with the children in the swimming pool with the young people in particular with the young boys in the swimming pool." Pastor Carol did not know my involvement with being a Youth Ministries Director, Camping Resource Person, and everything else I had accomplished in the area of Youth Ministries. She just saw a guy playing with the kids in the swimming pool.

"Then he went on internship and I was very happy that he wasn't involved with my children anymore." How is this relevant? I kept asking myself. All she is doing is giving credibility to a bunch of lies.

A PASTOR'S PROFESSION

"So, he came back after his internship and I had an after school program and if he liked he could tutor in the after school program. And I was still uncomfortable." This was my work-study program. It was either this or work downtown filing papers at the regional office.

Then she went into the tutoring program where I ended up tutoring two sixth-graders outside of the program because I was personally asked to do so and Pastor Carol knew this. Her tutors didn't even know how to do sixth-grade math. Three weeks before the end of the school year, she asked for a meeting with me and the Director of Contextual Education. She did not want me back to finish the year, even though I had done nothing wrong.

And that was the extent of Pastor Carol's testimony. I felt that it served no purpose at all to prove the allegations of this trial. Then my lawyer cross examined her.

"His choice was to be involved with the youngsters in the swimming pool," she said.

"If you like swimming, that is the logical place, isn't it?" My lawyer asked her.

"Yes. But he didn't teach the children how to swim," she answered. That was odd, I thought, I never said that I knew how to teach a swimming class.

"Then why did you keep him there?"

"Because he had a car." Really? You kept me around because I had a car?

"But when he came back the second time, you welcomed him in the program?"

"With reservations, because I knew I could watch him." Well, that would explain why she was always peeping around the corners and leering out the windows at me.

"Did anyone make a complaint to you about Mr. Thomas?"

"No."

"So, you had no information to go on other than what you felt?"

"Other than what I observed," she answered. And that's what makes this testimony irrelevant to any facts of the case, I thought. Certainly, it could be relevant if there was anything at all wrong. But there wasn't one shred of wrongdoing. And taken in the whole scope of everything I had already accomplished in the area of Youth Ministry, this testimony seemed absurd. But taken by itself, it was easily twisted into looking like I had evil intentions, and added to the lies already spoken, it just added credibility to the prosecutor's case against me.

The last witness for the day was Miguel. He had come across the state from the community of my internship site to add his testimony to the mix. His testimony was short.

His first inaccurate statement came when the prosecutor asked him when he first came to know the defendant.

"I was sitting at the park and he came up and asked if I wanted to play basketball with him." The truth was he had attended a community-wide multi-church youth program and then he and his brother, one year younger, came to visit me at the Parsonage. They had invited themselves.

A PASTOR'S PROFESSION

The lawsuit lawyer had gotten him to make it look as though I was out 'fishing' for victims. His memory was inaccurate on this point.

"After meeting him the first time, did you get up and immediately go to his house or did you see him in the park more?"

"I kept seeing him around." Of course you did, I thought, there are only five hundred people in this West Texas city, but the prosecutor was making it seem like I had been targeting him.

"At some point did he invite you to his house?"

"Yes he did." Another lie. He invited himself by ringing the doorbell. It was a small inaccuracy, but the prosecutor wants to paint a picture that I was in the community looking for victims.

Then came the alcohol, the two sips that he had originally said he had before I walked in and realized that he was drinking out of the wrong picture now had morphed. "Do you remember how much you drink?" The prosecutor asked.

"I know it was a lot," he replied. What happened to the 'two sips' that you originally said, I thought. We can show his interview video that the lawsuit lawyers made to show he's lying, can't we?

But this was nothing compared to the next line of questioning culminating on a statement that I had asked him to pull down his pants. With that the prosecutor passed the witness.

My lawyer started right off asking questions of this extremely delayed outcry.

"Did you tell your father about this?"

"No. I didn't."

"Did you ever tell your brother about this?"

"No."

"You know he has said that nothing happened?"

"Yes, I know."

"Who is the first person that you told about this?"

"A lawyer I have." The lawsuit lawyer strikes again.

"Well, how long did he know you?"

"About a year."

"How much of that year were you all friends?"

"Pretty much most of it."

"You didn't do it?"

"No."

"Did he hit you?"

"No."

"Did he tell you he was going to tie rocks around your neck and throw you in the lake?"

"No."

"Didn't put a gun to your head?" My lawyer was trying to show how absurd Mark's story was.

"No."

With that my lawyer passed the witness. The prosecutor had nothing further and the witness was excused.

"If there is no objection, I think this is a good place to stop for today," Judge Leggat announced. "It looks like we will finish up tomorrow. Be

A PASTOR'S PROFESSION

back tomorrow at Nine O'clock." Then she rather sternly said, "I want to see the attorneys in my chamber, immediately." She seemed to be unhappy about something and it seemed to me like she had just called two school kids who had been in a fight down to the principal's office.

######

WRAPPING UP THE TRIAL

The next day there was one more witness called on to testify for the state. She was a licensed marriage and family therapist who would testify about theories in child sexual abuse. While she testified as to how child abusers choose, groom, and condition a child towards the abusers ultimate goal, I then realized why all of the teenagers seemed to have tweaked their stories. Small lies that by themselves didn't amount to much on their own, together the lies showed a uniformity that would match this expert's testimony about how a child abuser operates. In other words, the witnesses had been coached. Now their stories fit neatly into the theories of this witness.

"Do you look for consistencies in what children have told you?"

"Yes, sir."

"Did you find that the statements that the children have given in this case are consistent?"

"Yes, sir." Of course they are, I thought, all of their stories have been altered to appear that way.

The expert witness continued on, tying up all of the loose ends, making everything fit together into one neat-and-tidy package. Finally, the prosecutor asked her, "Are you aware of at least one of the individuals attempted to commit suicide?"

"Yes, sir." Objection, I thought, how is she aware of this if she didn't even interview any of these people? This can't be right, I thought, the prosecutor is twisting everything around again.

Then, it was my attorney's turn. "Can't you make a better judgment had you gone out and talked to these individuals?" He asked.

"To formulate an absolute opinion, yes, sir. It would be necessary to interview the child."

"So did you do that?"

"No, sir." Of course not, I thought, the lawsuit lawyers would never have allowed it.

My lawyer hammered the point home. "So, actually, you don't know anything about those, other than what you read in the file of the District Attorney?"

"That's correct." But then she admitted to viewing the one-hour broadcast-quality video that was produced and paid for by the lawsuit lawyers. Yes, even this witness had been influenced by the lawsuit lawyers.

"Now, tell the jury what a 'street smart kid' is."

"One who knows how to work things, how to get his way, how to manipulate things, how to make the most of situations."

"Do street smart kids usually come from disturbed backgrounds?"

A PASTOR'S PROFESSION

"They may."

"Children who are involved in crimes, not going to school, can do anything they want?"

"Children who are street smart often skip school, are truant, do not do well in school. That's correct."

Finally, my lawyer wrapped it up. "Do children sometimes tell a story?"

"Yes, sir."

"Can you always believe them?"

"You cannot one-hundred percent believe anybody, sir."

That's a good place to end and that's exactly where the trial ended and the jury was sent out.

I had one character witness who was still willing to testify for me. The school counselor had bailed on me on the first day. I thought she might be able to give some insight into the two mentor students, how neither of them had ever complained to her about me. But she had told my lawyer that she wanted to see me fry. Other witnesses didn't show up because they were not subpoenaed.

So rather than put on the witness stand one sole character witness who knew little about the facts of the case, I chose to spare him from testifying. I chose to call no witnesses.

My lawyer then petitioned the court to instruct the jury for a verdict of Not Guilty due to being insufficient evidence, which was quickly denied by the judge. Both sides then rested and closed and we went into closing arguments.

After bringing the jury back in and reading the charging papers to them, the prosecutor began to run through how he felt the presentation of the testimony proved each of the charges. If what these witnesses were saying was true, then I'd be about the worst person in the world. But I knew it wasn't true. That's what allowed me to sit there peacefully. There was nothing I could do about it. I was simply along for the ride. I would hold my head high and walk straight into whatever the outcome would be.

Composure. Integrity. Faith that God would see this through to the end. God has yet to speak, I thought. But God will speak. In the end, God always gets the last word!

After the prosecutor ran through his version of the facts, my lawyer made his closing argument that there was not enough evidence to prove the charges.

"How many times did I ask a question," my lawyer asked the jury, "and they would say, 'I can't remember. I don't know.' No one ever came forward."

"Did Mr. Thomas ever tell y'all to do that on the computer? 'No.' Why did you do it then? 'We were just clowning around.'"

"I did ask each one of them, did you talk to your lawyer about this and they told you they had."

"Can you believe Mark? Was he the kind of witness that you want to believe?"

A PASTOR'S PROFESSION

"We've got two kinds of evidence. We've got the experts with the computers and then we have street smart kids. And they are street smart. When I asked her what street smart kids were, she said, 'somebody that knows how to work the system.'"

Finally, he asked the jury to take the charges back there and read the charge and make a decision based on the application of the law.

The prosecutor then had the closing words. "I guess the theory is, it's a big conspiracy. These kids didn't have the motive to make this up." Yes they did, I thought, but you wouldn't allow my lawyer to talk about the lawsuit and the lawsuit lawyers' involvement. Remember?

"I can tell you this," he said, "Mark sat right here and told you the truth. He wasn't faking that. He wasn't making it up. He wasn't pulling facts out of the air." Yes, he was, I thought, and it was an award-winning performance at that.

"We brought to you what happened in Ohio." Yeah, I tossed some kids around in the pool. No crime there. "Here it is in Wilson." No crime there either, until the lawsuit lawyers showed up.

"And then as the police approached them independently of everyone else so that it matched the criteria." So why weren't any police called to the witness stand? Because it wasn't independent at all. The police had to have some reason to go to them. But we couldn't talk about that. The common denominator was the lawsuit lawyers. They were pulling the hidden strings, and the jury would never hear about it.

"I submit to you things happened to these boys that we don't even know about." Can you say that? I thought, let's just get everyone's imagination involved.

"When Mark testified up here he brought tears to the eyes of a lot of people in this courtroom. Me, you, the defendant." Yeah, but our tears were for different reasons. He had the jury feeding out of the palm of his hand and they were buying into it all. Me, I just couldn't believe someone could lie so much and make up such horrid stories about me. It hurt deeply.

"Don't let him get away, ladies and gentlemen, he did it." Well, so you say. And with that the trial ended and the jury went into deliberations.

But the jury didn't need too much time to deliberate. It took a total of nineteen minutes. This time included the time it took to file out of the jury box until they filed back in. It included the time it took to choose a jury foreman, sit down and deliberate on eleven charges and then sign eleven separate verdict sheets, one for each charge. It was as though they couldn't sign the verdict sheets fast enough. They were so sure that I was simply the most hideous person on the face of the earth. Guilty on all eleven charges.

######

THE SENTENCING PHASE OF TRIAL

It was now time to enter the punishment phase of the trial. It was obvious that the jury had bought into every single lie and my lawyer couldn't turn things around. We came close a few times, but my lawyer's cross-examination alone wasn't enough to shed some light on what was really going on. The lawsuit lawyers were like the Wizard of Oz, pulling strings and making a bunch of smoke and nobody bothered to pull back the curtain. The fact was, the prosecutor wouldn't allow us to pull back the curtain. Every time we got too close, the prosecutor would object. The prosecutor wouldn't even put the police detective on the witness stand for the fear of us pulling back the curtain. The detective would have revealed how it came to be that he went to talk to their witnesses in the first place.

The prosecutor put on one piece of evidence for the sentencing phase by reading into the record my federal sentence. That's not fair, I thought, he's treating the federal sentence as if it were a whole different sentence, but it was part of this very case. Now, the jury thinks I had a prior sentence when in reality it's all part of the same investigation. Can they do that? It didn't seem right. With that, the State closed and then the defense closed.

After reviewing the instructions for imposing sentence, the range of time for each of the eleven charges and the potential fines, closing arguments began.

"This case is not about money," he started, "the state is not going to ask you to worry about fines in this case."

"Pastor Carol saw what was happening, he was training himself with his grooming process in Ohio." Really, I thought, when did it become a crime to play with kids in the pool? I had done nothing wrong. "Chance number one."

"Chance number two," he continued, "he went to Wilson. Reverend Carol says, 'don't come back to Ohio.' So they sent him to Wilson." Well, that's a stretch. Reverend Carol didn't say that, he's got it all mixed up to make it seem like there was a cover-up but there wasn't.

"Chance number three he comes to Marshall, Texas. He can ask God for forgiveness for what he has done," Shall I ask for forgiveness for playing with the kids in the pool? There was never anything to seek forgiveness for. "He has chosen to separate himself from the family of God, from the family of law abiding citizens that we have in our community." He was painting me as the outsider that I was. I wasn't from around here.

"How can we make sure that this predator doesn't fall on any other children in the world? I challenge him to get up here and guarantee you that that man will never do it again, what he has so heinously done in our community. Put him in prison for as long as possible." I'm just here for the ride, I thought to myself.

Then my lawyer spoke. "Take this charging paper, read it carefully and discuss it all and come up with some kind of sentence that you would feel alright about. Vote with your heart. Talk to each other and come to an amount that you all feel is just and right in this particular instance. Thank you for your time and effort and I know you will do what you feel is right." That's it? Oh man, I thought, I'm screwed. Point out to them the lies. Do something. Voting with their heart is a bad idea, I thought.

A PASTOR'S PROFESSION

Then the prosecutor finished. "You know what scares me to death is that on Sunday morning this individual sat in front of a congregation and supposedly spoke the voice of God to his congregation, while on Monday, he acted with the heart of the devil." Oh that's rich, I thought. "I want to send one message to him, that we ain't gonna tolerate that anymore. Because any day less than life is not fair to these boys."

The jury was then told to retire to the jury room and begin deliberations. It wasn't long before a note with questions to the court was sent out to the judge. "What's the difference between ninety-nine years and life?" and "Where will the fine go to – can the fine go to counseling for the victims?" and "Will the sentence be consecutive or concurrent?" Oh great, I thought, the jury has bought into each and every lie. Besides, where did they think the fine money was going to come from if I'm in prison for life? They didn't get the fact that the lawyers referred to throughout the trial were civil lawsuit lawyers. Now they thought that this was the civil trial. It might as well have been. That's where all of the evidence came from. "People," I wanted to say, "this isn't the civil lawsuit trial!"

It wasn't long before another note came out. The jury had reached their verdict. Once they entered the courtroom, the judge warned everyone to not make any sound in voicing an opinion of the verdict in any manner. To do so could result in a charge of Contempt of Court. The judge then asked the jury if they had reached a verdict in sentencing. One of the jury members answered that they had indeed reached a verdict.

I was instructed to stand and my lawyer stood with me as the punishment verdicts were read. No surprise by now, maximum sentences and maximum fines on each of the eleven counts. Then the judge pronounced the sentence. "I propose to assess each sentence on each count to run consecutively." We added it up. Three hundred ninety-seven years and one hundred-thousand dollars in fines. These people fell for it all, I thought. The joke was on them, though, I'd never be able to do that much time.

"It is the opinion of this court," the judge barked, "that no more just verdict has ever been handed down than this verdict here this afternoon. You have as good and as well have murdered and killed and maimed with what you have done with these lives." I felt a little sorry for them to have been fooled so easily.

Don't show them any emotion, I told myself. They don't deserve it. I went to trial because I was innocent, not because I was guilty.

They made a big scene of handcuffing me in front of the jury and escorting me out; a Texas tradition. I was stopped in the back hallway by a newspaper reporter and photographer. The jail guards told me I could make a statement if I wished to. I did. The reporter wrote frantically as I spoke until I said something she didn't like. She stopped writing instantly when I began to tell her that my conviction was based on lies and greed for settlement money from the civil lawsuit that was already pending. But she had the story already written; She was just looking for a sound bite to fit into her story.

A PASTOR'S PROFESSION

At the jail they put me on suicide watch. Standard procedure when someone gets more time than they could ever do. Innocent people don't commit suicide, do they? I wasn't about to give them the satisfaction.

God will speak when God is ready to speak. I've preached on this before. On Good Friday, when Jesus was crucified, all signs pointed to this as being the end for Jesus. But on Easter Sunday God spoke loud and clear. Jesus was raised from the dead. It wasn't the end at all but the beginning of a whole new era. I knew that God was yet to speak on my behalf. Note to self: Must be patient, God will speak.

I also remembered another thing that I preached on. Praise God at all times. In good times and in bad times. The ancient Old Testament story of Job came to mind. Job was doing pretty well for himself. He had land, thousands of animals, a big family, all of the things that made for a successful man in those days. Then, one by one, Job lost everything. First, the Sabeans stole the oxen and donkeys and killed the servants. (Job 1:14) Then fire fell from heaven and burned up the sheep and servants. (v. 16). Then the Chaldeans stole the camels and killed the servants. (v. 17).

Finally, a great wind knocked over the house and killed his sons and daughters. (v. 18). But instead of cursing God, verse 20 tells us that "Job fell on the ground and worshipped God. 'The LORD gave, and the LORD has taken away, blessed be the name of the LORD.'"

But Job was not finished with hardship yet. In Chapter 2, Job is "inflicted with loathsome sores from the sole of his foot to the crown of his head." (v. 7) Job's wife looked at Job's misery and told Job to "curse God and die." (v. 9) but Job replied, "Shall we receive the good at the hand of God and not receive the bad?" (v. 9).

Verse 10 says that "in all this, Job did not sin with his lips." We often refer to Job as being a 'patient' man. But I would suggest something different. It's not so much that Job was patient because he had no idea how this string of calamity would end, or even if it would end at all. Instead, I suggest that Job endured faithfully throughout his entire ordeal.

In the end, God did speak and God replenished Job with more than he had in the first place. Chapter 43, verse 10 says that "The LORD gave Job twice as much as he had before." Note to self: Keep the faith.

######

SHADRACH, MESHACH, AND ABEDNEGO: THE FURNACE OF FIRE

The Old Testament story of Shadrach, Meshach and Abednego is found in the book of Daniel. The three friends were first mentioned at Daniel 2: 49 and their story continues through Chapter Three. The four young men, probably no older than eighteen, were taken into captivity with other Hebrews as a result of the Babylonian conquest of Jerusalem in 597 B.C.E. Daniel had found favor with King Nebuchadnezzar by interpreting the king's dreams. For Daniel's achievements, the king rewarded Daniel with "many great gifts, and made him ruler over the whole province of Babylon and chief perfect over all the wise men of Babylon." (v. 48). Daniel requested that he bring his three friends along, so the king also "appointed Shadrach, Meshach, and Abednego over the affairs of the province of Babylon." (v. 49).

The four young men remained faithful to God, but King Nebuchadnezzar decreed that all should bow down to a very large golden statue. Shadrach, Meshach, and Abednego refused to worship the golden statue, saying to the king, "we will not worship the golden statue that you have set up." (Dan. 3:18).

As punishment for their refusal, the king ordered them to be burned alive in a furnace that would be "heated up seven times more than was customary." (v. 19). The furnace was so hot, "the raging flames killed the men who lifted Shadrach, Meshach, and Abednego into it." (v. 22). Even so, the three young men "were not harmed." (v. 27).

"Blessed be the God of Shadrach, Meshach, and Abednego, who has sent his angel and delivered his servants who trusted in him," (v. 28), the king said. Then King Nebuchadnezzar made a decree. "Any people, nation, or language that utters blasphemy against the God of Shadrach, Meshach and Abednego shall be torn from limb to limb and their houses laid in ruin for there is no other God who is able to deliver in this way." (v. 29). Finally, the king "promoted Shadrach, Meshach and Abednego back to their original positions of stature in Babylon." (v. 30).

The story of Shadrack, Meshach, and Abednego is not a story about how to survive a fiery furnace. Not literally. Rather, it is a story about keeping a strong faith alive in situations that test the foundations of our faith. Shadrach, Meshach, and Abednego's faith was tested by the pressures of the king, but their faith did not falter in their adversity. They trusted God to get them through, and God did pull them through. As a result, the three youth were given back their original positions in the foreign Kingdom, but now they have the King's blessing and protection to worship the God of Israel.

For the people also held in captivity in Babylon, this is a story of hopeful redemption. Be faithful to God and God will be faithful to us. Keep the faith through this adversity and God will deliver us out of captivity.

Eventually, God does deliver the Hebrews from captivity and in 538 B.C.E., under new leadership, the Hebrews are allowed to return to their homeland. God delivers on God's promises. The story of the Hebrew's return from captivity can be found in the books of Ezra and Nehemiah.

But the story of Shadrach, Meshach and Abednego also reminds us of our own struggles in keeping a strong faith in adversity. The story of Shadrach, Meshach and Abednego serve as a model still today, that God will prevail and God will deliver on God's promise to remain faithful to those who remain faithful to God.

In my case, the heat was about to become more intense, a test of faith. But I was determined to remain steadfast in my faith and steadfast in my innocence.

######

A PASTOR'S PROFESSION

CHAPTER SIX

THE PURSUIT OF INNOCENCE

THE NEXT STEP

Jail personnel looked in on me every fifteen minutes throughout the rest of the day and night, but I was fine. This would all get ironed out eventually. The next day I was told that there was someone here to see me. They took me up to the front of the jail to meet a man, who was already there waiting for me. He wore cowboy boots and blue jeans and I did not know who he was.

"I'm your appellate attorney," he introduced himself. "I'll be doing your direct appeal." He was appointed by the trial judge to work the next part of the process.

The direct appeal is a review of the decisions made by the judge throughout the trial. When one of the lawyers objects, the judge's decision to overrule or sustain the objection will have an adverse effect on one of the parties. The direct appeal will look at the decisions the judge made to be sure that the decisions were proper and based on sound legal principles.

"What if my lawyer didn't object to something he should have objected to?" I asked.

"Well, if there was no objection, the appeals court can't consider it," he said, "but you can bring those kind of issues up later on your habeas corpus."

"How long will that take?"

"A year, maybe more. First we'll have to wait for the court reporter to transcribe the trial. That's at least six months. Then I'll go over the trial and see if there are any issues we can use."

"O.K."

"So just sit tight. In the meantime, write down some things you think you want me to look at. I can't guarantee anything, you never know how the court will go."

"I can do that." I said. I already had some ideas about how things went wrong. So at least now, I had some direction, something I can do to help my lawyer fight my direct appeal.

After my meeting with my newly appointed appellate attorney, I went back to my cell and contemplated the things that went wrong at my trial and wrote it down for him. I had plenty of questions. Where were my witnesses? Why didn't we show them the polygraph test that I passed? Why was Pastor Carol able to testify against me when I didn't do anything wrong? Why did they allow the prosecutor to places three bottles of alcohol on the witness stand for the duration of trial when the federal judge said they were not admissible at all? My head was swimming in questions.

By the time I was finished ranting about the trial on paper, I had produced 8 pages of things that I was not happy with. Unfortunately,

A PASTOR'S PROFESSION

there is a big difference between what you're mad about and what is legal, and I didn't have a clue about the law. The following week my appellate attorney visited again and I proudly presented him with my eight-page complaint. I would not hear from him again.

A week later, my appellate attorney sent a secretary to see me at the jail. "He's a great attorney," she said. "He's the highest biller in the firm." That should have been my first clue that things would not go well. "He wants you to sign these papers." She handed me what appeared to be a typed copy of the eight pages of notes that I had hand written for him. It was written up as an affidavit. I signed the oath on the last page.

######

BACK TO FEDERAL PRISON

Two more weeks passed by before it was time to head back to the federal prison in Milan, Michigan. This time a husband and wife team employed by the Sheriff's Office would transport me. They saw transporting prisoners for the county as a way to see the country. They'd do their transport and then take a leisurely trip back, stopping along the way to enjoy the sights. I would take up the back seat of an unmarked police cruiser. We ate well along the way, stopping at all-you-can-eat restaurants. I was of course shackled and handcuffed with a leg-iron chain around my ankles, but I didn't mind hopping into a restaurant. It was the best food I'd eaten since my brother and I stopped at the restaurant before I turned myself in six months earlier.

GERALD THOMAS

We arrived back to Milan a day after we left the county jail. I had stayed in a fairly nice jail at the half-way point for the night somewhere in Kentucky. They called the prison when we were five minutes out to let them know we were almost there. They were expecting us and a group of prison personnel were in the front of the prison when we drove up. They opened the back door of the police cruiser for me to get out and when I stood, one of them took me by the arm.

"He got 397 years," the husband told the prison guards.

"Jee-zus!" He answered back, shaking his head in disbelief.

"O.K. then, Thomas," the wife said.

"We'll be happy to transport you anytime," the husband said. Then he told the prison guards, "he was no problem. No problem at all," as if that would help.

The prison guard had a file with him. "What's your prison number?" He asked me.

"0-8-0-7-8. No that's not right," Not enough numbers, I thought. "0-8-4-0-7-8." No, that's not it either. "I can't remember." I said. I had been gone for six months and I had only known this number for a month prior to that. Did that mean I couldn't come in?

"0-8-0-7-8. I know that's not the whole thing." They prompted me on the part I couldn't remember. "0-8-0-4-0-0-7-8" It finally dawned on me.

"Close enough," he said and they escorted me through the front doors.

######

A PASTOR'S PROFESSION

NO LONGER A LOW-SECURITY PRISONER

There are essentially five security classifications in the federal prison system. The least restrictive is the Camp. There aren't even any fences around most camps to keep the prisoners in. Then there is a Low, like Milan is, non-violent, white collar crimes, and then a Medium. The Lows and Mediums are called F.C.I.'s or Federal Correctional Institutions. Then there is the High Security prisons, called U.S.P.'s, United States Penitentiary, and finally there is the Super-Max. There are only two Super-Maxes in the country, one in Florence, Colorado and another in Indiana. The security levels are not mixed into the same prison, but each is separate from another.

There is a point system to determine a prisoner's security level. Points are generated based on the violence of the crime, gang affiliation, criminal history, and disciplinary cases accumulated while in prison. If a prisoner is in trouble a lot, their points could rise to the point of getting transferred to a higher security prison. Likewise, a prisoner can lose points for staying out of trouble for a year and then go to a lower security prison.

At the time, it took ten points to go to the High-level security prison, seven points would put a prisoner at a Medium, four points was considered low. Less than four points could make someone eligible for the Camp. I had zero points. No criminal history, non-violent charge, the month I had been at Milan I did not get a disciplinary case and I self-surrendered. I was eligible for the Camp. Then, there is the "Management Variable." I now had a State Detainer with multiple Life sentences. I was no longer considered a Low. I would be transferred to a higher security federal prison and until that happened I was no longer eligible to stay on the yard in general population at Milan.

My prison case manager would do the paperwork for a transfer and the Regional Office would decide where to send me. Meanwhile, I was locked up in the prison's jail.

######

THE TRANSFER

Another four weeks passed by before the transfer papers were approved and one morning I was woken up at three a.m. and told to get ready to leave. There were five of us on transfer for one reason or another and by seven a.m. we were on the prison bus on our way to the airport. We weren't told our final destination; that was kept a secret for security reasons.

The U.S. Marshal Department is in charge of prison transport and because the federal prison system is spread out over the entire country, they operate two mid-sized jets, large enough to accommodate about one hundred twenty to one hundred fifty people. Prison buses from the area would meet up at an airport, always a cargo airport or an Air Force Military airport, to make the prisoner exchange. Each prison would be

A PASTOR'S PROFESSION

dropping people off while picking up others from off the plane to bring back.

The prison jet, familiarly called "Con-Air" was on a route just like a bus route only in the air. It would land and take off again five or six times all over the country until it returned to the transfer center in Oklahoma City with a completely new set of prisoners who were now 'in transit.'

After the jet landed, a team of U.S. Marshals surrounded the perimeter of the jet to guard it carrying M-16 rifles. Then prisoners were directed off the buses, identities rechecked, while some of the prisoners who were headed to the prisons in the area came off the jet, and the exchange was made. The buses fled back to their respective prisons with new inmates while we boarded the jet headed back to Oklahoma City Transfer Center.

The jet was not officially marked with any Federal identification. This one was apparently bought second-hand from a tour operator. The Marshals decided to keep the old paint scheme in order to stay Incognito. It was called the "Vacation Express." Oh, that's humorous, I thought to myself. The Vacation Express.

We made three more stops on the Vacation Express somewhere in Minnesota, then down to St. Louis, then to Memphis before the jet returned to Oklahoma City. The jet landed with a completely new group of "in transit' Federal prisoners at the Oklahoma City International Airport. The airport was on the left of the runway but the jet passed the terminals and turned to the right and up to the Federal Transfer Center, an eight-story building complete with its own jet docking area. This is where we would stay until the next leg of our trip, wherever that might be.

People were leaving and new people were arriving every day. Now they could disclose to us where we were headed. I was told that I was going to Beaumont, U.S.P., Beaumont Texas, High Security Federal Penitentiary. They skipped me right over the Medium. I told some people I had met who might be able to give me some information about my destination. I only had one month of federal prison under my belt. Some of these guys have been around.

"I'm going to Beaumont U.S.P." I told someone.

"Dang, man, what did you do?" he asked with a concerned look on his face.

"Got a lot of time in the State." I said.

"I feel sorry for you!" he said, my attention now in full swing.

"Why?" I asked.

"Beaumont U.S.P. is one of the most violent prisons in the country, man," he told me, "they don't call it Bloody Beaumont for nothing!"

"Oh, just great," I thought, "they're sending me to a place they call Bloody Beaumont."

######

A WHOLE DIFFERENT KIND OF PRISON

It was a six-hour bus ride from Oklahoma City to Beaumont, Texas, which is in the Southeast corner of the state, close to the Gulf of Mexico.

A PASTOR'S PROFESSION

U.S.P. Beaumont is actually part of a prison complex made-up of four separate prisons. Beaumont is home to a Camp, a Low, a Medium and a High. The bus dropped off a group at the front door of the Medium. Then dropped off another group at the front door of the Low. What was left was a group of us going to Bloody Beaumont. We weren't dropped off at the front door. Instead, the bus drove around to the back and into a tight walled-in area. We got off the bus and were directed into the building.

Inside, the floors were highly glossed. The walls seemed to be freshly painted. This prison was well maintained, probably less than ten years old. We went through the intake process which took a solid four hours and included being issued new clothes and boots. Then, one-by-one, we were taken into a small room to be interviewed by the warden and another member of his staff.

I was called into the room and was invited to have a chair. The warden looked at me, then looked at the file again. After more reading, looking back at me, he finally spoke. "Why are you here?"

I shrugged my shoulders and said, "I don't know. This is where they sent me."

"But you don't even have any points," he said, "I don't see why they would send you here."

"I got a lot of time in the State. A detainer. Maybe that's why."

"What's your story?" He asked. He knew my charges and he wanted to know what I was going to tell the other prisoners.

"I don't know. At Milan I was a CEO who embezzled company funds, but I don't think that'll work here." I answered.

"No, no, that won't work," his assistant chimed in. He was sitting at the other end of the table.

"How much Fed time do you have?" The assistant asked.

"Sixty months."

"Okay." He was thinking of a workable alibi. "You robbed a bank with a note. That would take care of the sixty months. And you robbed some convenience stores with a gun, so you have a violent state detainer for that. That should take care of it."

"Don't ever tell anyone what your charges are," the warden warned. "Never, never."

"Okay," I said, "I'm a bank robber."

"And if they ever find out why you're really here, let someone know and we'll get you off the yard immediately."

They were trying to keep me safe. There were three kinds of people that were not tolerated on the prison yard at Bloody Beaumont: Snitches, law enforcement who had Federal charges, and child molesters. It would be easier to say that I was a bank robber than to plead my case with these people that I was not a child molester. There was a guy back at Milan who had robbed nine banks with a note in the Detroit area before getting caught, and he loved to talk about it. Thankfully I was listening and now I would adopt his story as mine in order to stay alive. There was always someone who wanted to make a name for himself by killing someone

A PASTOR'S PROFESSION

undesirable. I couldn't allow that to happen. I was still in the courts and I was innocent. *Dear Lord, please keep me safe. AMEN.*

######

WALKING THE YARD

These men were not the white-collar criminals that were in Milan, far from it. Many were affiliated with gangs. These people had shoot-outs with the police, killed someone on federal property, or trafficking large amounts of drugs or robbed a bank with a gun, or had disciplinary issues at the Medium level prisons. There was a lot of gang activity and there were many people who suffered mental illness.

But not everyone was in these categories. There were a handful of people who, like me, seemed to be out of place here. They weren't difficult to spot. Michael, for example, was an honorably discharged Marine from New England. Unfortunately, he came out of the Marines with a new hobby. He enjoyed making and detonating small pipe-bombs. He never had any intentions of using them for any reason other than making big holes in the ground or blowing up an ice-chest cooler, but, well, pipe-bombs are volatile and sometimes unpredictable and extremely dangerous. Other than this odd hobby, Michael was a pretty normal guy and now he found himself doing federal time at Bloody Beaumont. He and I hung out together often, him thinking that I was a bank robber. I hated the fact that I couldn't tell him or anyone else the truth about my case, but it was necessary in order to survive.

One day I was walking the track on the rec yard with another inmate who also seemed to be out of place here. He was a few years older than me. "Thomas," he said, "What are you here for?"

"I robbed a bank with a note." I said going through the details in my mind if my friend pushed for more details. He had a doubtful look on his face.

"You don't seem like the bank robber type," he said, questioning my story.

"Well, what does a bank robber look like?" I said with a laugh, "if you need the money, you need the money." I wanted to say that I would never even think of robbing a bank, but I stuck to the prepared script, relying on the story I knew from the bank robber back in Milan.

It usually worked, but this time I was really having to work the story. He still had a puzzled look on his face and said, "I don't know, you don't seem like the bank robber type."

"Well," I answered becoming uneasy, "desperate times call for desperate measures, right?"

He still had a confused look on his face, but didn't know where to go with it and dropped the subject. That confusion is what I would rely on for the eighteen months I was held at Bloody Beaumont. They may or may not believe my alibi story, but they had nothing else to go on and they had nothing to prove me wrong, so they accepted my story. I often had to add a few more details to the story but I would keep it short,

A PASTOR'S PROFESSION

simple, and would rely on the details of the story as told by the real bank robber in Detroit if more details were necessary. Not realizing it at the time, God had been supplying me with the exact answers I needed.

One evening on the rec yard, not too long after I arrived, I was walking around the track with one of the other inmates when it sounded like shots were being fired. "Pow. Pow. Pow. Pow. Pow." It was a string of shots seemingly fired in a fast progression.

"What the heck," I said in confusion, "They're shooting at us!"

"No, it's just a concussion grenade. They threw it from that guard tower to get our attention. Something's going down," my walking partner said.

It certainly got my attention. Then, they played a pre-recorded message on the loud speakers. "All inmates on the yard. Get down on the ground. Face down on the ground." Then in Spanish, then in English and Spanish again.

Simultaneously and in unison, everyone on the rec yard began to lower themselves to the ground, everyone looking around to see where the commotion was coming from. As everyone on the yard lowered to a sitting position, they didn't enforce the face-down directive, it became apparent. Two inmates were left standing, trying to stab one another with a home-made weapon, a Shank, made of any metal that could be filed down to a point, and the handle put on it, usually made of tape.

Then prison officers, stationed around the yard came running to the scene to tackle one or both of the fighting inmates. This was a common occurrence, sometimes happening two or three times in a week. The two fighters would be led off in handcuffs. Sometimes one of the two men didn't get up and a Gurney was called for. They would pick the down man up off the ground, place him on the Gurney and wheel him out. He would never be seen again. Whether he was hurt, killed or just transferred to another unit, we would never know.

######

SETTLING IN

One of the first things I did after arriving at 'Bloody Beaumont' was call my appellate attorney to let him know that I had been moved.

"I'm sorry, he's not in," the receptionist said, "do you want to leave a message?"

"When do you expect him to be in?" I asked.

"Well, he just usually calls in for messages every morning."

Odd, I thought, is he not ever in the office? But instead of asking the question, I said, "This is Gerald Thomas. He's working on my direct appeal. I need him to know that I've been transferred to Beaumont U.S.P. If he needs to get a hold of me, that's where I am. They moved me." I gave the receptionist the new mailing address.

"I'll tell him," she said. I could only hope so.

Since my appellate attorney had already warned me that it would take a year or more for a final decision on my direct appeal, I decided to make the best of a situation. I first got a job at the library as a janitor in the evenings. My only responsibility was to sweep the outside corridor once each night, a job that took twenty minutes, even though I was to be at the library from six until ten p.m. The library had an incredible video library with hundreds of educational videos including P.B.S. specials on the Civil War, Outer Space, and National Geographic Specials on virtually every culture and nation in the world. I spent three and a half hours watching these educational videos and twenty minutes doing my janitorial duties. They paid me thirty dollars a month for this, with an extra fifteen dollar bonus for just showing up.

In the federal prison system, everybody works and everybody is paid. There are maintenance jobs in plumbing, air conditioning, electrical, and painting. There are jobs in the kitchen and dining hall, janitorial jobs, yard crews; there are jobs in virtually every area of the prison. Each job came with a pay grade ranging from thirty to a hundred dollars per month.

Then there was the prison factory. The garment factory employed three hundred people and U.S.P. Beaumont made army camouflage pants, also known as B.D.U.'s or Battle Dress Uniforms. I quickly learned that I had to get on a waiting list for a job in the factory. The longer waiting list was for people without a G.E.D. or High School Diploma. It was a full page long, about a two-year wait. Fortunately for me, most people at Beaumont U.S.P. didn't have a high school education and were required to go to school to earn a G.E.D. The short list was for people who had at least a G.E.D. That list had eight names on it. It was only a two-month wait.

We boxed up twelve hundred pair of army pants a day. The Gulf War was in full swing and the army needed uniforms. A sewing machine operator would be responsible for one stitching operation. Then the batch of thirty pair would move to the next operation throughout the factory. We were paid by the piece. I learned how to operate the double-needle sewing machine, making a six-inch stitch which pulled the finished product together. It paid 1.6 cents each. But it added up to about three hundred dollars a month.

######

A SURVIVAL GUIDE

For the most part, inmates just want to do their time and be productive in some way. The prison factory allowed them to earn a living and the time working ate up most of the day. There was always the danger of violence in the air, but two things I learned early on were important for survival here. One, mind your own business and two, respect others. All anyone wants here is a sense of dignity and self-worth. Abide by those two rules, and everything will be fine, provided they never knew my real charges.

Part of respecting others includes always keep your word to people. If you promise someone something, a favor or a loan, always keep your promise. As people would tell me, "Your word is all you really have in this place." Don't let your word become tarnished. Never talk bad about other people. You never know who their friends are, whose friends are who's.

How you live these 'rules' forms your reputation. A man either had a good rep or a bad one, and a bad rep is tough to shake. A good rep meant you would be respected. I decided early on that I would be a good listener. If someone wanted to talk, then I would give them the gift of a listening ear. I listened more than I talked most of the time.

One day for lunch they served a wonderful fried-chicken dinner with mashed potatoes and gravy, and two wonderful biscuits. I was looking forward to a nice meal. I went through the line and saw an open seat in the crowded dining hall. My buddy Michael was at a table with an empty seat next to him. Across the table were two other men who I did not know.

Before I even sat down on Michael's side of the table, the man sitting across from me said, "You gonna eat them biscuits?"

"Yes," I said in a not-so-nice tone. I was a little put off at this biscuit vulture sitting across from me.

"Just asking," he replied sheepishly.

In my peripheral vision, I could see Michael was concerned and a little anxious. He looked at me with wide eyes, looked back at him, and back to me, then went on eating. Perhaps I was a little harsh in my response. I didn't like some guy asking for my food before I even sat down.

After eating, Michael and I both left together. He was also working at the factory and we had some time to walk around the track before being called back to work. It didn't take too long before Michael spoke his concern.

"Thomas," he started in with wide eyes, "do you know who that was?"

"No." I answered.

"That was Trigger, the enforcer for the Southern Mafia." Michael was checking me on my attitude. Perhaps I was a little too harsh in my response to Trigger.

"Well," I answered, "I bet he won't ask me for my biscuits again."

But Michael had a good point. It's so easy to get out of character here. Too easy. I must always remember. Respect, dignity, and always stay patient and tuned in to others. Trigger had no claim on my biscuits, but I could have been a little more professional in the way I answered him. He didn't mean any harm; he just liked biscuits. The situation could easily have gotten out of control and I would have been the one in the wrong for being disrespectful in my answer to him.

It would be at least a year before my appeal would be heard, so I enmeshed myself in working at the factory, took up handball on the rec yard. They even had guitars to lend out and I occasionally plucked out tunes. The atmosphere was always tense, sometimes violent. But it wasn't too difficult to steer clear of the chaos.

######

A PASTOR'S PROFESSION

LIVING IN A BAD NEIGHBORHOOD

It was a Saturday afternoon and I was sitting alone in my cell playing the guitar. There was a guitar on each of the housing units and it was my turn to have it for a couple of hours. It was a quiet day. Some people were in the common area watching football while others were watching a movie. There are about one hundred fifty people to a housing unit, the cells arranged on the outer perimeter on two floors, with a large common area in the middle. There are tables where people play cards, dominoes, chess or other board games and there are eight televisions located throughout the common area. The cells are unlocked at six a.m. and remain unlocked all day until 'rack-up time' at ten p.m. when everyone is locked in their cells for the night.

There was a knock on my cell door and then Michael entered with his eyes widened, indicating to me that he was anxious about something.

"Thomas," he stated, "You'll never guess what I saw!"

"What did you see?" I asked the obvious.

"I just saw two Mexicans, one on each side of another Mexican, the two were stabbing him over and over as they fell down the stairs." He was referring to the housing unit on top of ours. Each unit has two stories, but one was stacked on top of the other, with an outside concrete staircase leading up to the top unit.

"Oh, wow," I replied.

Michael shook his head. "I didn't see this much hand-to-hand combat when I was in the Marines!" He had been stationed in Japan and they were not allowed off the base.

After a few seconds of quiet reflection, Michael spoke again. "Thomas, we live in a bad neighborhood."

I chuckled. "Yes, Michael, I agree. We live in a bad neighborhood."

######

THE LAWSUIT

After eighteen months, still no word from my direct appeal attorney. So I plugged along, working in the factory on the double-needle sewing machine making army pants, trying to stay under the radar. I had earned a good rep and no one questioned me anymore about my case.

Then the lawsuit hit.

Two lawsuit lawyers represented ten teenagers altogether. Seven of them maintained that nothing ever happened, that I had never done anything remotely questionable. Three of them only said something after the lawsuit lawyers got involved in the case. These three plaintiffs would propel the civil suit forward. I would only read about it in the newspapers.

According to the news reports, they first approached the seminary threatening to take them to a jury trial for allowing me to complete my seminary education. I could think of nothing they did wrong. There was never a plausible complaint from either Pastor Carol's church or my internship church. There was no basis to toss me out of seminary. But

A PASTOR'S PROFESSION

the insurance company chose to settle out of court for eight million dollars rather than risk a trial.

Next, the civil attorneys went to Michigan having sued the Candidacy Committee, the group of people who were in charge of overseeing my progress throughout my seminary career. The same group of people who had sent me to a psychologist the summer before beginning school as part of the process to vet their candidates for ministry. They had done nothing wrong, they took their responsibilities seriously. Their insurance company also paid them eight million dollars to settle the claim.

Then, they traveled to Chicago and the headquarters for the nationwide church. These people don't even know me and had nothing to do with me either during my seminary career or with bestowing a pastorate upon me. They did nothing wrong, but their insurance company also paid off the claim of eight million dollars. The lawsuit had netted the plaintiffs twenty-four million dollars, but they weren't finished yet.

The next stop was the congregation, whose insurance company also kicked in eight million. Finally, armed with four insurance settlements totaling thirty-two million, they went to the Synod headquarters in Dallas. Talk about double dipping! The Synod overseas the placement of pastors in all of the churches in Northern Texas. They are the most 'hands-on' in managing the clergy roster, helping churches in the Synod find a qualified pastor.

The Synod told the lawsuit lawyers that they had done nothing wrong and they would go to trial to defend their position. I was proud that they would go up against this lawsuit, even though it was against the insurance company's advice. They went to trial and they lost. The jury awarded the lawsuit plaintiffs thirty-two million dollars. It was the civil trial that got the media's attention.

Sixty-four million dollars in all. Even if the lawyers took half of it for fees, expenses and awards, that still left thirty-two million to be split between ten plaintiffs, seven of which insisted that I had never done anything wrong. Three said so only after the lawsuit lawyers became involved and solicited their stories.

It seemed to me that they had just pulled off one of the biggest insurance scams in the history of civil lawsuits. They solicited abuse stories when the police failed to do so. It seemed like this was an obstruction of justice, and I was on the losing end.

I read the newspaper account in the prison library. The library subscribed to a number of newspapers from around the state for inmates to be able to read their 'hometown' paper. The Fort Worth Star Telegram was one of them. But this newspaper reporter for the Star Telegram went one step further than the rest. This reporter added one last sentence. "Thomas is being housed in federal prison at U.S.P. Beaumont." They might as well have put out a hit on me. Didn't they realize that people incarcerated here subscribe to their newspaper and so did the prison library? Didn't they know that this was a no-nonsense, very violent place? They obviously didn't care about my life.

######

A PASTOR'S PROFESSION

BORROWED TIME

It was just a matter of time before they figured out who I really was and what my incarceration entailed. It was up to the gangs of each race, White, Black, Mexican, to police their own people, even those who weren't affiliated, and rid the yard of the "undesirables." The White groups were not happy with me. I had eluded them for eighteen months and that made them look bad in their standing on the yard. They knew me, and even respected me, but they had no idea who I was. Now, they would have to make an example out of me.

Leaders of the White groups put the word out that my time was very limited, and after work that day my time on the yard would come to an end, one way or another. Word got back to me from people who I was friends with, and their advice was predictable. I needed to "check in." That meant to get off the yard and into protective custody, essentially, getting locked up and then transferred off the unit. I remembered the warden's words, "If they ever find out what your case is really about, tell someone and we'll immediately get you off the yard." After eighteen months at Bloody Beaumont, it was time to put the warden's statement to the test.

After work that day, everyone was required to go back to their cells for the 4:00 stand-up count. At 4:00 p.m. every day, inmates were locked in their cells, and remained standing while two correctional officers walked by the cells and counted. Once their count was complete they'd call it in. If the count matched what it was supposed to be, and count cleared, they would unlock the doors for the evening, which began with mail-call and then dinner followed. The lock-down normally lasted twenty minutes.

On my way to my cell, one of the leaders of the prominent White groups crossed my path. We knew each other from the factory. He stepped out in front of me and stood, glaring at me with a raging hatred. He didn't say a word, but he didn't have to. He had done his homework earlier that day, getting the word out to the people who would tell me what the score was. They had given me until after lockdown count to get off the yard. I wasn't about to disappoint them.

Before I went into the cell, I approached one of the correctional officers who was already locking in the cell doors. "Look," I said, "I'll go in the cell for count, but before you unlock the doors, you have to get me out of here. I need to check-in." 'Check-in' meant that my life was in danger and I needed to get off the yard. He seemed to understand. I could only hope that he would follow through. I went into the cell and he locked me in for count.

After they counted but before they reopened the doors, my cell door was unlocked and I was escorted out of the building and into the jail. The SHU, or Special Housing Unit. Essentially, it was Protective Custody. For the most part, I would be safe. Sure, they could reach me if they wanted, but they really only wanted me gone, off the yard. An investigation would ensue and transfer papers would be prepared.

######

A PASTOR'S PROFESSION

THE INVESTIGATION

"Here's what did you in," the prison detective said. Any incident that results in a 'check- in' would have to be investigated, "This was taped to your cell door after you left." He handed me a copy of the newspaper article about the civil lawsuit. "The Fort Worth Star Telegram put you out there."

I had already read the article in the library.

"Not much else you can do at that point," he added, "so I will concur that your check-in was valid. The next step is for your case manager to do the paperwork for a transfer to get you out of here to a place where they don't know you. It'll take about six weeks before you're reassigned. Any questions?"

"No, not really," I answered, and was then whisked back to my three-man cell in the SHU.

About a week later I was visited by my case manager who was responsible for doing the transfer. He brought me to an office and I sat at a table across from him. "I've been reviewing your file," he began, "and for the life of me, I can't understand why the regional office sent you here." As he thumbed through the file, he showed me some of its contents.

"Here's your transfer recommendation from Milan, Michigan," he said and I read it. My case manager in Milan had recommended that I be transferred to a Medium security prison, not a High. I had not been invited to view this paper before now.

"I have never seen this," I said. "It seems like the regional office took it upon themselves to bump me up from a Low to a High, skipping right over the Medium."

"Well, I'll get started on the paperwork," he said, "and I'll put in for you to go to a Medium."

"Very well, thank you. I appreciate you looking into this for me." They took me back to my cell.

Now, I would just have to wait for the reports and the paperwork to be done. I had to get a hold of my appellate attorney. I have not heard one word from him, but I realized that the lawsuit lawyers were waiting for the direct appeal to be complete before they moved on to the lawsuit trial. A criminal trial is not complete until the direct appeal has been decided. Obviously, it wasn't decided in my favor, which gave the lawsuit lawyers the green light to proceed with the lawsuit trial. There were no telephone privilege in the lock-up so I decided to wait until I got to where I was going to contact him.

Lock-down in the SHU is just that. Locked in a cell for safekeeping. Meals are brought in. There is a shower in the cell for the three people sharing the cell. There is also one hour of recreation, which consisted of an escort to one of the television rooms with five or six other individuals. Otherwise, the rest of the day is spent in confinement to a cell.

I took advantage of that one hour a day out of the cell. It was an opportunity to socialize with my assigned rec partners. One day there was a new rec partner in our group. It was the Mexican man who my friend Michael had seen being stabbed by two other Mexicans while falling down the outside concrete stairs.

"They said you were dead," I told him, amazed to see him here.

He smiled. "Me, no dead," he answered in his broken English. "Me live!" Still grinning from ear to ear, he lifted his shirt and revealed dozens of stab-wound scars, fifty or so on either side of his upper torso. Once a man is taken off the yard, there's no way of knowing whatever happened to him, so the rumors start to fly. Perhaps people believed that he shouldn't have survived. But he did, and he was now proud to show off his battle scars.

"Either you're a very blessed hombre, or those guys weren't trying so hard," I said, but I was sure he didn't understand English too well. Besides, he was too busy showing us that he had survived Bloody Beaumont, and had the scars to prove it.

The day finally came for me to leave. It was still dark when an officer came to escort me to the administration building to be processed out. It was pre-dawn and no one else was on the yard as we walked across the yard. It was quiet and peaceful. Never had I seen the yard like this.

My escort officer spoke first. "You were here for eighteen months?"

"Yeah, something like that," I answered.

"Well, no one ever expected you to last that long." I imagined the employees talking among themselves in the breakroom taking bets on how long I would last.

GERALD THOMAS

"Yeah, eighteen months isn't too bad." I said. I felt as proud as that hombre showing off his scars. I walked the front line at Bloody Beaumont for eighteen months. *Thank you Lord for keeping me safe. AMEN.*

Before too long, I was on the prison bus headed for the airport, and back on the Vacation Express. Up and down we went, dropping off and picking up before arriving in Oklahoma City. Final destination unknown.

######

THE SECOND TRANSFER

"Why are you here?" The warden asked looking up from the file at me and then back down to read more.

"Good question," I answered, sitting across from him at my intake interview. "I was supposed to go to a Medium." The regional office sent me to U.S.P. Atwater, California, another high-level security penitentiary, trumping the recommendation of my case manager at Beaumont.

"Well, you can't go on the yard here. Texas Federal Inmates and California Federal Inmates don't get along too well," his assistant said. Years later I learned that there was a long-running feud between the two groups, often turning deadly.

"I'm not really from Texas," I explained.

"Doesn't matter," he said, "you're not going on the yard here."

The matter was settled. I would be housed in the SHU, away from the general population. Atwater, halfway between Sacramento and San

A PASTOR'S PROFESSION

Francisco, in the Northern half of the state, had a special SHU. They could house an inmate in closed custody here for up to a year. Other SHU's were for short-term housing. This was a place to put people who needed to be forgotten about by the rest of the prison population.

It was a long-term solution and it was overpopulated. Often they had to put three men in a two-man cell, the third man sleeping on a mat on the floor. There were no vacancies here. I was first housed in a converted to t.v. room with no bunks, no plumbing, just find a spot on the floor until a bunk opened up. Then I was housed in a converted office. No bunk, no running water, just a mat on the floor.

It was three more weeks before I was invited to a cell with a bunk and running water, by an inmate who now had an empty bunk in his cell. He decided to be proactive in finding a cellmate and ascertained by my walk alone that I was not a threat and was perhaps as out-of-place here as he was. He figured he'd get me to be his cellmate before they threw someone in his cell who was either violent, mentally unstable, or both. He had good instincts.

My personal property, including legal papers and addresses was still in Beaumont. On a federal transfer property gets shipped separately taking six weeks or more to arrive at the new destination. When it finally arrived I had one objective. Find my appellate lawyer. I was pretty sure that the direct appeal was finished and I had yet to hear one word from him. There were no telephone privileges so I would have to rely on writing a letter to him and now that I was on the west coast, it would take much longer to correspond.

After three weeks from sending the first letter, it came back 'Return to Sender.' But I had requested an address correction and the post office gave me a new lead. In all, I sent eight letters, three weeks apart from one another, but got no response. Then I sent a letter directly to the direct appeals court. Their answer was not helpful either. "We've forwarded your letter to your appellate attorney." Still, I got no response. I had been officially abandoned.

Frustrated, I had to start thinking about the next legal step without the help of an attorney and without any legal resources. The Habeas Corpus is the next step in the process of challenging a conviction. Unlike the direct appeal, which relies on objections and decisions that the judge makes on those objections, the habeas corpus challenges the trial attorney and prosecutor, whether an objection was made or not. The jury made a determination of guilt based on what they had heard at trial. What if they didn't hear something that they should have heard? What if they heard things that they shouldn't have heard? Those are some of the questions that a habeas petition attempts to answer. Ultimately, was the trial fair? I didn't think so and now I had to convince the court that my conviction was unjust. Being locked up in a cell all day, I had plenty of time to think of the answer. But I had no access to legal books from the law library. I didn't know where to begin!

My trial attorney had argued after trial that there was not enough evidence to sustain a conviction. That's normally an issue for the direct appeal, that the State failed to meet its burden of proof. I didn't have my direct appeal brief and I didn't know if my direct appeal attorney brought it up in his brief. But even if I could prove that some of the charges failed to meet the burden-of-proof threshold, and got those charges dropped, it would do me no good because I had three life-sentences stacked one on top of the other based on the testimony of Mark and the law was clear that in a sexual assault trial involving a minor, the testimony of the minor alone was sufficient to prove the charge. In an effort to make it easier to convict people of these types of charges, the state legislature enacted this law. No other evidence was necessary outside of the testimony of a minor.

I would have to concentrate on proving that Mark had lied and what the jury heard that convinced them that I was guilty was improper. I had caught some of the lies at trial. He said that I directed him to make those illicit video clips when I wasn't even in the house; that the assaults occurred after the videos were made; that the first person he told was the police when he actually first told the lawsuit lawyers; that I put a gun to his head when I didn't even own a gun. If I could provide the proof and argue that had the jury been introduced to this proof then Mark would have been proven to be a liar. I could argue that the jury would have found me 'not guilty.' I could argue that my lawyer at trial failed to provide the evidence that the jury needed to hear in order to find me 'not guilty.' I decided that I needed to concentrate on this and if I was successful, the whole trial would have to be overturned.

GERALD THOMAS

As the days grinded by, I wrote my trial grievances only from my memory of what happened at the trial. It was at least a start.

#######

THE PERFECT JURY POOL

I learned that they intended to keep me here in lock-up for every bit of a year. There was no mistake in transferring me here, it was the plan all along. How could I prove my case if I was locked in a cell on the West Coast with no access to legal resources?

Someone on the wing subscribed to the USA TODAY and passed it around and I looked forward to reading about what was happening in the world. There was no other resource available in lock-up to know what was happening in the world. One article caught my attention. It seemed that the writer of this particular article had caught onto a new trend. All of the product liability civil lawsuits that originated in Dallas were mysteriously being moved to the Federal Court in Marshall, Texas, some one hundred fifty miles to the east of Dallas. A product liability lawsuit could be brought up anywhere the product is sold.

The author of the article questioned why this was happening. Why were all of the product liability class-action lawsuits finding their way to a small East Texas community one hundred fifty miles east of its origin? Her conclusion was that perhaps the lawyers had family in East Texas. Sitting in a prison cell in California, I knew the answer. The legal community in Northern Texas had found a jury pool of people who seemed to believe anything they were told and they loved to give away other people's money. The class-action lawsuit lawyers wanted their trials to be heard in East Texas.

I remembered back to my trial. While deliberating on a sentence, the jury wrote a note to the judge. "Can we give the fine money to the victims?" Even at a criminal trial, after the prosecutor told the jury that the state wasn't interested in a fine, the jury wanted to give away someone else's money. How did they expect that I could ever pay a fine, after giving me three life sentences? My trial lawyer even made the point of telling the jury in his opening statement that I had no money. He told them "When you have no money to hire an attorney the court will appoint one for him, and I've been appointed in this case."

Yes, the legal community had found themselves a perfect jury pool and now all of the class-action product liability civil lawsuits originally filed in Dallas were making their way east to Marshall, Harrison County, Texas. I knew the answer to this author's question and I had a good mind to write a letter to her, but I did not. I did, however, write a letter to the Editor of the Fort Worth Star Telegram. I knew a little about journalism and I wanted to know why they felt it necessary to publish my prison location in their story. It added nothing to the story. In my letter I told the Editor that I was innocent and I would like very much to live long enough to prove my innocence, thank you very much. I hope that they would at least question their practice of putting people's lives in danger while they were incarcerated. I didn't expect an answer back and I didn't get one.

I did receive a letter from a former pastor friend of mine, the one who was going to testify at trial but at the last minute I had spared him from the task. He was the one who provided me with the extra money I needed; what Mr. Salvador insisted on after he and his bondsmen pried me out of jail. He's the one who bought me some extra clothes and a bus ticket back to Florida after the judge unexpectedly released me on a P.R. Bond. He wrote to tell me that my trial attorney had died and he sent me a copy of the obituary. My attorney was in ill-health to begin with, I knew that. But now, my task of proving that he was ineffective just became exceedingly more difficult.

######

BORROWED TIME, AGAIN

One of the officers in the SHU continuously referred to me as "The Priest." It was a reference to my charges at a time when the Catholic Church was in the news regarding the sexual abuse scandal involving numerous priests and the cover-up by the church. I was not a priest, of course, but I was very uneasy because he was trying to put me out there in a very violent, high-security prison. But no one ever picked up on what I thought was so obvious. Why else would a priest be in prison? Certainly not for robbing a bank. Confusion again. I can only believe that this was God's way of keeping me safe. Why no one ever put two and two

A PASTOR'S PROFESSION

together, and figured out what this officer was referring to, will always be a mystery. It was the work of God, keeping people confused, again.

But three months into my one-year stent at Atwater U.S.P., my time ran out, and it wasn't due to the officer trying to throw me under the bus.

Rec-Time at Atwater is not simply going to the t.v. room for an hour like at Beaumont. The t.v. rooms here are strewn with sleeping mats. At Atwater, we were taken to rec cages that were semi-outside. At least the sky was visible overhead. Six oversized rec cages held four to six people each and I was put in a cage with three other inmates. This was the only opportunity to be "outside." Even though we were walled in, the sky and the fresh air was a welcomed change from being otherwise locked in a cell all day.

I didn't know these guys and they didn't know me, but one of the three started up a conversation with me. I hadn't gone to rec to socialize, I just wanted to walk around in the outside air for an hour, but if someone wanted to talk, then I'll listen.

He wanted to talk about his crime. This was not unusual. But he went on with a sense of pride for having killed a young couple and stealing their car. It was a carjacking. I listened patiently, but this guy had no remorse for what he had done. He wore his crime on his sleeve like a badge of honor. All I could think of to myself was, "Dude, you belong here. The world is a better place with you locked away in here." Of course I didn't say that. Instead, I smiled and nodded.

Shortly after my encounter with the carjacking killer, someone from the other cage next to mine recognized me from Beaumont. He pointed at me and made a big ruckus. He knew my charges and he let everyone know it. Why he was here, he wouldn't say, but my cover was blown.

One of the other two inmates in my cage called for the guard to get me out of their cage. "You picked the carjacking killer over me?" I thought, but there was a crime hierarchy in these places. Murder and theft was O.K., just a business transaction, as long as it wasn't against the elderly or a child. Even killers have their standards. A sexual assault, especially against a child, was inexcusable. They weren't even interested to hear my side of the story. So I was escorted out of the rec cage and back to my cell. I knew it wouldn't be long before word of me got around. There was an undesirable among them and they finally understood why the SHU Officer kept referring to me as The Priest.

I wouldn't go to the rec cage again, but my safety was still in question. One evening an officer came to my cell door. "There's a Charlie over in 28-cell. He says he knows you," he told me. "He Says he wants to be the third man in your cell. O.K. with you?"

"No, no, no." I shot back. "I don't know anyone here named Charlie. In fact, I don't know anyone here at all. I've never been on the yard here." It appeared that this Charlie guy was trying to maneuver himself and I was pretty sure that he was up to no good. I was thankful that the officer checked it out with me first, before they moved Charlie or anyone else into the cell to be the third man. They were gunning for me.

A PASTOR'S PROFESSION

Two days later, my case manager showed up at my cell door. She told me that I was on an emergency transfer. My year stay here had been cut short.

"In my two years of doing this," the case manager said, "I've never seen anybody jump from a Low to a High."

"My last case manager put me in for a Medium. Try and get me to a Medium," I said.

"I'll see what I can do." She answered.

An emergency transfer could only mean one thing. There was a confirmed death threat on my life. They wouldn't say one way or the other. But it was a blessing as well. I had been working on my habeas corpus application and I needed time in the law library to do some legal research. I wouldn't be able to do that here.

I was on the next transfer out, after four months of first setting foot in Atwater High-Security United States Penitentiary. I enjoyed a beautiful sunny California day riding on the prison bus to an Air Force Base to make the transfer to the unfriendly skies of Con-Air. This time, before boarding the jet, they Black Boxed me. A Black Box is a device that fits around the chain of the handcuffs. The effect of the Blackbox is that you can't bend your wrists. "What did I do to deserve this?" I thought. *Thank you, once again God, for keeping me safe. AMEN.*

######

GERALD THOMAS

STUCK IN A VIOLENT RUT

At five thousand feet above sea level, the air was thin. But the tension in the air was so thick at U.S.P. Florence, Colorado, you could cut it with a knife. Florence was in a beautiful mountainous setting, built on a slight slope. At the top of the slope was the dining hall, and on a clear evening, you can stand in front of the dining hall and look down and over the wall to see the small cities lit on the mountainside. To the West was snow-capped Pikes Peak at fourteen thousand feet above sea level. A beautiful sight.

The facility was also beautiful. It was well maintained, always freshly painted. Paint crews went around continuously touching up scuffs and scrapes on the wall surfaces. The windows along the glass corridors were washed daily. But it was all a façade. Underneath the beauty of the facility and the mountain setting, it was pure ugliness. This is where the Regional Office had sent me next.

There were White Skin-head groups from the West Coast. There were Mexican Families and organizations and Blacks had their groups and associations. One of the Skin-head groups approached me. The Welcome Wagon at U.S.P. Florence for the White guys.

"Why are you here?" The leader asked me.

"I got transferred to get closer to home." I shot back.

"Where were you before?"

"Atwater."

"I was at Atwater, don't remember seeing you there."

"I wasn't there long, before my transfer went through."

A PASTOR'S PROFESSION

"What building did you stay on?"

I had to think quick because I was already getting myself in a bind. He knew his way around Atwater and I was never on the yard.

"Six-A," I said.

"I was on Six-A," he said.

Oh, great, I thought, I'm getting in trouble already. What were the odds of him having been on Six-A?

"Where did you work?" He continued the 20-questions game.

"In the library." I figured they didn't get down there too often.

"Who did you work with down there?" I was right. He probably never set foot in the library.

"Well," I thought quickly, "there was Fred and Joe. I hung out with them down at the library."

I could see that he was trying to place who Fred and Joe were, two names that I had just made-up. I knew he couldn't know everyone who was there.

"Who do you know?" He then asked me point blank. He was getting tired of playing this run-around game. What he wanted to know was which of his home-boys at Atwater could vouch for me. My goose was cooked. I didn't know any of his associates at Atwater. I was at the end of my rope. I should have kept the story simple to begin with. I should have said that I had been on the East Coast, away from anyone he could have known. Now, this guy was losing his patience with me.

Then I suddenly remembered a seemingly insignificant event. Back at Atwater my cell was on the first floor near the corner. There was a young bald guy up on the second floor. His cell was situated in a way that he could look out of his cell and right onto the door of my cell. I noticed that he was at his door looking out the window of his cell door often. He must have seen that my cellmate subscribed to a newspaper that he was interested in reading, so he sent a note down to our cell.

"Hey," the note started, "I'm up in 42 and I saw that you get a newspaper. If you don't mind, I'd really like to read it when you're done with it." He signed it, "Casper."

I didn't know Casper, and he didn't know me, but I possibly had a name of one of his associates and I used his name like he was one of my best friends at Atwater.

"Well, I wasn't at Atwater too long, but I knew Casper," I said.

It was a hit. "Yeah, Casper got in a little trouble over there." Of course he had. That would be the only reason he would have been in the SHU with me. Casper left before I had, and I was banking on him not being here!

It worked. They had to let up on me now, at least until they verified me with Casper. That would pose another problem, Casper didn't know me, but it would buy me some time.

Thank you, Lord, for giving me the right answer. AMEN.

######

A PASTOR'S PROFESSION

DIVINE KNOWLEDGE

God often bestows upon us knowledge of things that we otherwise wouldn't know. Divine knowledge is a piece of knowledge that you could not have learned on your own, but still, it has been somehow given to you; revealed to you. It is special knowledge and it is knowledge that can be used to thwart off an ungodly plan.

The Birth Narratives of Jesus found in the Gospels of Matthew and Luke are surprisingly different. But as different as the storylines are, there are some underlying similarities. Both gospel accounts announce the birth of the Messiah. Both gospel accounts teach us about how God revealed divine knowledge to people.

In the Gospel of Matthew, angels in dreams are a common way that divine knowledge is received to thwart off danger. "An angel of the Lord appeared to Joseph in a dream," to communicate God's plan to him. (1:20). Then in Chapter Two, the Magi, astronomers from the East, follow a star and out of courtesy they stop in to check with King Herod to tell the king that they are looking for the newborn King of the Jews. (v. 2). Having found Baby Jesus, they are "warned in a dream not to return to Herod, they left for their own country by another road." (v. 12). King Herod is up to no good.

Then, "an angel appeared to Joseph in a dream. 'Get up, take the child and his mother and flee to Egypt, for Herod is about to search for the child and destroy him.'" (v. 13). When King Herod dies, "an angel of the Lord appeared in a dream to Joseph in Egypt and said, 'Get up, take the child and his mother, and go to Israel, for those who were seeking the child's life are dead.'" (v. 19-20). In Matthew's Gospel, divine knowledge is given through dreams in order to warn of pending danger.

Luke's gospel doesn't employ dreams at all, rather angels and the Holy Spirit bestow divine knowledge. "An angel of the Lord stood before [the shepherds] with a message of Good News of great joy. . . to you is born this day in the city of David a Savior who is the Christ, the Lord." (2:8). Then, "Simeon, righteous and devout. . . the Holy Spirit rested on him. It had been revealed to him by the Holy Spirit that he would not see death before he had seen the Lord's Messiah." (2:25-26).

Herod had an evil plan, an ungodly plan that went against God's plan. Knowledge was revealed to Joseph and the Magi, knowledge that they otherwise lacked. This divine knowledge was given to them so that they could thwart off Herod's ungodly plan. In Luke, Shepherds are given knowledge of a newborn king by angels. Simeon and Anna are given knowledge of who Jesus is by the holy Spirit.

God still bestows divine knowledge upon us. God can still employ dreams, but God may also use circumstances as well as other people of God to communicate to us knowledge that we otherwise couldn't have known. I believe that God had now provided divine knowledge to me twice in order to thwart off an ungodly plan against me. There was no way that I should have known a name of an associate of the skinhead group. But because of a seemingly unimportant circumstance, I could give them a name and stay safe.

A PASTOR'S PROFESSION

The same happened when the lawsuit lawyer planned a staged demonstration for the t.v. cameras. It was an ungodly plan, but my seminary friend happened to tag along at the last minute. He wasn't trying to hear, he said, but it was as though the lawsuit lawyer announced his plan over a loudspeaker so that the plan was revealed to him. He reported it to my lawyer and me, and by the time the lawsuit lawyer arrived to set me up, I already knew the plan and we were able to thwart his staged demonstration. Another ungodly plan, thwarted by divine knowledge.

In both circumstances, it was divine knowledge that kept me safe from danger. I couldn't have thwarted off pending danger except through special knowledge. On the prison yard, God used circumstances to communicate knowledge that would keep me safe. At the courthouse, God employed other people of God, my pastor friend, to communicate knowledge of an ungodly plan. It, too, was thwarted.

God communicates to God's people, even today. Through other people of God and through everyday circumstances, information is revealed to us that we otherwise couldn't have known in order to keep us safe from harm and to thwart off ungodly plans.

######

STAYING UNDER THE RADAR

"This place is like Beaumont, but on steroids," I thought. The next day I had an appointment with my case manager. We met in his office and as I sat across from him, he read my file.

"Why did they send you here?" He asked me.

"I don't know, but this is crazy! Every warden, every case manager that I've had asks me the same question. But the regional office keeps sending me to high security U.S.P.'s."

"This isn't just a High," he said, "it's a Disciplinary High. All the disciplinary problems from around the country come here. Give me six months and I'll get you out of here."

I sighed. "Look, I'm filing." That was code for 'I'm filing a grievance.' "I should have filed in California, but I didn't think they would send me here." I had his attention now. "It's not against you," I assured him, "but I have to start with a BP-8, which goes to you. It's really the region I would want to file on, they're the ones who keep sending me to these high security places, but I'll have to start with a grievance against you." After a BP-8 I could file a BP-9 to the warden, then a BP-10 would go to the regional office and a BP-11 would go to Washington D.C., to the Bureau of Prisons. It was a long process but I had to start at the beginning, a BP-8 to my case manager, the same person that I was currently sitting across from.

I could see that my case manager was thinking. It was a problem that he hadn't created but it was now his responsibility. Then he spoke carefully. "You have a right to do that, and I encourage you to do that. But before you do that, give me two weeks. I'll e-mail the Region and see what they say."

A PASTOR'S PROFESSION

"Fair enough," I said, "Two weeks." He didn't want any grievance on his record, and I was going to hold him accountable to his two-week deadline.

Meanwhile, I picked up a job at the library, cleaning the windows. The whole library, including the classrooms, were glass panes from floor to ceiling. There were no hiding places in here. It would be two more months before my property arrived. In the meantime, I signed up for a class on legal research. The Education Department put on classes from time to time, paying an inmate to teach a ten-week class. At Beaumont I took a class from an inmate who taught Japanese. Can't learn too much in ten weeks, but it was stimulating. The legal class was not too helpful, though, our instructor feeding us with a bunch of Federal cases. Then he wanted us to share our cases with the class. I couldn't do that and I ended up opting out.

Just like at Beaumont and Atwater, I wasn't the only person who was out-of-place here. There were five of us on my building who found each other and often commiserated with one another about the situation we found ourselves in. One man had been a truck driver who was moving drugs along the highways. My cellmate was a jovial fellow who rode a Harley, sold some drugs and end up in a shootout with D.E.A. Agents. A young man who came in after I did was a low-level drug dealer who put his drug proceeds in his bank account. This alerted the bank manager, who called the F.B.I. and D.E.A. They tailed him and finally busted him for possession and distribution of a small amount of drugs.

Then there was Jose, who was a fireman with a family. But in his younger days he was heavily associated in a Mexican organization. Now his past had caught up with him. These were my friends at Florence USP. They were normal people with not-so-normal situations. Jose and I met while we were still at Oklahoma City transfer center. We realized that we were both headed to the same place. We ended up on the plane together, then ended up on the same housing unit once we arrived. There was a built-in friendship just in that. And even though he wasn't active in his organization anymore, he was still in-the-know. He would often tip me off to trouble brewing. "Thomas," he would say, "don't go on the rec yard today."

I asked no questions and thanked him for the advice. Something was going down and he wanted me to stay clear of it. It's good to have friends in-the-know.

The bus showed up every Tuesday with a new set of inmates and the various groups knew who was on the bus who needed to be taken care of. Usually, the various groups had word that someone on the bus was a snitch who had testified against one of their associates. That person would get off the bus, onto the yard, and often leave in an ambulance that same day.

Two weeks had passed, so I knocked on my case manager's office door. "Remember me?" I started. "Two weeks ago you and I talked about getting me transferred to a Medium."

A PASTOR'S PROFESSION

"Oh, yeah, come in," he said, "Have a seat." I sat down in front of his desk. He thumbed through the computer. "I sent an e-mail, but haven't got a response."

Here we go again, I thought, the start of another run-around. But then my case manager did the unexpected. He said, "Let me make a call." He picked up the phone and dialed the number to his supervisor at the regional office.

"I've got this inmate sitting here in my office," he told someone on the other end, "I just don't see why he's classified as a High Security. He has no points, he's functional."

I'm functional. Wow. The difference of being transferred out was based on whether or not I was 'functional.'

"He even self-surrendered," he added. "The only thing is he has a bunch of time in his state case in Texas. Otherwise, I don't see why he's been classified as a High."

There was a pause as he listened. "Gerald Thomas," he answered. "His Number? 0-8-0-4-0-0-7-8." Another pause. "O.K. thanks," and he hung up and turned to talk to me. "O.K. You are going to a Medium." And just like that, my tour of high security federal prisons was over.

"Thank you," I said in a great sigh of relief.

"Let me know where you want to go. Choose three places. Chances are good you'll get one of them. I'll start the paperwork. Plan on about six weeks tops."

"Wonderful!" I said, a heavy load immediately taken off of my shoulders.

I was finally on my way out and my new friends were happy for me, even though they couldn't understand why they had to stay. But obstacles presented themselves. Checking with my case manager on the progress of my transfer four weeks later, he revealed that the secretary misspelled a crucial word in the report and the region sent it back to be retyped, resulting in a thirty-day delay. Then someone on my building came down with the chickenpox, of all things. There would be no one leaving this facility for thirty days. We were on quarantine.

The fellows on the yard let me make it, and I would be fine so long as Casper didn't show up. He never did. So while I waited for the transfer to go through, I worked on my habeas corpus application and by the time I left I had a pretty good rough draft, but I would need some help from some people at the church back in Marshall. I would need proof that I was at the nursing home visiting a church member at the time that Mark had testified that I was directing him to make those video clips. I would need to present the evidence that he lied, hoping that by doing so, the court would see things my way, by seeing that he was a big liar.

One last time, I was on board the Vacation Express and even though I was finally headed to a Medium-Security federal prison, the U.S. Marshals blacked-boxed me again.

"Why?" I protested when they signaled me out for this extra security measure, "I'm going to a Medium."

"Doesn't matter," the Marshal responded, "You're on the list."

A PASTOR'S PROFESSION

CHAPTER SEVEN

LISTENING FOR GOD

LIFE AT A MEDIUM

I finally arrived to a prison where people weren't trying to kill one another. Greenville Federal Correctional Institution, F.C.I. for short, is just east of St. Louis on Interstate 70. We weren't walled in like at the High-Security penitentiaries, so there was some scenery. The interstate traffic was visible from the yard, a reminder of the world passing by on the other side of the double razor-wired fencing. There were no guard towers, just small pick-up trucks constantly circling the perimeter. The inmates here were likely short-timers waiting for their release date. Many would go home from here. Although I couldn't let my guard down altogether, I could at least breathe a little easier now.

My habeas corpus application was nearly complete but I needed evidence. I decided to write a letter to a man who was a member of my former congregation and ask him if he would be my legs on the ground. I needed an affidavit signed by the woman in the nursing home who I was visiting at the time that Mark testified that I was directing him to make elicit video clips on my home computer. John wrote back stating that he would help me.

Meanwhile, I settled in at Greenville FCI. The prison here also had a factory and the inmates here made army jackets. I had already made army pants at Beaumont U.S.P. The problem was that even the short list, the list for people who at least had a G.E.D. or high school diploma, was a two-year wait. Unlike Beaumont's inmates, who mostly didn't have a G.E.D., inmates at Greenville had some education. But I learned that there was another list called the short-short list. It was for people who had experience at another UNICOR factory and transferred here. Inmates on the short-short list jumped in front of everyone else. So in just a few weeks I was employed again sewing the bottom-hems of army coats. We boxed up nine-hundred coats a day. I was paid one-point-four cents for each bottom-hem that I sewed.

While I worked at the factory during the day, I spent the evenings at the library typing up my final draft of my habeas corpus application. My grievances regarding my trial included my trial attorney failing to investigate and call an alibi witness, failing to prove that Mark was never in my house after that date, so the assaults never could have taken place since he testified that the assaults occurred on a date after the videos were made. I also complained that Pastor Carol's testimony should not have been admitted being that I had never done anything wrong and no one ever said that I did, and the polygraph test that I had passed should have been admitted so the jury would know that I was telling the truth.

All I lacked now is a signature on the affidavit that I had typed up and sent to John to present to my alibi witness and when John sent it back to me signed, I added it to the appendix as my exhibit. After saying a blessing over it, I signed, sealed, and mailed the eight-and-a-half by eleven-inch envelope containing my habeas corpus application to the trial court in Marshall, Texas. The ball was now back in their court.

It wasn't long before I received an answer from the District Attorney. "We deny all allegations in part and in whole." They were going to stand behind their conviction at all costs. Thankfully, they didn't have the last word on the matter. After someone is convicted of a felony, jurisdiction over the sentence and conviction shifts from the trial court to the Court of Criminal Appeals, an arm of the State Supreme Court which handles all criminal cases, and the Texas Court of Criminal Appeals wasn't ready to sign off on the conviction so fast.

The Order from the Court of Criminal Appeals came six weeks later. "The Petitioner has alleged claims that we believe, if true, may entitle him to relief." The Order continued, "The trial court is to make findings of fact and conclusions of law and recommendations to this court within ninety days." The High Court designated two issues that they wanted the trial court to focus on, my Alibi witness claim and my claim that Mark was never even in my house after he made the videos, contrary to his testimony.

Every ninety days thereafter, the D.A. petitioned the higher court for another ninety-day extension. In all, the Court of Criminal Appeals granted four ninety-day extensions. My court date would still be over a year away. In the meanwhile, I did the remainder of the Federal sentence at Greenville F.C.I. But I was headed back to court!

GERALD THOMAS

The rec yard at Greenville was nothing like the high-security prison rec yards. It was park-like in comparison. Greenville had a half-mile track around the perimeter of the rec yard right up to the fences behind the prison itself with views of the free world and the interstate traffic. Inside the track was two baseball diamonds, basketball and tennis courts, a soccer/football field and horseshoe pits. There was a weight-lifting room and an inside gym. Inside, there was a pool hall with about fifteen pool tables, an art room for those who painted and a music room with a drum set and guitars.

I spent time on the rec yard, jogging around the track, playing handball and shooting pool in the pool hall. I also started playing the bass guitar, taking lessons from the bass guitar player in the rock band. It wasn't long before the bandleader came looking for me.

"Thomas," the lead guitarist and singer of the premier band said, "I've been looking for you." He was a professional musician in the world, performing concerts and selling CD's of his own original music. Now he was doing federal time for a drug-possession case. "I heard you've been learning the bass guitar."

"I have," I answered.

"I need a bass player. Ours got transferred." It was his bass player who was teaching me.

"I don't know if I'm ready for you guys yet," I said. I had been to one of their concerts. These guys were very good. They were professional musicians and I was just learning the bass.

"But you've been playing guitar all your life, right?"

A PASTOR'S PROFESSION

"Pretty much." My tutor had been reporting on me.

"Well, don't worry. I'll teach you the songs." It was a gracious and generous offer. At the same time, there was no one else even close to being able to step up to the challenge. So, I agreed to be the bassist in a three-man classic/southern rock'n'roll band. Soon, I was playing with them in the concerts they put on in the gym and on the rec yard. People actually came out to hear us play. Inmates who loved classic rock music were coming out to escape the daily grind of prison. On practice night, people lined the small practice room walls, sitting on the floor shoulder-to-shoulder just to listen to us practice. I couldn't believe that I was playing with these guys. They were patient and gracious as I caught up to a respectable level, learning the songs that would make up our playlist. Our Lead's method of teaching paid off and soon I was able to keep up with them without missing a note. Even twenty years later, when I hear one of our songs on the radio, I whip out the air guitar and start jamming out the bass lines. It always brings a smile to my face; I played bass guitar in a real rock band.

A year went by quickly as I waited for the court to hold a hearing on my case. Finally, I received another one of the D.A.'s motions for an extension of time. His plea to the higher court was that since I would be transferring to state prison to begin my state sentence, and would be passing through the county jail anyway, and to "promote judicial fiducial responsibility," they would hold a hearing after my federal sentence was finished.

Of course it was granted, but I couldn't help remembering a time when these same people had me arrested in Florida after saying that they wouldn't do that, just to travel two-thousand miles round trip to bring me in. Where was the judicial fiduciary responsibility then? The D.A. had managed to put my hearing on hold now for a year since the order came from the Court of Criminal Appeals. But I was going back to court and this was a very big deal. It could overturn my state conviction.

On the day after Christmas, 2006, I was discharged from Federal prison. But in order to have picked me up on time, the Texas Sheriff deputies would have to have left Texas on Christmas Day to travel up to Greenville to meet me at the front door. No one expected them to do that, so they made arrangements with the local sheriff in Greenville to pick me up and hold me in his jail until the next day. Arrangements were already made for me to go to court once I arrived in Marshall in order to plead my case and an attorney had been appointed to represent me at the hearing. I would meet him when I got there.

I didn't have to wait long for the local sheriff to arrive.

"How big is your jail?" I inquired.

"It's on the small side," he answered.

"Fifty, a hundred?" I pried.

"I think we currently have eight."

He secured me with the standard leg chains and belt chain which connected to the handcuffs. It was cold outside so the prison gave me a coat and a duffel bag for the possessions I would take with me, consisting mostly of my legal work and papers. The appellate attorney had finally

A PASTOR'S PROFESSION

sent me a copy of my trial transcripts and the clerk's file. Too late to be useful in preparing the habeas corpus application.

After asking me some security questions to be absolutely certain that I was the right person to be leaving this day, we walked out to the sheriff's waiting patrol car. As I hobbled to the car in chains, I looked back towards the front door. Parked next to the front door was one of those pick-up trucks that constantly circle the prison. Standing next to the truck was a prison guard holding a shotgun.

I laughed, "look," I said to the sheriff, "I have a send-off party."

The sheriff looked back and then responded to me, "And you didn't think they cared."

######

ON THE ROAD. DESTINATION: COURT

At 5:30 a.m. the next day two sheriff deputies from Marshall, Texas, met me at the small jail in Greenville, Illinois. "Hi, Jerry," one of them greeted me, seemingly happy to see me. The sheriff's deputies and jail personnel always treated me well. The jail deputies often gave me words of encouragement and hope. These deputies had traveled here merely to provide the transportation back to the county jail in Texas. The case belonged to the city detective.

By 6:00 we were headed back to Texas in a marked S.U.V. I had the whole back seat to myself. We passed the prison on the Interstate and I looked back as we sped by. The prison was just getting started for the day. It looked so different under the lights from the outside.

"We're so fed up with the feds," one of the deputies said to me.

"Why?" I asked.

"They were supposed to get you closer so we wouldn't have to pick you up this far away. They said they would transfer you closer and they didn't."

"Oh, you've been listening to the D.A.'s office, haven't you?" Neither answered so I continued. "You know I'm going back to court, right?" No answer again. They had been kept in the dark about my habeas corpus court order, but they were listening now, perhaps realizing that there was more to the story. "Let me tell you what really happened and I know this because my case manager told me about it two weeks ago.

"The Court of Criminal Appeals ordered a hearing on my habeas corpus application. That was more than a year ago. That's when they first called the prison and asked my case manager about getting me closer. My case manager said that they could do that, but he never heard back. The prosecutor had motioned for an extension every ninety days since then. Two weeks ago they called again and told my case manager, 'O.K., you can send him now.'

"My case manager told them, 'it's too late now, there's not enough time.' There's paperwork to be done, reports to be made and a whole lot of logistics – a seat on the bus, a seat on the plane, a bed at the transfer facility and a bed wherever I end up. There just wasn't enough time to do it."

A PASTOR'S PROFESSION

"They were gonna just let you go!" One of the deputies said.

"They had to," I said, "they can't keep me one day past my out-date, or they could be liable for ten thousand dollars a day. I've read the cases on it. Besides, you ought to be glad that I'm not still in Atwater, California, or Florence, Colorado."

"You were in California?"

"Yes I was." I could see that they were thinking that maybe this wasn't so bad after all. A trip to Colorado was a four-day round trip and California was a six-day round trip. A two-day round trip to St. Louis didn't seem so bad after all.

Now I had their attention so I continued. "Your prosecutor is a spin-doctor. That's why your Sheriff's Department wouldn't come to get me in Florida. The prosecutor told my lawyer that they wouldn't rearrest me and then turned around and had me arrested anyway. Your supervisor picked me up and took me to trial. He told me that they said, 'if you want him, you go get him.' That's why the Marshall police detective had to come get me. You guys wouldn't do it. Then when I got back to Texas, the judge just threw me back out on a P.R. bond. They just play these little games."

I hoped that my deputies now realized that they were given only part of the story, just enough to get them to believe what the prosecutor wanted them to believe. But now they knew that they had been misled from a lack of knowledge of the whole story. Just like the jury was misled in my trial. We were like pawns in a chess game being moved around the board by a higher authority. The prosecutor, the lawsuit lawyer, the judge had one thing in common that we didn't have. A law degree.

Hours later we stopped in Arkansas to gas up and eat a late lunch. I was very hungry. That little jail in Greenville didn't feed well.

"Get whatever you want, Jerry," the deputy told me, "the county's paying." Well, I knew I wasn't paying. I ordered a one-third pound black Angus beef hamburger with mushrooms and Swiss cheese, a large order of fries and a large soft drink. We sat down at a booth. They uncuffed me so that I could eat and I enjoyed the last meal from the free-world. On the way out, I refilled my soda and we got back into the S.U.V. for the remainder of the trip. They allowed me to ride the rest of the way without handcuffs restraining my wrists.

We sped back the rest of the way in record time. It wasn't long before the deputies were on the radio announcing their presence in their home county. When we got closer to the county jail, the deputy said to me, "Jerry, you're gonna have to put your handcuffs back on now. It wouldn't look so good going into the jail without you being in handcuffs."

"Yeah, you're probably right about that." I thought that maybe they just forgot to cuff me back up, but they knew and I was grateful for the privilege. I cuffed myself for the rest of the ride. Then I was booked into the county jail for the fifth time. I was due in court the next week.

######

A PASTOR'S PROFESSION

PREPARING FOR COURT

The next day my newly appointed lawyer came to visit me to talk about the case. He had already motioned the court for an extension so that he could prepare for the hearing. He sat on the other side of a Plexiglas window while we talked through the telephones on either side. He was thumbing through my habeas corpus application while we talked.

"If it's true that your lawyer didn't contact an alibi witness," he told me, "you win."

"It's true, it's all in the notes. I wrote a ton of notes. Typed them up – about eighty pages worth. The alibi witness and everything. It's in there."

"Well, there's a problem with that."

"What?"

"The notes, and everything pertaining to your case, they lost your entire case file."

"What?" I couldn't believe what I had just heard.

"Yeah, it sounds a little fishy to me, but they say they've looked everywhere, and they haven't found it."

"How do I prove that my trial attorney knew about the alibi witness without the notes I gave him?"

"I don't know," he answered.

"Well, you know, he did mention it at trial, so it's actually in the transcript that he knew." I said after a long pause.

"O.K."

"And my first lawyer had those same notes. She had them first and when I found out that I'd be going to trial, she gave them to him. Maybe she'll testify to it."

"That could be helpful. I'll look into that."

"I didn't do it," I told him. "Everything they said is a lie, especially Mark. He's the worst one. I don't know which is worse, him saying all those things or the fact that everyone believed him."

"I picked up your trial transcript from your appellate attorney. I'll read that."

"Yeah, well he's another one." I said. "He never told me about the appeal. I just now got a box of stuff from him just about six weeks ago. Then there was my attorney's second-chair assistant, his daughter. Sneered at me throughout the trial. When Mark was putting it on real heavy, had everyone crying. I was crying but for a whole different reason. I just couldn't believe someone could lie like that about me. My lawyer's daughter looked over at me and said, 'Oh, don't even,' real nasty-like."

"She said that?"

"Yep."

"In front of the jury?"

"Yes, in front of the jury, but I don't think they knew it."

"Well, you know, she got disbarred."

"Really?" I had no idea.

"I'll put her on the stand," he said, "I'll do what I can. Anything else?"

"I can't think of anything right now." I said.

A PASTOR'S PROFESSION

"O.K. then, I'll be in touch." Then he hung up the phone on his side of the plexiglass divider, pulled all the papers together into one file, turned around and left. A jailer retrieved me a few minutes later.

Later in the week, John stopped by. I had sent him a letter letting him know that I was in town. I owed him at least that much for being my legs on the ground. Without him I wouldn't have had the statement signed by my alibi witness, the reason I was headed back to court.

John had prepared a list of questions, and he read them off one-by-one and I gladly answered them. Then he told me about a memo taped to the door at the church. It was from the Bishop of the Synod Office in Dallas. It said that in no way was anybody allowed to help me fight my case. John scoffed at it. The Synod really had no authority to tell the congregation what to do and what not to do. But the thought was hurtful. I was just trying to get to the truth, something that hadn't happened yet. The church, though, wanted to put me into the distant past, truth or no truth.

I also instantly knew how the Synod Bishop knew what was happening. I had written a letter a month back to the former colleague at a neighboring church, the same colleague who had been so very helpful to me. The same pastor who was going to testify on my behalf at trial. The same pastor who had helped me with the extra two-thousand dollars when Mr. Salvador demanded more money than I had when they worked to pry me out of jail. The same pastor who I called on for help when the judge threw me out of jail and I was penniless. I had written him a letter letting him know that I was going back to court and that John helped me get the affidavit signed by my alibi witness.

The person who had been so helpful was now acting like a spy, telling the higher-ups in the church what I had told him in the letter. I was saddened by this news. John wouldn't know how this Synod Directive had come about, but it was directed at him, indirectly. The church was no longer interested in the truth, they only wanted me to be a thing of the past. And I knew at that point that I could no longer trust anyone associated with the church hierarchy. I would now have to be careful in what I said, if I said anything at all, to people associated with the church. And, I would have to cut ties completely with someone I thought was my friend.

######

BACK TO COURT

The day I had been waiting for had finally arrived. Exactly four years after my trial I was back in court for a fact-finding hearing, one that could turn the tides in my favor. The hearing would determine what my trial attorney knew regarding an alibi witness who could have testified that I was visiting her at the nursing home at the same time Mark was using the computer to make a lewd video, saying at trial under oath that I was present in the room with him and directed him to make the videos. Why hadn't my trial attorney questioned and called her to testify four years ago?

A PASTOR'S PROFESSION

"Where is the trial file?" My new lawyer asked his first witness, my trial attorney's wife, who ran the law office.

"I just don't know. We looked for it everywhere." She answered.

"Did your husband hire an investigator to help on the case?"

"No, he liked to do the investigation himself."

"As your husband's legal aid, it was in the regular course of your business to prepare legal files, true?"

"Yes it was." She answered.

"And it was in the regular course of business to keep or store legal files?"

"Yes. I remember taking the papers out of the notebooks that I prepared for trial and putting them in a storage box, but after that, I don't know where that box went."

Next, my attorney called my trial attorney's daughter, the one who sat in at trial and subsequently got disbarred from practicing law.

"Isn't it true that you sat second chair in Mr. Thomas's trial?"

"Yes."

"How long had you been working on this case prior to trial?"

"I only began with the case two weeks prior to trial."

"Where's the case file on the trial?"

"I have no idea."

"Did you destroy it?"

"Of course not!"

"Put it in the trunk of your car?"

"No. We looked for it. I don't know where it is."

"Did you investigate an alibi witness?"

"No. If anyone would have, my father did, but I don't know. It was his case, I was just helping out for trial."

"Why didn't you call any witnesses?"

"Nobody wanted to testify at trial. Next question?"

"Oh, I will ask the next question, ma'am. You can count on that!" My attorney went on with a few more questions, but the answers didn't amount to much. The trial notes had mysteriously disappeared and nobody knew where they were.

The attorney who bought the building from the family testified about the missing box of trial notes. "On the third floor," he said, "every case he ever worked on to the beginning of dirt is there. But the Thomas trial box is not there."

After hearing testimony from my appellate attorney, who said that he last saw the box of trial notes at his old office but was told to leave them there, my attorney then called my first attorney, the one who had represented me for the federal case. This hearing had become a meeting of attorneys.

"Did you know about a possible alibi witness?"

"Yes I did," she answered. "There was a woman in a nursing home that Mr. Thomas told me about. That's where he was at the time Mark was at the house and made some videos."

"How did you know about this?"

"Mr. Thomas had prepared a considerable amount of notes to work from. We didn't go to trial in federal court. But if we had, I would have called her to testify that Mr. Thomas was not in the house and therefore did not direct the teen to make the videos – contrary to what he said – that Mr. Thomas directed him to make them."

"O.K. What did you do with those notes?"

"When I was informed that he would be going to trial for the state case, I gave all the notes to his new attorney."

Bingo! I thought. We established that there was a possible alibi witness and the witness could have testified contrary to Mark's testimony, that my trial attorney knew about it through my written notes, and had possession of those notes, which have now come up missing.

In closing arguments, the prosecutor waived around a stack of subpoena applications my trial attorney had written and called off each name. "And look, your honor, all these people and no one wanted to even testify for him."

One of the names the prosecutor read off was my seminary classmate, the same one who had shown up at federal court and ruined the lawsuit lawyer's plan for that staged demonstration for the t.v. news cameras.

"He's here," I whispered to my attorney.

"What?"

"Yeah. The prosecutor said he didn't want to testify. He's here and he'll testify that he never received a subpoena, or a phone call or any communication from my trial attorney."

"Really? Which one is he?"

"Third from the door in the first row with the clerical collar on."

"The judge isn't going to let him testify, but I'll call him anyway. I'll talk to him at the break."

During a short break my seminary friend disappeared into the hallway to wait for his name to be called. He would have to be called from the hallway outside the courtroom because my lawyer had invoked The Rule, which meant that anyone who is to testify cannot be in the courtroom while other people are testifying.

"Ready to proceed?" The judge asked after the break. Both the prosecutor and my attorney agreed that we were ready to proceed. Boy were we ready! We had a surprise witness to refute the prosecutor's argument that nobody wanted to testify. The truth was, nobody was even asked. For a second time, my seminary friend was going to stir things up in the courtroom.

"Do you have any witnesses?" The judge asked me attorney.

"Yes we do, your honor. We call John Carlson to the stand." The bailiff was at the door, opened it, and called my witness' name.

When John walked into the courtroom, the prosecutor immediately jumped from his seat. "What?" What's he doing here?" he barked, his eyes wide with surprise. John walked in from the side door, making the short walk to the witness stand. He had made it as far as the prosecutor's table when the judge stopped him in order to sort this new mess out. The judge looked at my attorney with scolding eyes. This wasn't supposed to happen. John stood waiting to be told what to do next.

A PASTOR'S PROFESSION

"He can't testify," the prosecutor said. "He was sitting in the courtroom!"

The judge looked back at my attorney for a response as John continued to stand in mid-path to the witness stand.

"I wasn't going to use him judge, but the prosecution brought it up," he said innocently.

"He invoked The Rule, your honor," the prosecutor said, trying to find a way out of the mess he had unknowingly created.

"It's your rule, counselor," the judge said to my attorney. He shrugged, satisfied with the situation he knew he would lose in the end.

Still standing mid-way to the witness stand, John shrugged as well. "I'll tell the truth," he said.

"Get back over there, Sir," the judge commanded him. "You won't be testifying." John shrugged again, turned around and walked back out the way he came in. I smiled with delight. We threw them a good curveball. But they weren't interested in the truth anyway. They merely wanted to get through this and find a way to dismiss my writ of habeas corpus.

There was still one more problem that they would have to deal with. Even without the help of my trial attorney's case file, we were able to establish an alibi witness had been available who could have refuted trial testimony. The next day a sheriff's deputy took me to the nursing home for an out-of-court deposition of my alibi witness. The nursing home where I had visited my parishioner had closed down and now she was living at a nursing home some thirty miles away. I rode in the back seat of the police patrol car, handcuffed and shackled. My attorney carpooled with the prosecutor and we all met at the nursing home for court.

The deposition lasted twenty-nine minutes, thirteen seconds for examination by my attorney, sixteen minutes for cross-examination by the prosecutor. No one had talked to her about being a witness for the trial. Yes, I had been her pastor and visited her frequently. Yes, there were times when she would call me, especially after October of that year when her husband filed for divorce. Yes, I often helped her deal with depression during that time. Yes, she signed the statement but couldn't remember the exact date. "I'm bad with dates," she acknowledged.

"But I remember now what computer game I was playing when he came to see me." She said eluding to a sentence in her affidavit. "It was Wheel of Fortune," she smiled, "He bought it for me."

I did, didn't I? I thought back to trial when the prosecutor made a big deal about buying baseball gloves for two boys who needed them. Elaborate gifting, he called it. I didn't think it was that elaborate. I wondered if they would use this gifting against me too.

I had decided early in my ministry that I would be generous. One day while I was at the church office, a gentleman came in and said that he needed some gas money to get home. As I often did, I had him follow me to the gas station down the road and had him pull up to the pump. I walked into the convenience store/gas station. It was not a busy time of the day. I introduced myself to the cashier and then put five dollars on the counter.

"Put five bucks on that man's pump." I said.

"OOH, You're going to get a special blessing for that," she said.

"No, you see, I'm already blessed. That's why I bless others. I don't give in order to receive a blessing. Rather because I'm blessed, I bless others."

My attorney thought that we had won the case, and I would likely get another trial. But without being able to pin down the exact date of my alibi, I wasn't so sure. It wasn't my alibi witness's fault. Who can remember an exact date for a seemingly insignificant event that happened five years ago? No one ever investigated or talked to her until now. My attorney had done the best anyone could hope for under the circumstances.

We met back in the courtroom later in the day to finish up the hearing. By then, the judge had viewed the video of the deposition. My attorney passed out a copy of his proposed findings to the judge and District Attorney.

"What's this?" The judge asked him.

"It's my proposed finding of facts." He answered. They all read over the one-page of findings, obviously slanted in my favor.

"And your honor, for the record, I checked the court's files and there's not one single return on any of the subpoena applications, which would indicate that no witnesses received subpoenas."

"That doesn't necessarily mean that," the prosecutor shot back.

"We're not going down that road again." The judge said. "We've already been there."

"Yes, your honor." My attorney said, but he made his point.

"Mr. Prosecutor, I was going to ask you to do the same. Would you write up your proposed findings?"

"Yes, your honor, I will do that." He answered.

"Have it on my desk by the end of the week."

"Yes, ma'am, and your honor, I see no reason to hold over Mr. Thomas. He's already been accepted at Texas Department of Criminal Justice. He can go there while he waits for the final answer from the Court of Criminal Appeals on his writ of habeas corpus."

"Alright. I see no reason to hold him. Go ahead and make arrangements with them. Anything else?" She asked with no response. "Alright, court is adjourned."

"Do another writ," my attorney whispered to me. On what grounds, I had no idea.

######

ON 'THE CHAIN'

Three weeks after the habeas hearing I was on "the chain," slang for 'prison bus,' with roots back to when they actually chained everyone together in a single line. Today they just handcuffed one prisoner to another in pairs, but the lingo still lives. The destination was Huntsville, the prison capital of Texas. After two weeks at the intake facility, new prisoners would be farmed out to prisons across the state. I had still not received a final answer from the Court of Criminal Appeals, but I didn't expect good news. I knew that I had not met my burden of proof.

A PASTOR'S PROFESSION

I hit the unit that I was assigned to in March 2007 and in April I received a postcard in the mail from the High Court of Texas. "On this date your writ of habeas corpus has been denied." No other explanation.

I signed up to go to the Law Library. Every prison is required to have one. I would get two hours a day, Monday through Friday. Where to begin.

I quickly learned that the next step in my legal process was to petition the federal courts. So I wrote a shortened version of what I had already written for the State. But under the rules of Federal Procedure, I was already time-barred from having my complaints heard under a strict one-year time limit that begins after the direct appeal is decided. My Federal application was denied on procedural grounds because the court-appointed direct appeals attorney failed to tell me that my appeal was denied. The clock was ticking away and I didn't even know it.

Next I wrote to the Fifth Circuit Federal Court of Appeals, telling them that it wasn't my fault that I had missed the filing deadline. My direct appeal attorney that the trial court had appointed to me had totally abandoned me. I even included copies of all the letters that were returned because he had moved four times. How could I keep up with that? How could I meet the federal deadline if my appellate attorney failed to tell me the outcome of the appeal?

The Fifth Circuit Court of Appeals wrote back, "just because you had a bad attorney does not justify a time-limit extension." I was at the end of the legal line, frustrated with nowhere to turn.

GERALD THOMAS

"Is this it, God?" I prayed. "It's hard for me to believe. You know I didn't do it, can this be the end? Is this where I will die? For something I didn't even do? How can this be?"

######

SERVING A LIFE SENTENCE

I slowly gave into the routine of daily life in prison. I wasn't the only one serving a life sentence here. Most of these men would never get out. Was I one of them? But still, I was somehow sure that God wasn't finished with this yet. The story was not over. God would speak, I was certain of it.

They assigned me to work in the kitchen and I quickly realized that I didn't like working behind the serving line or on the chow hall floor cleaning tables. There was an opening in the bakery and I jumped at the chance to work behind the scene. Texas doesn't pay prisoners to work, unlike most States and the federal prisons who pay their inmates something. But being a baker had some privileges. We ate well for one thing. We could make our own food and because the officer's meals were made in the bakery, we could eat the officer's food, which was prepared much better than the meals served to the inmates. I never went hungry in the bakery!

But baking for three-thousand people is not easy work. We served a dessert once a week. Cake, brownies, peach cobbler, pear or apple crisp. When I and four other bakers were tasked with making cake, for example, we made seventy sheet cakes. First we'd mix and pour out the

A PASTOR'S PROFESSION

batter for ten at a time. After pouring out seven batches, baking them, cooling them, we'd make the frosting, three batches. Then frost all seventy sheet cakes and cut them. It was a day-long no-break task, just so that everyone could enjoy a small square of cake. Few people realized the immense work involved in being a baker, but everyone looked forward to the one dessert they got each week.

When we weren't making dessert, we were making biscuits and cornbread. We had cornbread at most meals. It was hard work in a very hot bakery and I often left exhausted. But when I would hear people commenting to one another on how great the dessert was, I could hold my head up high and be proud. "Yeah," I would say, "I made that."

Pastor Dave was still sending me crossword puzzles that he cut out of the newspaper. I'd receive a large batch of them three or four times a year, and I got in the habit of bringing out one at a time and share working it with my new crossword buddies. The three of us would work a puzzle together to pass the time when I wasn't working at the bakery.

"You're going to be a great writ writer," one of my puzzle buddies said after I figured out a tough answer.

"How do you figure?" I asked in response.

"You can think outside the box." He said. In crossword puzzling, especially the tougher ones, the answer is always the not-so-obvious one. The easy answer, the one most people go for, is nearly always the wrong answer.

Little did I know, my crossword pal did a lot of legal work for people and he had lost two of his partners before I arrived. Now he was doing the work by himself. "Do you have a typewriter?" He asked me.

"No, but I can get one," I said. I still had some money that I brought with me, money I made at the Federal prison sewing army clothes.

"I need a good typist," he said, "and at the same time, you can learn how to be a jail-house lawyer and even make some money by typing."

The next time they called for us to go to the prison commissary I became the proud owner of an electric typewriter and very soon after that I was typing legal work that my crossword friend wrote for other prisoners and I started to learn how to find legal issues in a trial by reading the trial transcripts.

My crossword friend was very pleased with my work. "You make me look good," he would say, as I did slight editing of his work, never changing it but strengthening his wording and grammar. At the same time I was learning all of the issues that can come up at trial. Before long I was reading other people's direct appeals. I noted that my own direct appeal didn't look like any of these. Now I knew what a direct appeal was supposed to look like and I realized that my direct appeal was a frivolous piece of rubbish. All my appellate attorney did was copy my notes to him and turn them in as his own work. I hadn't received a fair appeal.

Pretty soon, my crossword/legal partner was working in the craft shop making money in metalworks and he began to send everyone who asked him for legal advice to me. "Make sure you talk to Thomas," he told them, "he's the only one I trust." That was because there were a lot of people trying to do legal work but most couldn't write a paragraph. I saw some of the work others did, masquerading it as legal work. How could anyone mess up someone's only opportunity for legal relief by turning in trash? It was a question I also wanted to ask my direct appeal attorney. They were ruining other people's lives.

As I learned legal issues for other people I amassed a long list of grievances on my own trial, mostly based on things that my attorney failed to do or failed to object to at trial. Pastor Carol should never have been allowed to testify. My hunch was right. She just muddied the waters. She had no first-hand knowledge and everything she said was pure conjecture. It was called third party extraneous testimony. The CD-ROM used by Luke was inadmissible as an illegal private search and seizure. It was improper to limit my defense that the lawsuit lawyers were behind the whole investigation. I learned that I had an absolute right to a defense called 'Frame-Up.' My trial attorney had sold me out by not standing up for my constitutional rights.

But there was one huge problem. In trial law, procedure is king, and the procedure is clear. Once a prisoner goes back to court on a habeas corpus, there are very few exceptions to the rule: You can't go back. 'One bite from the apple' is what they call it. Even if I found a hundred legitimate complaints about why my trial was unconstitutional, I couldn't go back. I tried to go back to court two more times. Both times

GERALD THOMAS

I was "DENIED as a subsequent writ." The court didn't want to hear from me again.

One exception existed, however, that the court would have to look at. A claim of actual innocence based upon newly discovered evidence. But if there was no evidence to begin with, how could I find evidence to prove my innocence?

######

PRAYING TO GOD FOR HELP

There was one way, as I saw it, and I'd read cases that were overturned because of it. At church each week, I prayed for it. "God," I prayed, "touch their hearts. Let them see the error of their ways and see to it that someone writes me a letter apologizing to me for lying." I had given God a task that didn't seem like it would be such a difficult assignment . . . for God. It was called a recantation letter and it would be newly discovered evidence of actual innocence that would get me back into court. *Touch their hearts, Oh Lord, set the record straight. AMEN.*

I prayed the same prayer every week for two years. I had found a way out and all I needed was for God to do God's part. But finally, the answer came in the most unexpected place.

I was up for parole on the first charge and had an appointment to see the parole counselor. Even though I had too many charges that were stacked one on top of the other to ever get out on parole, the first charge was a ten-year, third-degree and I was eligible for parole on it after three years. If I were to parole, the second charge would begin. So even though

A PASTOR'S PROFESSION

I had three hundred ninety-seven years and would never see the streets, I still had to go through the parole process every time each charge called for it.

As the counselor looked over my file, she asked me what was I doing in the courts.

"Well," I said, "I've been through the courts already. I even had a hearing on my habeas corpus. The only way I can get back in is to find new evidence, maybe a recantation. These guys are older now. Perhaps one of them will come to their senses, and realize the wrong they've done and recant their testimony."

She continued reading the file while she listened and finally, after a period of silence, she spoke. "That's not going to happen," she said matter-of-factly.

It was an answer to my prayer. It wasn't what I wanted to hear, but it was an answer all the same. Maybe I just needed to hear it out loud, but she was telling me in her professional opinion that I was barking up the wrong tree. It was a direct, clear answer to my prayer.

When we ask God for something in prayer, sometimes we forget to look for the answer. But there it was, as clear as a bell ringing in the silence. Who did I think I was, anyway, to tell God how to do His job? "That's not going to happen."

From then on, my prayer at church changed. Instead of telling God what I needed Him to do, my prayer was, "What do you want me to do, Lord God?"

GERALD THOMAS

I waited for the answer.

GOD SETS UP THE ANSWER

It was now 2015, eight years since I set foot on the unit. It had been four years since I last attempted to access the courts. As far as I could tell, they had succeeded in silencing me. My appeals were completed. I was shut out of the federal courts even before I began thanks to an appellate attorney who not only wasted my only direct appeal, but because he never contacted me afterwards, he also got me time-barred in the federal court. I had gotten a little action in the state courts, but that was very limited because I had to write my state habeas application while I was in federal prison where I had no access to state law resources. I was beat down by the system.

Then I hurt my ankle. It wouldn't seem like a hurt ankle would have anything to do with the legal process, but the outcome of having a hurt ankle is what gave me new hope.

My ankle had mysteriously swollen up and I couldn't walk on it. I ended up having to use crutches to get around. When the doctor asked me how I hurt it, I had to tell him that I honestly didn't know. I just woke up one morning to a painful, swollen ankle. The doctor signed me up to see a podiatrist. That meant a road trip to the prison hospital in Galveston.

A PASTOR'S PROFESSION

The night before I was scheduled to go on the prison bus, I packed up all my personal belongings to put in the Property Room while I was gone. The next morning I was on the bus headed back to the transfer unit in Huntsville. It had been eight years since I saw the outside world, and I enjoyed the view from the bus window.

The next morning we got started at two a.m. to eat breakfast and process out onto another bus for the three-hour ride from Huntsville through downtown Houston and to the prison hospital at University of Texas Medical Center. U.T. Medical held the contract to provide all medical treatment for Texas state inmates.

University of Texas Medical Center is a huge building in Galveston. We didn't enter through the front doors though. There is a side entrance for the prison buses and a specially built area to accommodate prisoners. Fully loaded buses emptied out into the specially designated area by six a.m. for the day's patient load. Inmates from all over Texas would see specialist for whatever ailed them.

Little by little, the large groups were separated into smaller groups based on medical issues. Hands, arms, and shoulders went to one department. Cancer treatment went to another. Knees, legs, and feet went yet in another direction. This was assembly-line medicine and the system was designed to see as many people as possible with maximum efficiency. My name was called and I went with the knee, leg, and feet group. But there was one glitch in this well-oiled medical machine that day. The podiatrist didn't show up.

"If you're here to see the foot doctor," the prison guard announced, "it's cancelled. You'll be rescheduled."

People were not happy and some expressed their dissatisfaction.

"I'm sorry," she said, "we keep telling them how much trouble you guys have to go through to get here, but the doctor's not here. Nothing we can do about it."

The inmates slowly realized that this poor woman was just the messenger. There was really nothing any of us could do but come back another time. It was a dry run.

By six p.m., everyone else had been seen and the smaller groups reformed into the larger groups, ready to make the three-hour bus trip back to Huntsville. I was finally in a bed by midnight. It had been a long day. At three a.m. I was woken up. "Bottom bunk, get ready. You're on the chain. I'll be back to get you in twenty minutes."

As I awoke from my three-hour nap, I couldn't help but think of the logistics involved in getting everyone to where they were supposed to be. When the cell door opened, I walked out, ate a quick breakfast, was processed out, and on a bus and back to the unit by seven a.m.

######

ANGELS DON'T HAVE WINGS

By July my ankle had seemed to have healed by itself, but when I was told that I was on the medical chain again, I figured I'd go anyway. This time I would be stuck at the transfer unit in Huntsville over the July Fourth weekend.

People from all over the Texas prison system would come and go, each on their own separate schedule. But with the buses idle on Friday, everyone was on standby until Monday. At the transfer unit, that meant that we would be inside a small cell all weekend long, coming out only for meals. My cellmate was an older Black gentleman originally from Georgia, living in Texas and doing some time for a parole violation on a drug charge.

He told me his story and I listened. The gift of listening is rare in prison and I put my listening skills to the test. He told me about how he had become a Christian, how he had been really working on some personal issues and coming to some understanding about how he got to where he ended up – again.

"When I get out this time," he said, "I'm going to look for a good woman – in church!" Part of his problem was that he had been looking for love in all the wrong places – strip clubs. It always led to disastrous consequences. I knew he was serious in his Christian walk now, and when he finished this sentence, he would probably stay out of trouble for the rest of his life.

Then he asked me a curious question. Curious because all I did was listen. I hadn't revealed anything about myself or my case. "Are you going to the law library?" he asked.

"No, they don't want to hear from me anymore." I responded.

"Go to the law library," he said sternly.

"I'm pretty much out of time, procedurally barred."

"I don't care," he said. "Go back. You never know what you're gonna find."

"I guess," I said half-heartedly.

The next morning was Saturday. There were no buses running, so I was surprised when the guard came to the cell to tell my cellmate that he was leaving. "Twenty minutes, step out when the cell door opens," the guard told him.

People come and people go around here, that's the workings of a transfer unit. I didn't know my cellmate's name and he didn't know mine, and in twenty minutes he'd go his way and on Monday I'd go mine. As he readied to leave I lay on my bunk giving him the space he needed to prepare before the cell door opened. Just another prisoner encounter. Here today – gone tomorrow.

That's what made what happened next so odd.

The cell door opened and my soon-to-be ex-cellmate made his way out. Then he stopped in the doorway of the cell and turned around. "Promise me, you'll go back to the law library." He said.

"What?" I asked as I put down a book that I had brought with me to read on what I knew would be a long weekend locked in a cell.

"Promise me you'll go back to the law library," he repeated. "I'm not leaving until you promise."

Is this guy for real? I thought, he'll never see me again once he leaves this cell and he wants me to make a promise.

A PASTOR'S PROFESSION

"Promise me," he said one more time while I thought this strange encounter through.

"Yes, I promise, I'll go back," I answered, and meant it.

"Alright." He said, seemingly content with my answer. Then he turned back around and walked out of the cell as the cell door closed behind him.

Isn't that something, I thought. I made a promise to a guy that I'll never see again. But promises are promises and I had every intention to keep my promise, even though it was totally unenforceable. It's a prison thing. Say what you'll do and do what you say. I believe even then that this was the answer to my prayer. "What do you want me to do, Oh God?"

"Go to the law library. Let me worry about the details," was the answer and it was loud and clear as though God Himself had spoken it.

God uses our circumstances and other people of God to tell us things we need to know; to provide the answers to our prayers. Angels don't have wings. They are the ordinary people of God who often provide extraordinary insight, information, and yes, even answers to the questions that we pose to God in our prayers. If you're looking for guidance or even an answer from God Most High, be open to the people of God. One of his Saints, his angels, might just be holding the answers to your prayers.

######

GERALD THOMAS

GOD THE PATHMAKER

On the Tuesday after Fourth of July weekend I arrived back to the unit with a new sense of purpose. I wasn't sure how God would pull it off, being I was procedurally barred from going back to court, but I now sensed that the answer was somewhere in the law library waiting to be found.

I remembered a story I used once in a sermon about a man in the midst of a flood. The water was up to the windows and he was standing on the roof of his house praying to God for help. An hour passed by and a man in a rowboat stopped to help. "Get in, I'll row you to higher ground," the row boater shouted to the man on the roof.

"No, that's O.K., God will save me," the stranded man on the roof shouted back. He prayed again for God to save him.

The water rose higher, now to the eaves, and someone in a canoe stopped by. "Get in and I'll paddle us to safety," the canoe paddler shouted.

"No, that's O.K. God will save me," the man on the roof shot back. Once again he prayed for God to save him.

Two hours later, the water was at the top of the roof, swishing at the man's feet and a helicopter hovered above with a rope ladder dangling in front of him. "Climb on," a voice shouted from the helicopter. "We'll fly you to safety."

"NO, that's O.K., God will save me," he yelled back. The helicopter moved on. Needless to say, the man drowned.

A PASTOR'S PROFESSION

Now standing before God, the man asked God, "I prayed that you'd save me three times. Why did you let me drown?"

"Yes it is true that you prayed three times for Me to save you," God said, "and I answered your prayer three times. First I sent a rowboat, then I sent you a canoe and the third time I sent you a helicopter."

I didn't want to be that man on the roof. Just like the man stranded on the roof, God wasn't going to plop a hand out of the sky and take me to higher ground. God wanted me to go back to the library even if I couldn't see how I would ever get back into court. It was time to trust God again and believe that God will find a way. God wanted to speak but I would have to do my part.

"There's only one problem, God," I prayed. "I know you want me to trust you and go back to the law library even though I see no way of getting around the procedural hurdles. But my bakery job is getting in the way. I've tried to quit but they won't let me." Once I missed a session at the law library because of work, it would take three more days to get back on the list, only to miss another day because we had to make a cake, a day-long project. I couldn't get any quality work done in the law library.

Thursday of that week, I was called down to the administration building. I walked into a meeting room with the Major and two other staff people. I was offered a seat across from them. The Major had my file in front of him and he read it while I sat there.

"I see that you have stacked sentences," he said, breaking the silence.

"Yes." I answered.

"Well, there's a new policy and I'm meeting with everyone who is in this category. I'm afraid that we're going to have to reclassify your custody level. Instead of being a G-2, you'll be a G-3." A G-3 status was a more restrictive level of custody.

"But I didn't do anything wrong," I said wondering why I was being punished with a more strict custody rating.

"No, no, it's nothing like that. It's a new law. I'm not even happy about it myself. What job do you have?" he asked.

"I'm a baker."

"Oh, no, you're not doing that anymore. G-3's don't work at all." Then I realized that this was God's answer to my prayer; my complaint to God that my bakery job was preventing me from going to the law library and it must have shown on my face.

"I'm sorry," he said, "but my hands are tied."

He had no idea what I was thinking, but his tied hands just freed mine.

By the time I got back to the housing building, staff had already been looking for me with a housing change. "Pack up," one of the staff told me, "you're moving to the other side of the farm." I would be housed with other inmates who were serving life sentences in a more secure area of the prison. I wouldn't be returning to the bakery the next day. I was free to devote all my time to studying law.

I didn't know what I would find and I didn't even see a way back to court, but it was time to trust God again. God had forged a path for me to follow and nothing could stop me now. I was on a mission from God. My hope had been restored.

######

MOVING FORWARD

Because I now had no job, my designated law library session was from 4:00 a.m. to 6:00 a.m. I had to be up and ready to go by 3:00, and my group of lifers and inmates who had life-without-parole were escorted to the law library for our session.

Legal research is slow and time consuming and I started with what I already knew was wrong with my trial. By reading court opinions of cases with those same issues, other issues would present themselves. Without knowing how I would overcome the procedural hurdles, I studied as though there were no procedural hurdles at all, trusting that God would reveal a solution to that problem later.

I found many cases that supported what I had already learned, including the United States Supreme Court rulings which stated that it was unconstitutional to limit my defense from discussing the pending lawsuit at trial. I found cases to support the issue that the CD evidence was obtained illegally and illegally seized evidence can never be used against a defendant at trial. I also found more cases to support the issue of third party testimony. Pastor Carol's testimony was illegal and my trial attorney didn't object to it. Had he objected to these issues at trial my conviction would have been overturned on direct appeal.

Then I began to find even more issues. The prosecutor had used my silence during the initial interrogation against me by twisting my Miranda rights into sounding like I was hiding something and not being truthful, even though there was nothing to lie about. I found numerous issues with the prosecutor's closing argument. The prosecutor vogued for the witnesses truthfulness. He told the jury that those kids had no reason to lie, even though he knew they had a motive to lie because the lawsuit was already pending.

In all, I found and developed fourteen different issues where my trial attorney did not object to the prosecutor's tactics, when an objection would have resulted in a reversal of my conviction on direct appeal. Because I didn't have access to the state cases in federal prison, I hadn't brought these issues up on my original state habeas corpus. I could have gotten a reversal when I went to court on my alibi witness issue. But without access to state legal resources, I couldn't know that these issues even existed.

By the middle of 2016, ten months after I began, I had a winning habeas corpus on what is called ineffective assistance of trial counsel. But for these errors of my trial counsel, by providing little or no adversarial challenge, the jury would probably have arrived at a different conclusion on guilt.

But even as good as it was, I still didn't have a way to overcome the procedural hurdles. A second habeas petition would have to show actual innocence. The bar is exceedingly more difficult after an original petition has been presented.

A PASTOR'S PROFESSION

I wasn't going to give up this time. God would provide me with the next step. God wants to speak and I would do my part to provide the platform for what God will do.

######

WAITING FOR THE ANSWER

It was November 2016, and I had been going to the law library every weekday for my two-hour session since July of 2015, when I got back from the road-trip from Galveston. I was satisfied with the issues. Everything was backed up with the case law, or opinions from the courts from other cases with the same issues. If only this were my first go around, I knew I would be successful. But now I had a great habeas writ application and nowhere to go with it.

Then, out of the clear blue, someone sitting at the same table as I was asked me a question. "Hey, Thomas, do you know anything about that new Supreme Court case regarding ineffective assistance of counsel?"

"No, I'm sorry, I don't," I answered, my ears perked up. "New case?"

Then another guy at the table piped in. "Yeah, it's the one where the court has to give you a lawyer for ineffective assistance cases."

"Really?" I said with interest. That's exactly what I needed. "Can you give me the case citation on that case?"

The next day he did, and although he wasn't totally accurate on what the case was about, it seemed to be even better. The Supreme Court stated that a Federal Court would review an ineffective assistance of counsel claim even if the claim hadn't been brought up on an original state habeas corpus application. Could this be used to overcome the procedural barriers put in place to bar a prisoner from ever going back to court with a complaint about his trial?

I started to read every case I could find about this new Supreme Court precedent. The case was decided in 2012. Then another case was decided a year later that made this exception applicable to Texas cases. I read everything I could find regarding this new exception to reviewing trial issues.

By early 2017, I had made the decision that I would attempt to go back to federal court rather than state court under the new exception. I had also found another Supreme Court decision with an issue just like mine. This defendant was also abandoned by his court-appointed direct appeals attorney. The Supreme Court determined that in a situation where the petitioner is abandoned by his attorney on his direct appeal, the one-year time limitation would not apply.

The High Court reasoned that it was unfair to hold someone accountable to a strict deadline when it wasn't their fault that they didn't know when the time-clock began. I certainly fell into that category. Could I use this new decision to get back into federal court? I was certainly going to give it a try.

On April 10, 2017, I mailed my written application to the Federal District Court in Marshall Texas. It was received and filed by the clerk on April 17. The waiting began.

######

A PASTOR'S PROFESSION

PART THREE
A PROFESSION OF HOPE

GERALD THOMAS

A DEFINITION OF HOPE

In Matthew 19:26, Jesus tells his disciples that "through God all things are possible." Although extreme miracles really do happen, we often are required to put in a little 'elbow grease' in order to provide God a platform from which God will speak.

Hope it can be a dangerous commodity and is frequently leveled as an advantage. Politicians have based their entire election campaigns on the platform of hope. Something better is yet to come. Bill Clinton ran for and won the presidency employing the theme of hope. "There's a place called Hope," was his main theme. He was referring to Hope, Arkansas, his hometown to portray the idea that as a nation we could attain a better standard of living. The future was brighter than the nation's present state of affairs.

President Barak Obama penned "The Audacity of Hope." Donald Trump ran his presidential campaign under the theme, "Make America Great Again" calling the nation to hope for the country of the past. The concept supposes that the country was great at one time in its history and we can return to that greatness again; to something we once were but lost somewhere along the way. Hope is an expectation of something better than what we are presently experiencing.

Television evangelists often sell us hope. Many base their sermons on the Theology of Entitlement. "Receive your blessing." They tell us that as a child of God, you have a blessing coming. Sometimes your blessing is tied into sending them a love offering for a promise of hope in something better to come your way.

A PASTOR'S PROFESSION

In Greek mythology, Jupiter gave Pandora a box and was told to give it to her husband, Epimetheus. As soon as he opened it all of the diseases and evils of the world escaped and spread out over the world. Quickly shutting the box, Hope was left inside lying at the bottom. Pandora was left with the dilemma as to whether or not she should go ahead and let Hope out of the box as well. It had its good points and bad points. If she opened the box and let hope out, the world would have something to live for, something to keep her human subjects happy and content. Her subjects would live for what the future could bring them, rather than simply living in the present suffering that life offered them.

On the other hand, it could give her people a sense of false hope. They would always expect something better in life, an expectation that could never be realized. Pandora ultimately chose to open the box and let hope out, for better or for worse. Today we call it "Pandora's Box" when we are faced with a dilemma of opening up a certain issue or keeping it closed.

In Spanish, the word 'hope' and 'wait' share same root word, "I wait" is "Yo espero." "Hope" is "Esperanza."

Is waiting and hoping the same? We wait for our birthday because it is a fact that our birthday is coming. But we can only hope for a particular birthday gift that we may or may not receive. Whether we get a new car for our birthday is based on a number of factors.

But we must be careful not to confuse "hope" with "wishful thinking." Hope is something more. It is much deeper than a wish. The Old

Testament Book of Lamentations is exactly what you would expect. It is a lament over the destruction of Jerusalem by the Babylonians, who broke through the walls of the city in 586 B.C. Destroying the city, they took the captives to Babylon. The poetry of Lamentations yearns for a life and culture lost to the present situation of captivity. There seemed to be no end in sight for the captives.

In Lamentations 3:19-24, there is a glimmer of hope, and that hope is tied to the LORD God, and God's saving power.

> 19 The thought of my affliction and my homelessness
>   is wormwood and gall!
> 20 My soul continually thinks of it
>   and is bowed down within me.
> 21 But this I call to mind,
>   and therefore I have hope.
> 22 The steadfast love of the LORD never ceases,
>   His mercies never come to an end;
> 23 they are new every morning,
>   great is your faithfulness.
> 24 "The LORD is my portion" says my soul,
>   "therefore I will hope in Him."

Proverbs 23:18 pairs hope with the future:

> 18 Surely there is a future,
>   And your hope will not be cut off.

In the New Testament Hope is tied to the Resurrection. What seemed to be the end on the cross became the beginning of salvation grounded

A PASTOR'S PROFESSION

in hope and redemption. A situation that first seemed devoid of hope gave new meaning to human suffering. At once, all human suffering became merely temporary because in the Resurrection Jesus defeated death itself.

Paul's letter to the early church in Rome tells them in Romans 12:12, "Rejoice in hope, be patient in suffering, persevere in prayer." Paul tells them, "hope does not disappoint us, because God's grace has been poured into our hearts through the Holy Spirit that has been given to us."

The apostle Peter writes in his first letter, "By [God's] great mercy, [God] has given us a new birth into a living hope through the resurrection of Jesus Christ from the dead and into an inheritance that is imperishable, undefiled, and unfading, kept in heaven for you, who are being protected by the power of God through faith for salvation, ready to be revealed in the last time." (I Peter 1:3-5). "In this you rejoice, even if now for a little while you have to suffer various trials." (v. 6).

Finally, in the letter to the Hebrews, the writer says that "faith is the assurance of things hoped for, the conviction of things not seen." (Heb. 11:1). There is a great deal more written in the New Testament as well as the Old Testament, but these few verses and concepts provide the basis for my definition of hope:

Hope is waiting for something better to occur, and advance or improvement from the current situation of your human experience. Hope is a confident expectation in what God will do. It is knowing in your very soul that the current way that things are is not the way things are supposed to be. Hope is the confidence that God will make things right. In that way, hope is tied to justice. When justice is absent there is always hope for what things should be because justice fixes injustice in the same way that light always overcomes the darkness. Hope is grounded in justice because God is interested in what is right.

Hope is believing that something better than what you are presently experiencing is just over the horizon, out of sight yet not out of touch. Faith is hope in that which you cannot see. Hope is a deep conviction that God is not finished with your story. God will speak!

######

THE BEGINNING OF A LONG LEGAL PROCESS

A Federal Habeas Corpus goes through a lot more process than a State Habeas Petition. Once a petition is filed with the clerk, a federal Magistrate Judge takes over. If the Magistrate Judge deems that there could be issues, then an order is issued for the state to respond. The State Attorney General's office assigns one of their attorneys to answer the suit. Then, after an opportunity for the petitioner to respond to the Attorney General's answer, the Magistrate Judge makes a Report and Recommendation. If the Report and Recommendation is not favorable the petitioner has an opportunity to object to the Magistrate's Report.

After an objection is filed, the Federal Judge takes over and reviews everything, weighing heavily upon the Magistrates Report and Recommendation. Finally, the judge makes a decision.

A PASTOR'S PROFESSION

On December 8, 2019, thirty-two months after filing the original petition, the judge issued an order. "After carefully considering the issues, the Court has determined that it lacks jurisdiction to adjudicate the petition. Therefore, the writ is DENIED without prejudice to return after jurisdiction is granted by a higher court." The order came exactly twelve years and eleven months from the time I started my state sentence.

Sometimes what the court doesn't say is as important as what the court does say. The judge did not say that the issues had no merit. Only that because this was a successive petition, the court needed permission from a higher court before it could proceed in the district court. My argument that my first petition was wrongfully dismissed for being time-barred because my appellate attorney had abandoned me did not change his decision in my favor. But the opportunity was still open to return to this court to have the merits reviewed after receiving a favorable ruling on the jurisdictional issue. Procedure is king, merits only secondary.

Based on what I had read of opinions coming from the Fifth Circuit, I knew that my chances of a favorable ruling from them was minimal. But I was not deterred. God had taken me this far, from a point of despair and hopelessness to a new understanding of hopeful anticipation. I simply needed the courts to do their part. My conviction was unjust but God had shown me that I would be redeemed.

I had been continuing to study law faithfully, attending my law library session every day. Consequently, I had strengthened my legal arguments. On March 11, 2020, I appealed the district court's decision to the Fifth

GERALD THOMAS

Circuit Federal Court of Appeals in New Orleans. The Fifth Circuit Handles all Federal Appeals for Texas, Louisiana, and Mississippi. I waited in hopeful anticipation for a decision.

######

IT'S IN THE NUMBER

When an inmate is received into the prison system, prison personnel make an ID card with the new inmates' photograph and prison number on it and each prisoner is issued an "Offender ID Card." (In Texas a prisoner is identified as an 'Offender', a title meant to be dehumanizing.) The number is derived simply by adding one number to the person who is standing in line in front of you, so the numbering system is sequential, one number higher than the person in front of you and one less than the person standing behind you. According to Texas, I am the $1,415,141^{st}$ customer to the Texas prison system.

1-4-1-5-1-4-1. A pretty cool number I thought, as far as prison numbers go. It's a numerical palindrome – the same backwards as it is forwards. Not only that, but with the number "5" in the center, on both sides of the five is an identical mini-palindrome, 1-4-1. If I were playing Bluff Poker with this number I would certainly win with four aces and a pair of fours. But there must be more to the meaning of this number than it just being a pretty cool number. While many people over the years have also commented on my unique number, it would take years before I would unravel its significance.

A PASTOR'S PROFESSION

One day I was tasked with printing out my ID number onto a form which also directed me to fill in the corresponding 'bubbles' so that a computer could read it, and in doing so, I saw my number in a completely different light:

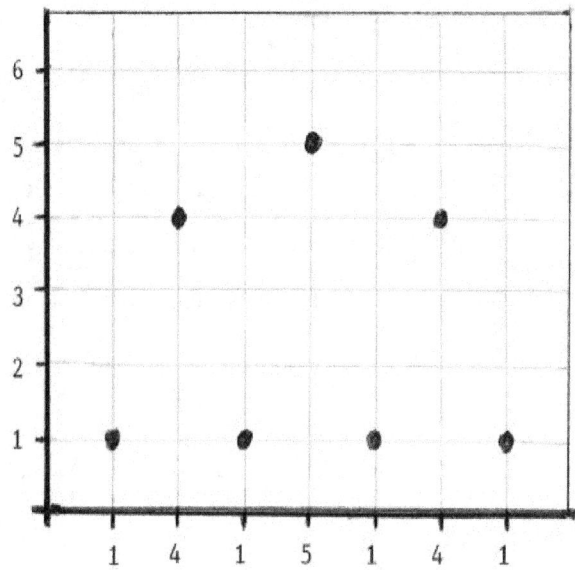

That was when I realized that I was supposed to interpret my number not in One-Dimensional, linear form, but rather in Two-Dimensional plane or graph form. In other words, a one-dimensional form was purely a physical realm. But a two-dimensional form was spiritual. When I saw my ID number in two-dimensional for the first time, I knew that I needed to study numbers in the Bible. Could the Bible give me some insight into understanding my ID number from a spiritual perspective?

After studying numbers in the Bible, I came back with some astonishing answers! First, I realized that the number was not only a perfect number in linear form, but it was also a perfect number in two-dimensional, spiritual form as well.

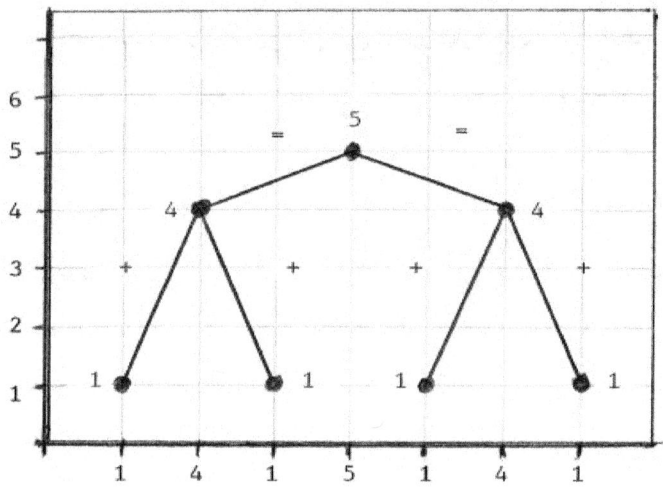

A PASTOR'S PROFESSION

On either side of the middle number five, each of the pairs of numbers, one and four, when added together equals the five. The number '14' is a significant number as well. In Matthew 1:17, it reads, "So all the generations from Abraham to David are fourteen generations, and from David to the deportation to Babylon, fourteen generations, and from the deportation to the Messiah, fourteen generations." The NRSV translation includes a footnote which reads, "Fourteen is the numerical value of 'David' in Hebrew." In two-dimensional form, the number fourteen comes up four times in my prison number.

There is another meaning for the number fourteen in the Bible. The number signifies "release and deliverance" and it's based upon the Old Testament story of Jacob and Rachel in Genesis 29. Jacob entered into servitude to Laban, his uncle, for fourteen years in order to take Rachel, Laban's second-oldest daughter, as his wife. Would the number fourteen have something to do with my sentence, release and deliverance? At this point I could only rely on conjecture and hope. I also know that it is dangerous to try and predict what God is doing. I'll just have to 'go with the flow' and see where it ends.

If we were able to transpose my prison number into my entire story something else happens when the five represents my trial, the middle of the story. When the five represents my trial, we are left with two identical triangles, one representing everything that happened before trial and another representing everything that happened after the trial:

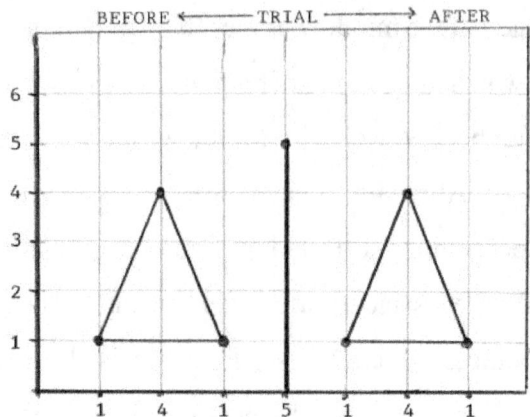

Two identical, perfect triangles on either side of the trial. In Christianity, the triangle represents the Holy Trinity – Father, Son, and Holy Spirit, the perfect presence of God.

In the first part of my story, (before trial) I told about having been asked to play the part of Jesus four different times, in four different places by four different groups of people, none of whom knew the others. (There's the number four again,) I was assigned the part of Jesus by my co-workers at camp while I was away. They had elected me to play the part of Jesus in our Passion Play up to and including the Crucifixion Scene starting on July 13, 1983.

Then in two other places, Emmanuel Lutheran Church in Mt. Pleasant, Michigan in 1985 and at Resurrection Lutheran Church in Saginaw, Michigan, in 1990, I was asked, both times by two women, to make a personal appearance as Jesus for their Vacation Bible School.

A PASTOR'S PROFESSION

Finally, in June 1996 at St. John's in Wilson, Texas, I was asked to play the part of the Resurrected Christ, a small part without spoken words, but not at all an insignificant part. The time that transpired between having portrayed Crucifixion Jesus at camp until I portrayed Resurrection Jesus in Texas was twelve years and eleven months. Not thirteen years, but precisely twelve years and eleven months.

Twelve is an important number in Biblical literature, as it means, "The Governance of God," or "God is in Control," or "The Order of God." The number twelve is found throughout the Bible. First, in the Old Testament there are twelve tribes of Israel. In the New Testament there are twelve disciples of Jesus. When Jesus feeds the five thousand, there are twelve baskets full of food leftover. (Mt. 14:20, Mk 6:42-43, Lk 9:17).

In his Revelation, John reveals, "Then the Angel showed me the river of the water of life, bright as crystal, flowing from the throne of God and the Lamb through the middle of the street of the city. On either side of the river is the tree of life with twelve kinds of fruit." (Rev. 22:1-2). This "twelve" is what is represented by the triangle "Before Trial", signifying the lapse of time between playing Crucifixion Jesus and Resurrection Jesus.

Then came the trial, another kind of crucifixion. Not a literal one, mind you, but a legal one indeed. The State's main witness against me was himself in legal trouble and he knew that he was headed back to youth prison. He couldn't fathom going back so with the help of his lawsuit lawyers, he devised a story that would portray himself as a victim and in doing so they would put the blame of all of his troubles on me. Instead of being the ' bad kid,' they would look at him as the poor, innocent victim, perfect and blameless, whereas I would be viewed with disgust, hatred and disdain as a violent predator. He would get off scott-free and I instead would go to prison with multiple life sentences.

Once more, for the fifth time and represented by the number "5", I would take on the part of Jesus. Once more I didn't ask for it. Instead it was thrust upon me. But isn't that what Jesus does for us? He takes on our sins so that we are blameless in the presence of God. And in the same fashion my accuser would go free, blameless for his criminal actions while I would receive life sentences for criminal acts that I did not commit. It would be the "best sentence ever handed down in this courtroom," the judge would say. But somehow I knew even then, standing in front of the judge while she pronounced my life sentences that God had yet to speak, and the number twelve would come up again in a very profound way.

As the triangle on the left side represented the twelve years and eleven months span of time I portrayed Jesus from crucifixion to resurrection before trial, the triangle on the right represents twelve years and eleven months after trial. The first decision by the Federal Judge came to me dated December 9, 2019. Calculating the time span from there back to when I began my state sentence, December 26th, 2006, it was exactly twelve years, eleven months into my state sentence! The triangles, the perfect presence of the Triune God – identical to one another represented an identical time span before and after trial.

It was the governance of God. God is in control. God's perfect presence before and after trial was absolutely real, as evidenced through my prison ID number. Two perfect triangles representing the exact time frame, twelve years and eleven months. But what about the trial itself? Where was God at my trial where I had to sit there as I was made out to be the most horrible, vile person in the history of that trial court. It seemed like God was nowhere to be found.

In the Gospel of Mark, before "breathing his last" on the cross, Jesus' last words were, "My God, my God, why have you forsaken me?" It is a quote of Psalm 22: 1. (also in Matthew 27:46). Did Jesus feel that he was abandoned by God? Where were all of the people that Jesus had ministered to? Where were all of those people whom Jesus fed or healed? Where were all the people who marveled at his teachings and sermons? Not at the foot of the cross. Where were his own disciples? Hiding away in some room trying not to be found. Yes, at that exact time on the cross, things looked very bleak. Where was God in the midst of such pain and suffering?

The cross is a very lonely place. A crucifixion is a very degrading, demoralizing, dehumanizing event. Was God nowhere to be found? Standing in front of the judge handing down "the best sentence ever handed down in this courtroom," I could only stand there while everyone looked on believing that I was the worst, most disgusting human being that ever walked into this courtroom. Is that what Jesus felt, with the sins of the whole world on his shoulders? Would God turn his head away for the time being only to speak three days later on Resurrection Sunday?

But in a paradoxical way, in a twist of fate, it is precisely at the cross where God meets us, as my prison ID number shows:

A PASTOR'S PROFESSION

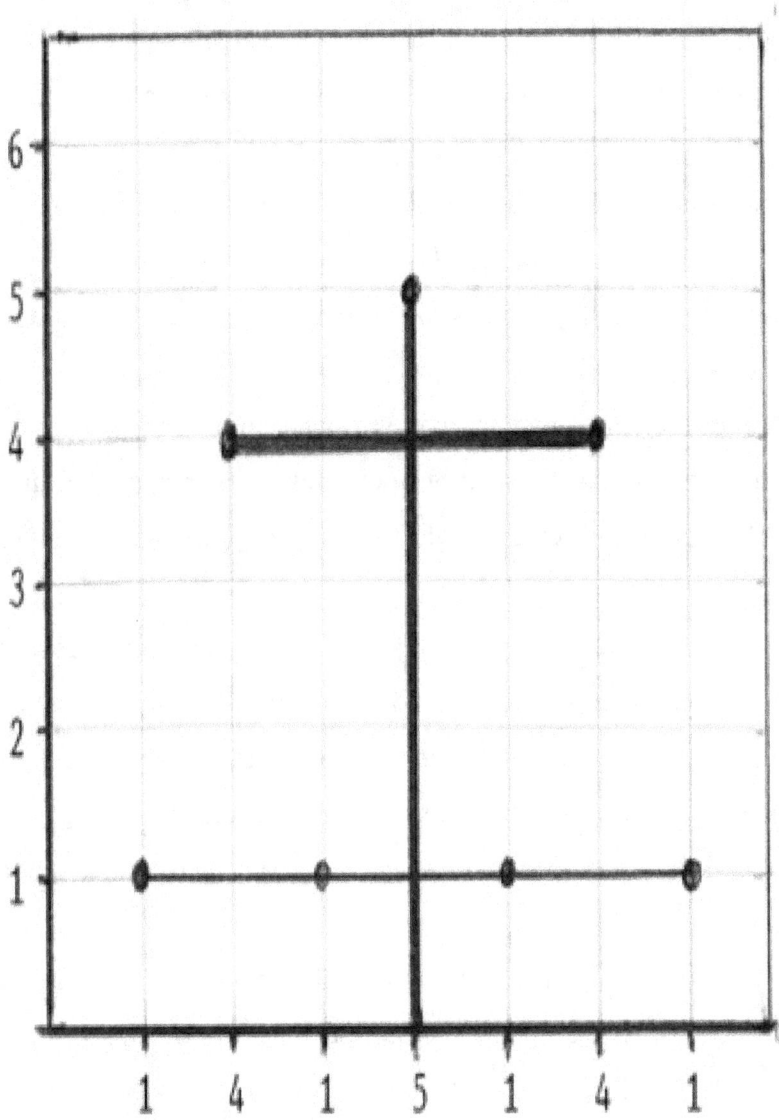

The empty cross has historically signified the Risen Christ, and there it was staring me in the face all this time! The resurrection of Jesus proves that God is present where the cross bar meets the cross post. In my case it was the trial. It was as though God was telling me through my ID number, "Sit tight, my child. You will be resurrected from the seemingly hopeless legal situation."

In the same way God wasn't speaking at Jesus's crucifixion, God was seemingly not speaking for me. Where were my witnesses? I would later find out that either they refused to testify or they weren't summoned to appear at all.

But even then, in the midst of a legal persecution, I knew deep in my soul, that this was not finished business. Jesus was resurrected in three days. My legal resurrection would take twelve years eleven months to begin.

When I finally realized this, I knew as a fact that I could depend on that my wrongful conviction would be overturned. This is simply too perfect. Some Christian people say that they don't believe in coincidences, that everything happens for a reason. Personally, I don't totally rule out a coincidence because a coincidence is one of t'e possibilities of reality.

But too many coincidences is too much. This is designed. It is God ordering chaos because that is what God likes to do. This is way too perfect to be anything else but God's handiwork. I'm still not sure how the Court will rule in my case. But I already know the ultimate answer. I shall be redeemed from this legal crucifixion. It's all there in my prison ID number.

######

A PASTOR'S PROFESSION

A NEW PATH OPENS

On February 25, 2021, fourteen months after the final order was signed in Federal District Court, the Fifth Circuit Court of Appeals denied my appeal. I filed for a rehearing in an attempt to get all of the judges to look at my legal briefing, but that was denied one month later on March 25, 2021, twelve months after I first filed the appeal. I found it interesting, even peculiar, the number twelve and fourteen would show up again and again. I could only think that this was God's handiwork putting the chaos in order. That's what God likes to do.

While still waiting for the federal appeals court to respond, I wrote to the Supreme Court of the United States, the highest court in the land, and the clerk sent me a packet which included the Rules of the Court and a template that I was to use in order to write a Writ of Certiorari, a plea to the Supreme Court to hear my case. The Court lets you know up front that your chances of being heard are slim. The odds of my case getting chosen by the High Justices were one out of a hundred. For every hundred petitions received, only one would be chosen to be considered.

The highest court in the land had their hands full with issues of national significance. Voting Rights. Abortion. Gun control. Freedom of speech. Police violence and professional immunity issues. I knew going in that the Supreme Court was probably not interested in hearing my case, but I prepared and sent in a Writ of Certiorari on July 7, 2021.

But God was already opening a path for me to go back to State Court. I believe that God had told me to go back to the law library back in 2016 and God hadn't told me to stop going, so I had been faithfully studying law ever since, not missing a day unless to miss was out of my control. Now, I had found an exception to the One-Shot Rule other than proving actual innocence.

It was now easier to overturn a trial conviction by showing that the witness lied. No longer would a habeas petitioner have to prove that the lie actually caused the conviction. A habeas petitioner no longer had to prove perjury but only that the witness lied. Perjury is more difficult to prove because one must show that the witness intended to lie. But now, the standard was easier to prove. One would just have to prove the lie. A conviction cannot stand on false testimony. I fit into that exception for reviewing a subsequent habeas petition.

It was as though a new pathway had been forged. It was an important discovery and I began to study cases that had met this exception in the past. This new law could get me around the procedural hurdle. I prepared to go back to state court.

######

A MODERN PSALM

The Psalms of the Old Testament are a collection of poetry that was originally accompanied by music and used in a worship setting. Of the one hundred fifty Psalms in the collection, seventy-two are ascribed to King David. Tradition tells us that King David wrote the Psalms, but modern scholarship has determined that the authors are many and authorship spans hundreds of years. The Psalms attest to a variety of situations in life; complaints and cries for divine intervention.

The Psalms can be categorized by types. One category is called Hymns of Praise or Thanksgiving. One of my favorite Psalms in this category is Psalm 91. "Say to the LORD, 'My refuge and my fortress, my God to whom I trust.'" (v. 2). The Psalmist uses imagery of God as protector, as wings of a large bird under which the author finds refuge. (v. 4). "You will not fear the terror of the night or the arrow that flies by day." (v. 5). "For he will command his angels concerning you to guard you in all your ways." (v. 11). The Psalm's divine imagery is beautiful.

Another category of Psalms is Laments. Approximately one-third of the Psalms are Laments. A lament is God's people seeking God to intervene for them. The Laments are either corporate, a hardship of the community, or individual hardship, which is written in first-person. Personal Laments offer a wide variety of topics, from illness to protection from enemies or even help when others have lied or given false testimony. These are some of my favorite Laments and a few verses from each:

Psalm 26: Vindicate me, O LORD, (v. 1) But as for me, I walk in my integrity; redeem me and be gracious to me. (v. 11) . . . I will bless the LORD." (v. 12).

Psalm 43: Vindicate me, O God, and defend my cause, against an ungodly people, from those who are deceitful and unjust, deliver me! (v. 1) Why must I walk about mournfully because of the opposition of the enemy? (v. 2) Hope in God; for I shall again praise him, my help and my God. (v. 5).

Psalm 54: Save me, O God, by your name, and vindicate me by your might. (v. 1) For the insolent have risen against me. (v. 3). With a free will offering I will sacrifice to you, I will give thanks to your name, O LORD, for it is good. (v. 6).

Psalm 55: Attend to me; and answer me, I am troubled in my complaint, I am distraught by the noise of the enemy . . . For they bring trouble upon me and in anger they cherish enmity against me. (v. 2). But I call upon God and the LORD will save me. (v. 16). He will redeem me unharmed from the battle that I wage, for many are arrayed against me. (v. 18). Cast your burdens on the LORD, and he will sustain you. (v. 22). But I will trust in you. (v. 23).

Psalm 59: Deliver me from my enemies, O my God, protect me from those who rise up against me . . . Even now they lie in wait for my life; the mighty stir up strife against me. (v. 3). But you laugh at them, O LORD (v. 8). O my strength I will watch for you, for you, O God, are my fortress. (v. 9). But I will sing your might . . . I will sing praises to you. (v. 16-17).

Psalm 62: For God alone my soul waits in silence. (v. 1) How long will you assail a person? (v. 3). They take pleasure in falsehood, they bless with their mouths, but inwardly they curse. (v. 4). For God alone my soul waits in silence, for my hope is from him. (v. 5). Trust in him at all times, O People, pour out your hearts before him; God is a refuge for us. (v. 8).

A PASTOR'S PROFESSION

Psalm 69: Save me, O God, for the waters have come up to my neck. (v. 1). I am weary with my crying; my throat is parched. My eyes grow dim with waiting for my God. (v. 3). Many are those who would destroy me, my enemies who accuse me falsely. (v. 4). I am the subject of gossip for those who sit at the gate. (v. 12). Answer me, O LORD, for your steadfast love is good. (v. 16). Let the heavens and earth praise him, the seas and everything that moves in them. (v. 34).

Psalm 86: Incline your ear, O LORD, and answer me, for I am poor and needy. (v. 1). Be gracious to me, O LORD, for to you do I cry all day long. (v. 3). In the day of my trouble I call on you for you will answer me. (v. 7). The insolent rise up against me. (v. 14). But you, O LORD, are a God merciful and gracious, slow to anger and abounding in steadfast love and faithfulness. (v. 15). Show me a sign of your favor, so that those who hate me may see it and be put to shame, because you, LORD, have helped me and comforted me. (v. 17).

Psalm 102: Hear my prayer, O LORD; let my cry come to you. (v. 1). All day long my enemies taunt me. (v. 8). But you, O LORD, are enthroned forever, your name endures to all generations. (v. 12). You are the same, and your years have no end. (v. 27).

Psalm 109: Do not be silent, O God of my praise. (v. 1). For the wicked and deceitful mouths are opened against me, speaking against me with lying tongues. (v. 2). They beset me with words of hate, and attack me without cause. (v. 3). In return for my love they accuse me even while I make prayers for them. (v. 4). So they reward me evil for good, and hatred for my love. (v. 5). But you, O LORD, act on my behalf for your name's sake; because your steadfast love is good, deliver me. (v. 21). With my mouth, I will give great thanks to the LORD; I will praise him in the midst of the throng. (v. 30). For he stands at the right hand of the needy, to save them from those who would condemn them to death. (v. 31).

Psalm 140: Deliver me, O LORD, from evil doers. (v. 1). They make their tongues sharp as a snake's. (v. 3). The arrogant have hidden a trap for me, along the road they have set snares for me. (v. 5). I say to the LORD, "You are my God." (v. 6). Do not grant, O LORD, the desires of the wicked; do not further their evil plot. (v. 8). I know that the LORD maintains the cause of the needy, and executes justice for the poor. (v. 12). Surely the righteous shall give thanks to your name, the upright shall live in your presence. (v. 13).

Psalm 143: Hear my prayer, O LORD: give ear to my supplications in your faithfulness; answer me in your righteousness. (v. 1). For the enemy has pursued me, crushing my life to the ground, making me sit in darkness like those long dead. (v. 3). Let me hear of your steadfast love in the morning for in you I put my trust. Teach me the way I should go, for to you I lift up my soul. (v. 8). In your steadfast love, cut off my enemies for I am your servant. (v. 12).

Each of these laments puts forth the author's complaint to God. It's not always clear what the exact issue is, but the authors use war-like imagery to paint a life situation that they are facing. Often, they are actually alluding to the enemies of war. But not always. Psalm 62

A PASTOR'S PROFESSION

specifically states that "they take pleasure in falsehood." Psalm 69 also states, "My enemies who accuse me falsely." This psalmist also complains that he is the subject of gossip. Psalm 109 complains that the wicked and deceitful mouths are opened against me, speaking against me with lying tongues. Psalm 140 speaks of evildoers who "make their tongues sharp as snakes." Yes, I can especially relate to these.

We ought to feel a sense of kindred to the Ancients who suffered. Suffering is not a new concept and as such, my story is a Modern Psalm. But there is one thing we suffering people can learn from the ancient people of God. Although each Psalm begins with a complaint of suffering, each psalm also ends with praise. The praise does not come because God has answered the Psalmist's complaint favorably, but simply because God loves and God deserves praise.

Suffering is not new to the human experience. There has always been, and there always will be iniquities, infirmities, and unfairness. It's part of the human condition. We can go to God with our complaints and laments, but let us not forget to sing praise to God, Creator, Protector, Redeemer, and Deliverer. That's what the Ancients did. The Psalms teach us to do the same.

Psalm 146: Praise the LORD, Oh my soul, I will praise the LORD as long as I live; I will sing praises to my God.

######

GERALD THOMAS

BLAZING NEW PATHS

On October 20, 2021, the United States Supreme Court denied my Writ of Certiorari. It only took three months for them to decide. At least the High Court didn't hold on to it for years before turning it down and I knew it didn't have anything to do with whether or not the issues were good. The Writ of Certiorari is completely discretionary as to whether or not the court takes up the petition.

But I was not deterred. God had blazed a new path. I learned that I would be able to go back to state court under a new state standard of showing that the witness lied to the jury. The first time I went back to state court I was trying to prove another lie, that Mark told the jury that I directed him to make lewd videos. I had an alibi witness from the very beginning because I wasn't even in the house when it happened. But I couldn't prove it because four years later my alibi witness couldn't remember the exact date. But now I remembered the other lie that he never told anyone about the alleged assaults until the police came to visit him.

I remembered the police report. The detective had written that he was called by the prosecutor who had been called by the lawsuit lawyer and in turn went out to the juvenile lock-up facility to obtain a statement that became the basis for three first-degree charges, which in turn amounted to three life sentences – stacked. It was the only evidence these charges were based on. But the detective's report proved that Mark had lied. He didn't tell the police first. He told the lawsuit lawyers first.

A PASTOR'S PROFESSION

I began to zero in on this issue in my legal studies. First I would need a copy of that report. So, I sent away for the report while I began studying the issue. I needed proof and the report itself would be that proof. No wonder why the prosecutor didn't call on the detective to testify. The prosecutor wanted the lawsuit lawyer's role to remain hidden from the jury. I might be able to expose a major conspiracy in keeping vital information from the jury.

There is a Supreme Court decision from 1959 called Napue v. Illinois. It's far from new. It's stated that the government cannot allow its witnesses to lie on the witness stand without correcting them. With the police report I could prove that the prosecutor actually knew that his witness lied and covered it up.

I would also have to prove that the lie was material. That would be more difficult. But without any additional proof that the assaults even happened, proving a lie goes back to Mark's credibility. Because the jury found me guilty based only on credibility, whether or not they believed him, exposing a lie on the witness stand goes directly to a witness's credibility.

The prosecutor knew his witness lied because the prosecutor had the police report. That's why he didn't call the detective to testify at trial; the lie would have been exposed at trial. Then in his closing argument, the prosecutor told the jury that his witnesses had told the truth and that they had no reason to lie. We all knew that wasn't true. As I saw it, Mark had plenty of reasons to lie. First, he would get out of the trouble he was in. Secondly, there was an active lawsuit against the church which he had a direct interest in the outcome. I had a constitutional right for the jury to know these facts and I had case law to support my position. There was a motive to lie and the court would not allow me to disclose this information to the jury.

The police department would not allow for me to have the police report, based on law that forbids them from disclosing information of child abuse to the public, including me, the accused. It is considered private work product of the department. But the law also states that with a court order, the department would still have to disclose the report. So I motioned the court to order the police department to disclose the report.

With the motion for disclosure and discovery, and my habeas corpus petition, I was ready to submit. I believed that I could prove a cover-up and conspiracy between the prosecutor, the witness and the lawsuit lawyer. The big question was whether or not I could convince the judge.

I said a prayer over the finished legal work and in April 2022, I sent the writ application to the trial court. The last time I was in court for my hearing was February 2007, exactly fourteen years and fourteen months had passed between time.

God is in control!

######

A PASTOR'S PROFESSION

THE GREAT WEAVER OF LIFE

Like many churches around the country at the time, my internship congregation in West Texas had a quilting bee. Usually consisting of older women, they met in the fellowship halls and basements of churches across the country to fellowship and to make quilts. Our quilting group met in the education building. Once a year these beautiful handmade quilts were collected and together with all the other quilts made throughout the entire country, were sent overseas for use in hospitals around the world. In that way the quilting groups performed a wonderful ministry.

It wasn't unusual to see our quilting bee assembling quilts and I often marveled at their work. Three-inch squares were cut from colorful fabrics, usually leftover scraps from other projects; hand sewn together. Then a border was sewed around the sewn-together small squares. Finally a batting and a bottom cover were quilted together to the top squares. Every inch was hand stitched. The finished quilts were beautiful, colorful creations.

So, in April I wasn't surprised to see our women assembling a quilt and, as my office was also in the education building, I walked over to greet them and watch as they worked their quilting magic. This quilt was especially beautiful with squares of reds, blues, greens, and yellows, all with different patterns to them. The scraps of fabric were cut down to size and sewn together into a brand new creation.

"It's beautiful work," I told them, and I wasn't kidding.

"It's for the school auction," one of the quilters answered.

I knew that was very plausible. The Band Boosters and the Athletic Club parents would hold an annual auction to raise money. Pies and cakes and quilts were among the items that the community would bid on. I had heard that a good pecan pie could fetch as high as two hundred dollars at one of these auctions. The bidding was fierce.

"Well, someone will be very happy to have this beautiful quilt." I said, and after watching them for a while I left thinking nothing more of it.

In May, towards the end of my internship year, we had a church potluck to celebrate my birthday; a gathering for fellowship and good food. And a gift for the intern pastor. They wanted me to open it in front of everyone.

I quickly unwrapped the large box and I was very surprised at what I saw. It was the beautiful quilt I had watched them sew together a few weeks prior. Smiling, I said, "Oh, this looks familiar."

Everyone watching me laughed. They all knew that I had walked in on the quilting bee making my birthday gift. Now they were all in on it.

"We had to have a story in case you walked in on us," one of the quilters confessed. "So we came up with the school auction."

"Well, it worked," I said. "I had no idea. Thank you. It's beautiful." It was a gift that I would treasure and I still do even though I've lost everything I owned.

This beautiful quilt was a metaphor for life itself. Each life is a beautiful, colorful, unique creation, hand stitched with love by the Great Weaver of Life. Each colorful square is a different pattern, texture, color, representing all of life's experiences, each and every life is a tapestry; a unique collection of squares, sewn together with the threads of life.

As we age and mature, we can look back at our unique 'quilt' and view it from a distance. Only then has our bad experiences lost some of its sting. But those are in there too. Woven into the human experience. Brokenness, and despair, strife, struggle, sewn together alongside happiness, victory, celebrations and fond memories. It's what makes each quilt so colorful and unique and what makes each life so remarkable, precious and beautiful.

Life is precious, a gift from the Great Weaver of Life. In the midst of the battles, sometimes it just doesn't feel that way. Faith is going through it anyway. Hope is knowing that the struggles are merely temporary.

God has never promised that we would live a trouble-free life. We are often the product of other people's bad choices. But as Psalm 23 reminds us at verse four:

> Even though I walk through the valley of the shadow of death, I will fear no evil;
>
> for you are with me;
>
> your rod and your staff - -
>
> they comfort me."

God's promise is to be with us through those valleys, to comfort, to guide, and to lead.

######

GERALD THOMAS

THE COURT'S ANSWER

It didn't take long for the court to rule on my newest complaints. The trial court quickly denied any and all claims in only two months, on June 22, 2022, the High Court of Criminal Appeals dismissed the writ application for being subsequent. Did they even read it? I believe that I gave them reasons for considering the application which were the same basis for their denial. I quickly asked the court for a rehearing, explaining to them why I felt I met the burden of seeking a subsequent writ, but that was also dismissed based on the rule that a petitioner does not have a right to seek a rehearing. I received that postcard on July 26, 2022.

It's nearly impossible to win a habeas corpus without legal representation. An incarcerated person needs someone to gather the needed evidence. I petitioned the court to provide me with the police report that would prove my case but they refused to provide it. The police department also would not provide it, citing the Family Code that expressly prohibited the police department from providing to the public, including the accused, a report that is the subject of child abuse. Petitioning the court for discovery was also fruitless. Once a defendant is convicted, rightfully or wrongfully, the court no longer feels obligated to produce discovery material even under new laws to the contrary. The trial court has once again prevented me from proving my case.

So without evidence to support my claim that I could prove that Mark had lied on the witness stand and that the prosecutor knew that he had lied, I had no way to show the Court of Criminal Appeals this conspiracy, and all my hard work rolled downhill very quickly.

A PASTOR'S PROFESSION

But I am not deterred. God had not communicated to me to stop going to the law library, so I have remained faithful to God's directive to "go to the law library." By December 2022, I was ready to try again, this time under a claim of Actual Innocence. I will do my part so that God may speak and right this injustice.

######

THE GREAT ORDEAL

There is a scripture passage from the Book of Revelation that I always liked to use at funerals. But even though the scripture fits well in a funeral setting, it also works for all of life's trials and tribulations.

Rev. 7:13-14, 17:

13 Then one of the elders addressed me, saying, "Who are these, robed in white, and where have they come from?"

14 I said to him, "Sir, you are the one that knows." Then he said to me, "These are they who have come out of the great ordeal; they have washed their robes and made them white in the Blood of the Lamb.

17 for the Lamb at the center of the throne will be their shepherd and he will guide them to springs of the water of life, and God will wipe away every tear from their eyes."

The Great Ordeal is Life itself, imperfect on this side of heaven. There is sickness and illness and disease. We encounter physical scars – the loss of an eye, hand, arm. Then there are the emotional scars, those scars that are invisible to the eye – divorce, the loss of loved ones, the loss of a job and betrayals, just to name a few. Yes, there are even legal scars.

But all of the sorrows of the Great Ordeal "will be washed clean by the Blood of the Lamb, and God will wipe away every tear from their eyes." This is our ultimate hope. But even in the midst of the storm, whatever the storm may be, Hope is never losing faith in how the story will end. Hope is that in the end God will prevail against every evil and every sin.

So life is about living in this ambiguity of the here and now versus the perfect future. The already but not yet. The certainty in the uncertainty. The calm amidst the storm. The beauty and the ugliness.

Each life is a different story – unique and beautiful in its own way. We have no choice but to live it faithfully – to see the story through because we are stewards of our own story "while we wait for the blessed hope and the manifestation of the glory of our great God and Savior Jesus Christ." (Titus 2:13).

Live life well. Live it faithfully. AMEN

######

A PASTOR'S PROFESSION

POSTLUDE

While waiting for the court to hear evidence of trial wrongdoings and rule on his actual innocence claim, Pastor Thomas resides on the Faith-Based living section of the prison, teaching Bible Classes and mentoring men who have come to the eighteen-month program to seek knowledge of God and to work on personal issues that have shadowed their lives thus far in order to become better Christian men in the process. He hopes that he will one day be released so that he can speak and preach about faith and his experience with God.

######

GERALD THOMAS

ABOUT THE AUTHOR

Gerald Thomas earned a Bachelor's degree from Central Michigan University in 1985, majoring in Broadcasting and has worked at radio stations in Michigan in various roles both on and off the air. In 1993 he answered God's Call to public ministry and graduated in 1997 from Trinity Lutheran Seminary, Columbus, Ohio, earning a Master's Degree in Divinity (M.Div). He has served in chaplaincy roles in hospitals, nursing homes, a domestic violence shelter, youth homes, and has served congregations in Texas. Currently, he is serving multiple life sentences in the Texas prison system, where he is once again learning how to serve God's people.

A PASTOR'S PROFESSION

GERALD THOMAS

Lightning Source LLC
Chambersburg PA
CBHW052131070526
44585CB00017B/1777

www.ingramcontent.com/pod-product-compliance